DAILY

POWER & Prayer

365-Day

DEVOTIONAL

Virginia Starke
410 625-3878

Dr. Myles MUNROE

DAILY POWER & Prayer

365-Day

DEVOTIONAL

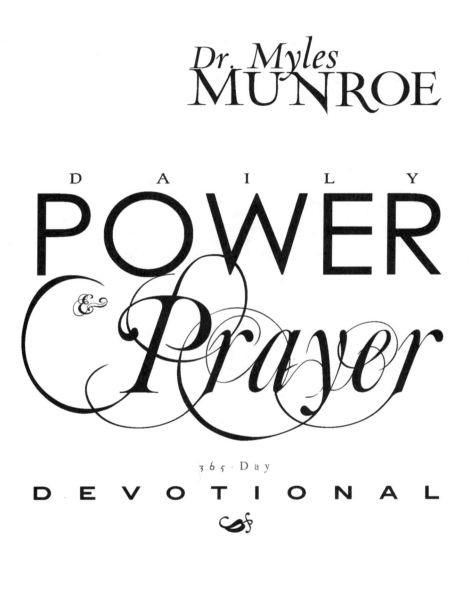

WHITAKER HOUSE

DAILY POWER AND PRAYER DEVOTIONAL

Dr. Myles Munroe
Bahamas Faith Ministries International
P.O. Box N9583
Nassau, Bahamas
e-mail: bfmadmin@bfmmm.com
websites: www.bfmmm.com; www.bfmi.tv; www.mylesmunroe.tv

ISBN-13: 978-0-88368-799-4
ISBN-10: 0-88368-799-2
Printed in the United States of America
© 2007 by Dr. Myles Munroe

1030 Hunt Valley Circle
New Kensington, PA 15068
www.whitakerhouse.com

Library of Congress Cataloging-in-Publication Data
Munroe, Myles.
Daily power and prayer devotional / by Myles Munroe.
p.   cm.
Summary: "A year-long, daily devotional focusing on two of the most important themes in the Christian life—prayer and having a clear vision for one's life; includes a program for reading the Bible through in a year"—Provided by publisher.
ISBN 978-0-88368-799-4 (trade hardcover : alk. paper) 1. Devotional calendars. I. Title.
BV4811.M75 2007
242'.2—dc22   2007032178

2 3 4 5 6 7 8 9 10 11 12 **ய** 15 14 13 12 11 10 09 08 07

Introduction

I n a world of instability, uncertainty, unpredictability, fear, terror, and global confusion, the need for anchors is imperative. The waves of our contemporary cultures make it difficult to navigate the challenges of each day, snaring the unsuspecting soul in a current of self-destruction.

Throughout history few things have remained stable and unshakable. Yet, without question, the most time-tested elements in the journey of mankind for the past seven thousand years have been the principles of the biblical text. The Word of God has been the sure foundation and source of hope and faith for millions of people over the years. These millions testify to the results of applying the Scriptures' powerful, eternal truths. God's Word is the source of vision, faith, confidence, peace, and salvation. Today, its principles are needed more than ever before.

In this devotional, I have isolated two of the most important themes of the Word of God: prayer and vision. Each of these areas can vitally impact life on planet Earth and must be understood, explored, and practiced for personal and corporate success.

I have battled the frustration of unanswered prayer and know the struggle many have faced in this crucial area of the human experience. Yet prayer is not difficult if you learn the principles by which it functions. I discovered these precepts and know that prayer works and can be achieved by anyone who is willing to embrace them.

I have also experienced the power of vision as I have captured the dream in my heart and pursued it with all diligence. I learned priceless principles that took me from where I was to where I am today and discovered that those principles are available to every human and will guarantee the same results to all who are willing to apply them.

In these daily devotions, I have labored to present the basic principles of these two vital subjects, along with practical instructions and advice.

Because the Word of God is essential for life, I have also included daily Scripture texts for reading through the Bible in one year, with one Old Testament and one New Testament passage for each day. Jesus said, *"Man does not live on bread alone, but on every word that comes from the mouth of God"* (Matthew 4:4), and the apostle Paul wrote, *"Let the word of Christ dwell in you richly"* (Colossians 3:16). It is imperative that we allow the God's Word to dwell richly in our hearts so that, as we meditate on it and absorb it, it truly becomes a part of our lives. Whenever we study the Word of God, we should also pray and ask God for wisdom. The Holy Spirit is our teacher, and we need to ask Him to illuminate the Word and to give us insight.

I challenge you to use this book to cultivate a lifestyle of prayer and visionary living that is destined to make a difference in your generation and the one to come, leaving an impact on the earth. Throughout the year, I will be with you as a life coach—helping, guiding, and motivating you to pursue your best and achieve your greatest potential in life.

May the Creator bless you as you pursue Him, enabling you to become all you were born to be. Let us begin the journey to greatness, and may each day's devotion take you closer to His perfect will for your life.

God bless you.

–Dr. Myles Munroe
Your Success Coach

Everyone Prays!

The President of the United States does it, the Prime Minister of Israel does it, the Chairman of the Palestinian People does it, and the Queen of England does it.

Jews do it, Muslims do it, Hindus do it, Buddhists do it, pagans do it, heathens do it, Christians do it. Few are sure it works; even fewer believe it is necessary. What is it? **Prayer!**

Prayer could be designated as the first product of global religion. No matter how diverse the religions of the world may be, they all practice prayer. Prayer is religion's neutralizer.

Yet prayer is still the most elusive and misunderstood practice of religious adherents. To understand prayer is the desire of every man's heart; even the pagan longs to connect with the divine and find comfort, access, and results. Understanding prayer, however, takes some work. We must first understand the source, principles, and purpose of prayer.

What is prayer? Why is it necessary? How should we pray? Why must we pray to God in the name of Jesus? Why are our prayers not always answered the way we expect? What role does faith have in the process of prayer? Does prayer affect or change destiny?

The questions go on and on; you can probably add many more to the list. To understand the foundation of prayer, we must understand the mind and purpose of the Creator Himself. Prayer is a result of God's established authority between heaven and earth, as well as a product of His faithfulness to His Word. *"Your word, O LORD, is eternal....Your faithfulness continues through all generations"* (Psalm 119:89–90). In the following pages, we will come to understand God's powerful, eternal purpose for man and prayer.

Prayer: Father, thank You for the gift of prayer.
Please open my heart to understand the purpose and
principles of prayer in the coming months.
In Jesus' name, amen.

Thought: When you understand the principles of prayer, you can
communicate with God with power, grace, and confidence.

The Greatest Common Denominator

Prayer is the greatest common denominator among all the great biblical characters and thousands of strong believers throughout history. Moses practiced it. Abraham practiced it. King David, Solomon, Esther, Deborah, Daniel, Joseph, all the prophets—and, of course, Jesus Christ Himself—had profound commitments to lives of prayer. The biblical record shows the direct impact of their prayers on the circumstances and situations they faced. The evidence affirms one thing: no matter what you may think about prayer, somehow it works.

Is man's role in prayer important? God believes so. God's actions in the earthly realm require human participation. To preserve humanity in the Flood, He needed Noah. To create a nation, He needed Abraham. To lead Israel, He needed Moses. To bring back Israel from captivity, He needed Daniel. To defeat Jericho, He needed Joshua. To preserve the Hebrews, He needed Esther. To secure the salvation of mankind, He needed to become a man.

Prayer is not optional, but necessary. If we don't pray, heaven cannot intervene in earth's affairs. We must take responsibility for the earth and shape what happens here by our prayer lives. *"Jesus told his disciples a parable to show them that they should **always pray** and not give up"* (Luke 18:1, emphasis added).

I invite you to discover your power, authority, and rights in the earth and to position yourself to become a faith channel for heavenly influence in earth's affairs. Heaven depends on you, and the earth needs you.

Prayer is meant to be one of the most exciting aspects of a life of faith. It has the power to transform lives, change circumstances, give peace in the midst of trial, alter the course of nations, and win the world for Christ.

Prayer: Father, thank You for providing biblical examples
of lives dedicated to prayer. Help me to have a prayer
life that brings powerful transformations.
In Jesus' name, amen.

Thought: The power of prayer is the inheritance of the believer.

Reading: **Genesis 1–3; Matthew 1**

An Effective Prayer Life

Consider this scenario: the day after he made a personal commitment to follow the Christian faith, Thomas was shocked to see a mere handful of people in the large building that had overflowed with worshippers the day before. "Where is everyone?" Thomas asked.

"I'm not sure," answered Cory, "but this is the way it is at every Monday night prayer meeting."

"But yesterday there were thousands here for corporate worship," Thomas said, bewildered. "I thought all Christians prayed. Why aren't they here? Why don't they attend prayer meetings like they attend the regular worship service?"

Does this scenario sound familiar? We can measure the average Christian's belief in the effectiveness of prayer by how few people attend prayer meetings in our churches. Prayer is not a priority for us. Other activities seem more exciting. We don't mind attending Bible studies, participating in ministry outreaches, or serving on church committees, but we avoid prayer—both individually and corporately—because we don't understand it.

Outwardly, we agree that prayer is worthwhile, but secretly we wonder: *Does God really hear me when I pray? Why does it seem as if my prayers just hit the ceiling and bounce back at me?* Unanswered prayer is a major obstacle to a life of true faith. Through the truths and principles we will share in the days ahead, you can change your outlook on God, yourself, and prayer. You can have an effective prayer life that will overflow into all the other areas of your life. The principles you discover will help to clear away the obstacle of unanswered prayer that has kept you from fulfilling your purpose, so you can enter into a new dimension of faith, deep love for God, and power for service.

Prayer: Father, I don't want to avoid prayer.
Please lead me into a life of powerful and effective prayer.
In Jesus' name, amen.

Thought: How would you measure your own belief in prayer?

Reading: **Genesis 4–6; Matthew 2**

God Is Faithful to Answer

God *is faithful to answer prayer.* Our understanding of prayer has become so distorted that we have developed a definition for the word that reverses its true meaning. When we believe something has no—or little—chance of happening, we say, "It hasn't got a prayer." Yet Jesus assures us that God hears and answers our prayers. He said, *"Therefore I tell you, whatever you ask for in prayer, believe that you **have received** it, and it will be yours"* (Mark 11:24, emphasis added). The answer is so sure that we are instructed to believe it has already happened.

God's *will and Word do work when they are understood and put into practice.* Whether or not you believe it right now, prayer *does* work, but you must first understand it. You must learn how to pray according to the truths and principles of prayer found in God's Word. True, biblical prayer builds intimacy with God, honors His nature and character, instills respect for His integrity, enables belief in His Word, causes trust in His love, affirms His purposes and will, and appropriates His promises.

Prayer is meant to be answered—otherwise, God would not ask us to pray. He won't waste your time and effort; He's too practical for that. He is interested in results, not just *"many words"* (Matthew 6:7) spoken in prayer. Jesus' approach to prayer was also very practical. He didn't pray without expecting to be heard. He said, *"Father, I thank you that you have heard me. I knew that you **always** hear me"* (John 11:41–42, emphasis added). We need to know how to approach God and to learn the kind of prayers God responds to. We need to pray as Jesus prayed.

Prayer: Father, I desire to learn Your heart concerning prayer.
Teach me of Your faithfulness to answer prayer.
In Jesus' name, amen.

Thought: Prayer is meant to be one of the most exciting
aspects of a life of faith.

Reading: **Genesis 7–9; Matthew 3**

Love

My dear friends, we must love each other. Love comes from God, and when we love each other, it shows that we have been given new life. We are now God's children, and we know him. God is love, and anyone who doesn't love others has never known him. God showed his love for us when he sent his only Son into the world to give us life. Real love isn't our love for God, but his love for us. God sent his Son to be the sacrifice by which our sins are forgiven. Dear friends, since God loved us this much, we must love each other.

1 John 4.7-11

This is a Selection of Holy Scripture in the *Contemporary English Version*. For a free catalog of other Scripture publications call 1-800-32-BIBLE, or write to the American Bible Society, 1865 Broadway, New York, NY 10023-7505.

Visit the ABS website! **www.americanbible.org**

AMERICAN BIBLE SOCIETY
NEW YORK

Eng. CEV Bookmark-107132
ABS-2/99-35,000–NE1

What Is the Purpose of Prayer?

What is the purpose of prayer? Doesn't God do whatever He wants, anyway? Why should we have to pray when God already knows everything?

These are valid questions. To answer them, we first need to understand essential truths about God's nature and His purposes for mankind that make prayer necessary. We will spend a few days looking at God's original intent for mankind and for prayer.

To begin with, God does everything for a reason, because He is a God of purpose. His actions are not arbitrary. *"The Lord Almighty has sworn, 'Surely, as I have planned, so it will be, and as I have purposed, so it will stand'"* (Isaiah 14:24). *"The plans of the Lord stand firm forever, the purposes of his heart through all generations"* (Psalm 33:11). *"Many are the plans in a man's heart, but it is the Lord's purpose that prevails"* (Proverbs 19:21).

God is a God of purpose, and everything He has created in this world, including men and women, has been created to fulfill His purposes. The Creator's commitment to His original intent for creation is a priority for Him that motivates and regulates all His actions. We can trust that God's purposes are steadfast and that they will guide us into His perfect will for our lives.

> *I make known the end from the beginning, from ancient times, what is still to come. I say: My purpose will stand, and I will do all that I please.* (Isaiah 46:10–11)

Prayer: Father, You are a God of purpose. Thank You
for including me in Your purposes for this earth.
Please use me to help fulfill Your plans.
In Jesus' name, amen.

Thought: Everything God does is driven by His purposed
desire, which never changes.

Reading: **Genesis 10–12; Matthew 4**

Let Us Make Man in Our Image

God said, *"Let us make man in our image, in our likeness"* (Genesis 1:26). What does this statement reveal about His purposes for humanity and for prayer?

First, God created humanity to reflect His character and personality. We were created to be like Him, having His *"image"* and *"likeness."* This means we were created to have His nature and moral character. God created mankind to establish a relationship of mutual love with humanity. He made mankind in His own image so love could be freely given and received between Creator and created. Man can have fellowship with God because God made man out of His own essence. He made man to be spirit, just as He is Spirit. *"God is spirit, and his worshipers must worship in spirit and in truth"* (John 4:24).

Although God is the Creator, He has always emphasized that He is man's Father. It wasn't His desire to be primarily thought of as an awesome God or a *"consuming fire"* (Deuteronomy 4:24). God wants us to approach Him as a child would a loving father: *"Is he not your Father, your Creator, who made you and formed you?"* (Deuteronomy 32:6). *"As a father has compassion on his children, so the LORD has compassion on those who fear him"* (Psalm 103:13).

Man was created out of God's essence, and he depends on God as his Source. As human beings, we are not self-sufficient, even though we would like to think we are. We cannot reveal God's image and likeness apart from a relationship with Him. No one will be truly satisfied until he or she loves God. God must be first in our lives because we were designed to find fulfillment and ultimate meaning in Him.

Prayer: Father, my ultimate fulfillment comes from You.
You are my all in all. Show me my dependence on You daily.
In Jesus' name, amen.

Thought: We cannot reflect God's nature apart from Him.

Reading: **Genesis 13–15; Matthew 5:1–26**

We Were Created for Dominion

G od created humanity to carry out His purposes on earth. When
God created man in His image, He gave him free will. Thus man
has the ability to plan and make decisions, and to take action to fulfill
those plans, just as God did in creating the world. Man is meant to carry
out God's purposes using his own will and initiative. He is to reflect the
God who formulates plans and carries them out through creative acts.
How is humanity to fulfill this vocation?

> Then God said, "Let us make man in our image, in our likeness, and
> **let them rule** ["have dominion" NKJV] over the fish of the sea and the
> birds of the air, over the livestock, over all the earth, and over all the
> creatures that move along the ground."
> (Genesis 1:26, emphasis added)

Man was created not only to have a relationship with God, but also
to share God's authority. "You made him ruler over the works of your hands;
you put everything under his feet" (Psalm 8:6). "The highest heavens belong to
the LORD, but the earth he has given to man" (Psalm 115:16).

The account of the creation of mankind shows that God never
intended to rule the earth by Himself. Why? It is because "God is love"
(1 John 4:8, 16), and He wants others to share in what He has. We must
understand that the *relationship of love* that God established with mankind is not separate from the *purpose* God has for mankind. Rather,
the relationship is foundational to the purpose. *Both are essential keys to
prayer.*

Prayer: Father God, I desire to have a relationship with You
and to be a part of carrying out Your purpose on this earth.
Please make this a reality in my life.
In Jesus' name, amen.

Thought: Man's vocation is to carry out God's purposes
on the earth.

Reading: **Genesis 16–17; Matthew 5:27–48**

Man's Dominion on the Earth

God has entrusted man with the care of the earth. Man is the proprietor of the physical earth, including all living things. In Genesis 2, Adam was placed in the garden of Eden to tend and cultivate it. This is what mankind is to do with the entire earth. God gave man the freedom to exhibit creativity while governing the earth and everything that dwells in it. Man is meant to reflect the loving and creative Spirit of God.

This brings us to an interesting fact that many believers overlook today. *God didn't originally create man for heaven; He created man for the earth!* God is the Ruler of heaven, and He made man to express His authority in this world. He said, in effect, "I want My rule to extend to another realm, but I don't want to do it directly. I want man to share My rule."

God's plan for creation was this: as God ruled the unseen realm in heaven, man would rule the visible realm on earth, with God and man enjoying continual communion through their spiritual natures. God made us in His likeness and gives each of us free will as a reflection of His own nature.

This does not mean that we are deity or equal to God. Adam and Eve could fulfill their purpose only by depending on and communicating with God. Similarly, we can fulfill our purpose only as we are connected to our Source. However, we must recognize God's high esteem and purposes for us. In essence, God said to man, "Let Me rule through you so you can appreciate, enjoy, and share in My governance."

Prayer: Father, it humbles me to know that You desire
man to rule with You on the earth. Please let me maintain
communion with You so I can fulfill my part in Your purposes.
In Jesus' name, amen.

Thought: God created man to express His authority
throughout the earth.

Reading: **Genesis 18–19; Matthew 6:1–18**

We Are God's Offspring

W hen God created Adam and Eve and placed them in the garden of Eden, He never intended them to leave. Instead, He wanted the *garden to be spread over the earth.* God wanted them to spread worldwide the character of the garden—God's presence, light, and truth. God said to them, *"Be fruitful and increase in number; fill the earth and subdue it"* (Genesis 2:28). This was the overarching purpose for man's dominion over the earth. Isaiah 11:9 says, *"The earth will be full of the knowledge of the LORD as the waters cover the sea."*

God shares His authority with humans because they are His offspring. He didn't create men and women to be servants, but to be sons and daughters who are wholeheartedly involved in running the family business. God has always wanted His children to help fulfill His purposes. Jesus told His disciples, *"I no longer call you servants, because a servant does not know his master's business. Instead, I have called you friends, for everything that I learned from my Father I have made known to you"* (John 15:15).

The Father wants to share His purposes with us. This means that He doesn't want man to work *for* Him, but rather *with* Him. The Bible calls us *"God's fellow workers"* (2 Corinthians 6:1) or *"workers together with Him"* (NKJV). In the original Greek, *"fellow workers"* means those who "cooperate," who "help with," who "work together." We should think of humanity's dominion as a joint purpose with God based on mutual love and the relationship of sons and daughters to their heavenly Father.

Prayer: Father, I can call You Father because of Your love
and Your creation of humanity as Your sons and daughters.
Thank You for sharing Your dominion with us.
In the name of Your Son Jesus, amen.

Thought: We should be working *with* God rather than *for* God.

Reading: **Genesis 20–22; Matthew 6:19–34**

What Is the Nature of Prayer?

Tragedy came to mankind when Adam and Eve turned their backs on God and desired their own wills instead of His will. Some people believe that prayer originated because sin separated us from God and we needed a way to reconnect with Him. That is one use for prayer; however, it is not the heart of prayer. To understand prayer's essence, we must realize that it began with the *creation* of mankind. It was not instituted *after* the fall but *before* it. Prayer existed from the beginning of God's relationship with man.

The nature of prayer can be understood only in the context of God's purposes for humanity, to commune and rule with God, which we have discussed in the last few days. The essence of prayer is twofold:

1. Prayer is an expression of mankind's unity and relationship of love with God;
2. Prayer is an expression of mankind's affirmation of and participation in God's purposes for the earth.

To pray means to commune with God, to become one with God. It means union with Him—unity and singleness of purpose, thought, desire, will, reason, motive, objective, and feeling. H. D. Bollinger said, "Prayer is *being* expressing relationship with *being*" (emphasis added). Therefore, prayer is a vehicle of the soul and spirit by which man communes with God.

Prayer is also the medium through which the human spirit affects and is affected by the will and purpose of the divine Creator. It is man cooperating with God's purposes for the earth. Therefore, prayer is the involvement of oneself (one's whole self) with the living God.

Prayer: Father, Your desire to commune with me blesses me.
May I walk with You in communion and unity with Your Spirit.
In Jesus' name, amen.

Thought: Prayer is the expression of man's relationship with God
and participation in His purposes.

Reading: **Genesis 23–25; Matthew 7**

Who Prayed the First Prayer?

W ho prayed the first prayer? I would say Adam, since he was created first and received God's instructions about tending the garden and the parameters of man's authority on earth. The Bible implies that God made a practice of walking and talking with Adam in the cool of the day. (See Genesis 3:8–9.) The fellowship between God and Adam formed the essence of the first prayer.

Since Adam was in God's presence, why did he need to pray? Adam needed to pray because the heart of prayer is *communion with God in a unity of love and purpose.* It is agreeing with God—heart, soul, mind, and strength—to bring about God's will. Adam communed with God and agreed with His purposes.

Ever since the fall of mankind, we have needed to pray to enter God's presence. Yet this is only for the purpose of taking us to the place of fellowship with God where Adam and Eve were before the fall—a place of purity before Him in which we reflect His nature and purposes and where our wills agree with His will.

This brings us back to an earlier question: Why do we have to ask God to do what He has already determined to do? When God gave man dominion, He placed His will for the earth on the cooperation of man's will. God did not change this purpose when mankind fell, for His purposes are eternal. *"The plans of the LORD stand firm forever, the purposes of his heart through all generations"* (Psalm 33:11).

Prayer: Father, Your purposes are eternal. Thank You for granting us dominion over the earth. Please help me to prepare my heart through prayer so I can enter Your presence.
In Jesus' name, amen.

Thought: Prayer is not optional.

Reading: **Genesis 26–27; Matthew 8:1–17**

Prayer Is Essential for God's Will

Our need to pray results from the way God arranged dominion on the earth. God made the world. Then He made men and women, giving them dominion over the works of His hands. When God said, *"Let them rule...over all the earth,"* He ordered the dominion of the world in a way that made rule by humans essential to accomplishing His purposes. He causes things to happen on earth when men and women are in agreement with His will. *Prayer, therefore, is essential for God's will to be done in the earth.* Since God never breaks His Word concerning how things are to work, prayer is mandatory, not optional, for spiritual progress.

God's plan is for man to desire what He desires, to will what He wills, and to ask Him to accomplish His purposes in the world so that goodness and truth, rather than evil and darkness, may reign on the earth. In this sense, by praying, man gives God the freedom to intervene in earth's affairs.

Even before God's plan of redemption was fully accomplished in Christ, God used humans to fulfill His will. We see this truth in the lives of Abraham, Moses, Gideon, David, Daniel, and many others. God continued to work with mankind to fulfill His purposes on earth even though man's part was limited by his sin and lack of understanding of God's ways.

As a man or woman created in the image of God, dominion authority is your heritage. God desires that you will His will. His will should be the foundation of your prayers, the heart of your intercession, and the source of your confidence in supplication.

Prayer: Father, I affirm that I am in agreement with
Your will. Your will is in Your Word. Please continue to reveal
Your will to me in the Scriptures each day.
In Jesus' name, amen.

Thought: Prayer is earthly license for heavenly intervention.

Reading: **Genesis 28–29; Matthew 8:18–34**

God's Purpose for Your Life

Praying does not mean convincing God to do your will, but doing His will through your will. Therefore, the key to effective prayer is understanding God's purpose for your life, the reason you exist—as a human being in general and as an individual specifically. This is an especially important truth to remember: *Once you understand your purpose, it becomes the "raw material," the foundational matter, for your prayer life.* God's will is the authority of your prayers. Prayer calls forth what God has already purposed and predestined—continuing His work of creation and carrying out His plans for the earth.

In him we were also chosen, having been predestined according to the plan of him who works out everything in conformity with the purpose of his will. (Ephesians 1:11)

The Father works out everything "*in conformity with the purpose of his will.*" In this way, your purpose in God is the foundational material for your prayers regarding provision, healing, deliverance, power, protection, endurance, patience, authority, faith, praise, thanksgiving, confidence, assurance, boldness, and peace, for the supply of all your needs.

Everything you need is available to fulfill your purpose. All that God is, and all that He has, may be received through prayer. The measure of our appropriation of God's grace is determined by the measure of our prayers.

Prayer: Father, I do not want to accomplish my will, but Your will. Lead me to conform my prayers and myself to the purpose of Your will. In Jesus' name, amen.

Thought: Purpose is the raw material for your prayer life.

Reading: **Genesis 30–32; Matthew 9:1–17**

Our Confidence in Prayer

S ome people say they do not know what to pray for. The answer is that we are not to ask God for anything outside of our purpose. *"When you ask, you do not receive, because you ask with wrong motives, that you may spend what you get on your pleasures"* (James 4:3). If we ask for what is contrary to our purpose, we will be frustrated. Jesus always prayed for God's will to be done, then worked to accomplish it.

One of the longest prayers recorded in the Bible is Jesus' prayer in John 17, where He said, in effect, "Father, before I came to earth, You gave Me people to redeem. I have protected them, I have kept them safe for that purpose, and now I am going to effect that redemption through My death and resurrection. I have fulfilled and am about to fulfill Your purpose for Me." (See John 17:6, 9–12.) Jesus knew the heavenly Father's purpose for His life, and He both desired to do the will of God and acted on it. *"'My food,' said Jesus, 'is to do the will of him who sent me and to finish his work'"* (John 4:34).

Jesus' assurance in prayer was based on His knowing and doing the will of God. As it says in 1 John 5:14–15,

> *This is the confidence we have in approaching God: that if we ask anything according to his will, he hears us. And if we know that he hears us—whatever we ask—we know that we have what we asked of him.*

Prayer: Father, I desire to be more like Jesus, my Lord.
Please help me to pray, from my heart, that my food
will always be to do my heavenly Father's will.
In Jesus' precious name, amen.

Thought: Assurance in prayer is based on knowing
and doing God's will.

Reading: **Genesis 33–35; Matthew 9:18–38**

Prayer Is Exercising Our Authority

Whean we know and obey God's will, and ask Him to fulfill it, He will grant our request. Whether we are praying for individual, family, community, national, or world needs, we must seek to be in agreement with God's will so His purposes can reign on the earth. This is the essence of exercising dominion.

Since the Lord has given humanity authority over the earth, He requires the authorization of mankind to act on the earth. When we stop praying, we hinder God's purposes for the world. Jesus taught His disciples *"that they should always pray and not give up"* (Luke 18:1). He said, *"I will give you the keys of the kingdom of heaven; whatever you bind on earth will be bound in heaven, and whatever you loose on earth will be loosed in heaven"* (Matthew 16:19).

We need to ask God to intervene in human affairs; otherwise, our world will be susceptible to the influences of Satan and sin. God will ultimately bring His purposes to pass in the world—with or without our cooperation. He will find someone who agrees with His plans, but when you neglect to pray, you fail to fulfill *your* role in His purposes. He does not want you to miss out on this privilege. James 4:2 says, *"You do not have, because you do not ask God."*

Prayer is necessary to fulfill God's purposes in the world and in our lives. As we embrace God's will, live in the righteousness of Christ, and seek to fulfill His purposes, nothing will hinder our prayers and we will begin to understand that *"with God all things are possible"* (Matthew 19:26).

Prayer: Father, I want to fulfill my role in Your kingdom.
Remind me daily of the importance of my prayers to You.
In Jesus' name, amen.

Thought: All that God is, and all that God has, may be received
through prayer.

Reading: **Genesis 36–38; Matthew 10:1–20**

Broken Relationship, Broken Effectiveness

God gave humanity a vast amount of freedom and authority on earth. Yet these gifts depend on man's using his will to do God's will. Using our will for anything other than God's will mars the image and likeness of God within us and hinders God's purposes for the world—purposes of goodness, fruitfulness, creativity, truth, joy, and love. Adam and Eve's rebellion distorted God's image in mankind and attacked God's plans for the earth.

How did this rebellion occur? Satan tempted Adam and Eve to disobey God, and they chose to agree with Satan's purposes rather than God's. In sinning, they cut off communion with God. Humanity no longer partnered with God to fulfill His purposes, leaving the world at the mercy of a renegade authority opposed to God's plans. In fact, man forfeited his authority to Satan, serving him instead of God. The fall introduced a new ruler on earth—one bent on its destruction rather than its growth. Because Satan usurped mankind's authority on earth, the apostle Paul referred to him as *"the god of this world"* (2 Corinthians 4:4 KJV).

When Adam and Eve broke relationship with God, their effectiveness in prayer was compromised. True prayer is maintained through oneness of heart and purpose with God. When we pray, we represent God's interests on earth, and representation requires relationship. Therefore, our difficulties with prayer are traced to the fall and the fallen nature of man, which estranges us from God. Even as redeemed believers, we must realize who we are in Christ and act upon the principles of prayer that God has established if we are to be restored to His purposes in the crucial area of prayer.

Prayer: Father, thank You that we are the righteousness of God in Christ Jesus. Please help me to pray in communion with Your will, in righteous standing with You because of Your Son. In Jesus' name, I pray, amen.

Thought: True prayer is maintained through oneness of heart and purpose with God.

Reading: **Genesis 39–40; Matthew 10:21–42**

God's Purpose for Us Is Eternal

The god of this world hath blinded the minds of them which believe not, lest the light of the glorious gospel of Christ, who is the image of God, should shine unto them. (2 Corinthians 4:4 KJV)

In the original Greek, one meaning of the word *"world"* in this verse is *"a space of time"* and *"an age."* In fact, some Bible versions translate the first part of the verse as *"the god of this age"* (NIV, NKJV).

Perhaps this term was meant to emphasize that while Satan may be the god of this world now, he won't be forever. His reign will endure only for a time. God's purposes are eternal, and He planned from the foundation of the world to restore mankind. *"God...has saved us and called us to a holy life—not because of anything we have done but because of his own purpose and grace. This grace was given us in Christ Jesus before the beginning of time"* (2 Timothy 1:8–9). *"He chose us in him before the creation of the world to be holy and blameless in his sight. In love he predestined us to be adopted as his sons through Jesus Christ, in accordance with his pleasure and will"* (Ephesians 1:4–5).

God planned to restore mankind and to renew the earth through a new Ruler—the Second Adam, fully human yet fully divine—who would be perfectly one with God and His purposes: *"the man Christ Jesus"* (1 Timothy 2:5).

Christ reestablished mankind's authority in the world and restored to us the God-given purpose and power of prayer.

Prayer: Father, You have given us the privilege to rule and reign with Your Son Jesus. May we exercise that authority, led and empowered by Your Holy Spirit.
In Jesus' name, amen.

Thought: God had a plan in mind from the foundation of the world to restore mankind to Himself.

Reading: **Genesis 41–42; Matthew 11**

Putting Prayer into Practice

I n the coming weeks, as we learn more about the powerful, God-given gift of prayer, you will need to ask yourself some thought-provoking questions. Be honest with yourself, because God wants to transform your mind concerning the power and the privilege of prayer.

Ask yourself today: Have I ever neglected to pray because I felt God would do whatever He wanted to do anyway? If the real purpose of prayer is to fulfill God's purposes on earth, how much do I know about those purposes? How can I learn more about God's purposes? Have I been resisting God's will in any area of my life? What can I do today to build a deeper relationship of love with God? What is one of God's purposes that I can agree with Him about in prayer today?

Now, let's go to the Lord together in prayer with the confidence that we are in His will and His purposes:

Prayer: Heavenly Father, You have said that the plans in a man's heart are many, but it is Your purpose that prevails. We ask you to fulfill Your word and make Your purpose reign in our lives. We all have plans and goals that we are pursuing. We ask you to establish whatever is from You—whatever is in line with Your purpose—and cause to fade away whatever is not from You. We honor you as our Creator and as our loving heavenly Father. We affirm that it is You who works in us to will and to act according to Your good purpose. Renew our minds so we may understand Your ways and Your plans more fully. We pray this in the name of Jesus, who is our Way, Truth, and Life. Amen.

Thought: How can I learn more about God's purposes?

Reading: **Genesis 43–45; Matthew 12:1–23**

Principles of Purpose for Prayer

Today, reflect on these principles of purpose:

1. God is a God of purpose, and His purposes are eternal.
2. God created mankind with a desired purpose, for a desired purpose.
3. God desired offspring with whom He could share a relationship of love, rule, and dominion.
4. God created mankind in His image, with His nature and moral character, and with a free will.
5. God gave mankind the freedom to function with legal authority on earth. He placed His will for the earth on the cooperation of man's will. This purpose never changed, even after the fall of mankind.
6. God's will is His purpose for mankind. To fulfill what we were created to be and to do, we must desire to do God's will.
7. Prayer is an expression of mankind's unity and relationship of love with God. It is also an expression of mankind's affirmation of and participation in God's purposes.
8. Prayer is the involvement of one's whole self with God.
9. Prayer is the medium through which the human spirit affects and is affected by the will and purpose of the divine Creator.
10. Prayer is not optional. It is essential for the fulfillment of God's purposes on earth.
11. By praying, man gives God the freedom to intervene in earth's affairs.
12. When we know and obey God's will, and ask Him to fulfill it, He will grant our request.
13. When Adam and Eve broke relationship with God, their effectiveness in prayer was compromised. True prayer is maintained through oneness of heart and purpose with God.

Reading: **Genesis 46–48; Matthew 12:24–50**

The Right to Pray

We know that God instituted prayer when He created mankind, and that prayer is our means of communion with God. It is the medium through which our spirits are to affect and be affected by the will and purpose of the divine Creator. That is the *purpose* of prayer.

Yet on what basis do you have a *right* to pray?

God originally gave us this right by virtue of our relationship with Him and our purpose of exercising dominion over the earth. Yet our first ancestors broke relationship with our Creator and forfeited our dominion authority. Satan, rather than man, became *"the god of this world"* (2 Corinthians 4:4 KJV).

As a result, people became estranged from God and His plans for them. This left them feeling isolated from God, unsure of where they stood with Him, unclear as to what God wanted to do for and through them, and without a sense of purpose.

Do these results sound at all like your own prayer life? If so, you must realize that your concept of prayer has been influenced by the effects of the fall. However, God wants to give you a new outlook on prayer—one that confirms your right to pray and reflects His purposes for redemption, as well as creation.

It was not until I understood God's principles of purpose and faithfulness that I began to grasp the nature, philosophy, and foundation of the concept of prayer and to experience the positive results of prayer in my own life. As we continue this devotional journey together into the heart of prayer, we will learn more life-changing truths about prayer's purpose and power.

Prayer: Father, open my spiritual eyes so that I may understand how vital my right to pray is to my Christian life. In Jesus' name, amen.

Thought: God wants to give you a new outlook on prayer.

Reading: **Genesis 49–50; Matthew 13:1–30**

God's Purposes Reflect His Character

G od's purposes are eternal. His plan from the foundation of the world was to defeat Satan and sin and to restore mankind. His purposes never changed.

Yet God's plan was not simply to come down and wrench control of the earth back from Satan. He *could* have done that, but He never *would* have done it. It would have been inconsistent with the integrity of His character and His purposes. Why?

God has all power and authority. However, He has given mankind free will and authority over the earth, and He will not rescind those gifts—even though man sinned, rejected Him, and deserves to be separated from Him forever. Romans 6:23 says, *"For the wages of sin is death."* What extraordinary respect God has for humanity! He continued to respect mankind's free will, even after the fall, for *"God's gifts and his call are irrevocable"* (Romans 11:29).

God restored man's relationship with Him and his earthly authority, even after he had thrown away these gifts. To do this, man's sin had to be dealt with, and man also had to desire to return to God and work together with Him of his own free will. This was possible only in Christ. As Jesus said, *"With man this is impossible, but with God all things are possible"* (Matthew 19:26). God's eternal plan for humanity was made possible through the obedience and sacrifice of Jesus Christ, who alone restores us to our purposes in God. *Only through Christ do we have a right to pray with authority.*

Prayer: Father, thank You that Your plans for mankind are eternal. Thank You for not giving up on us, and for sending Your Son Jesus to restore our right to commune with You. May we learn to pray with authority in Jesus' name. Amen.

Thought: God respected man's authority even when it lay dormant within his fallen nature.

Reading: **Exodus 1–3; Matthew 14:1–21**

God's Redemption through Jesus

F rom the beginning of creation, God planned to redeem and restore mankind through Jesus Christ.

> [God] *made known to us the mystery of his will according to his good pleasure, which* **he purposed in Christ**....*His intent was that now, through the church, the manifold wisdom of God should be made known to the rulers and authorities in the heavenly realms, according to* **his eternal purpose** *which he accomplished in Christ Jesus our Lord. In him and through faith in him we may approach God with freedom and confidence.* (Ephesians 1:9; 3:10–12, emphasis added)

To restore God's purpose, Jesus came as a Representative of the legal authority of the earth: man. He came as a *human being*, the Second Adam, the beginning of a new family of men who would be devoted to God—"*the firstborn among many brothers*" (Romans 8:29). John 1:14 says, "*The Word became flesh and made his dwelling among us.*" The second person of the Trinity voluntarily put aside His heavenly glory and came to earth as a man: "[Christ], *being in very nature God,...[took] the very nature of a servant, being made in human likeness*" (Philippians 2:6).

Coming as a man gave Jesus the legal right to reclaim humanity and the earth for God. To restore man's broken relationship with God, it was necessary for Jesus to live a sinless life and to *chose* to do God's will. Only a perfectly righteous man who desired to do God's will could redeem humanity. Second Corinthians 5:21 says, "*God made him who had no sin to be sin for us, so that in him we might become the righteousness of God.*"

Prayer: Father, thank You for sending Jesus as mankind's Representative in order to restore me to You. Help me to remember that because Jesus became sin for me, I have become the righteousness of God. In Jesus' name, amen.

Thought: The Father has accomplished His eternal purpose through Jesus Christ our Lord.

Reading: **Exodus 4–6; Matthew 14:22–36**

Jesus Is the Second Adam

As the Second Adam, Jesus reflected God's image, as Adam originally had. Jesus is called *"Christ, who is the image of God"* (2 Corinthians 4:4). The fullness of the *"image of God"* was revealed in both His humanity and divinity: *"God was pleased to have all his fullness dwell in him"* (Colossians 1:19). *"For in Christ all the fullness of the Deity lives in bodily form, and you have been given fullness in Christ, who is the head over every power and authority"* (Colossians 2:9–10). *"He is the image of the invisible God, the firstborn over all creation"* (Colossians 1:15).

Jesus also had a unique relationship of love with God the Father; it reflected the relationship God desired to have with Adam and Eve. *"The Father loves the Son and has placed everything in his hands"* (John 3:35). *"For the Father loves the Son and shows him all he does"* (John 5:20). The love between the Father and the Son enabled Jesus to say, *"I and the Father are one"* (John 10:30). Throughout the Gospels, Jesus revealed that His one purpose was to do God's will: *"Your kingdom come. Your will be done on earth as it is in heaven"* (Luke 11:2 NKJV). *"I can of Myself do nothing. As I hear, I judge; and My judgment is righteous, because I do not seek My own will but the will of the Father who sent Me"* (John 5:30 NKJV.)

Jesus still lives to do God's will, and He said that anyone who does God's will belongs to the family of God: *"Whoever does the will of my Father in heaven is my brother and sister and mother"* (Matthew 12:50).

Prayer: Father, I want to be one with You and Your purposes.
This is possible only because of my relationship with
You through Jesus Christ. Enable me to see and
pray for Your will to be done in my life.
In Jesus' name, amen.

Thought: Through Christ we are restored to our purpose.

Reading: **Exodus 7–8; Matthew 15:1–20**

Jesus Reigns with Authority

Just as Adam and Eve originally administered God's rule on earth, Christ exhibited God's authority when He lived on earth: *"The blind receive sight, the lame walk, those who have leprosy are cured, the deaf hear, the dead are raised, and the good news is preached to the poor"* (Matthew 11:5).

When Jesus returns to earth, the whole world will recognize His authority. *"At the name of Jesus every knee should bow, in heaven and on earth and under the earth, and every tongue confess that Jesus Christ is Lord, to the glory of God the Father"* (Philippians 2:10–11). *"On his robe and on his thigh he has this name written: KING OF KINGS AND LORD OF LORDS"* (Revelation 19:16). *"The kingdom of the world has become the kingdom of our Lord and of his Christ, and he will reign for ever and ever"* (Revelation 11:15).

Jesus has the authority to reign on earth and to ask God to intervene in the world since He was the perfect Man and Sacrifice. His prayers for mankind are powerful and effective. *"Therefore he is able to save completely those who come to God through him, because he always lives to intercede for them"* (Hebrews 7:25).

Jesus has given believers His Spirit so we can agree with God's purposes even if we are uncertain how to pray. *"In the same way, the Spirit helps us in our weakness. We do not know what we ought to pray for, but the Spirit himself intercedes for us with groans that words cannot express"* (Romans 8:26). We can pray with the same authority as Jesus did because the Holy Spirit dwells within us.

Prayer: Father, may I learn to pray with the authority of Christ in accordance with Your will, in the power of Your Spirit. In Jesus' name, amen.

Thought: Jesus has the right and the power to reign on the earth.

Reading: **Exodus 9–11; Matthew 15:21–39**

Jesus Transferred Authority

The position and authority that Jesus won have been returned to mankind through spiritual rebirth in Christ. (See John 3:5.) Because of Christ, we can live as true sons and daughters of our heavenly Father, having a restored relationship of love with Him, the ability to follow His will, and the right and privilege to pray.

It is God's will that every person be redeemed and rule the earth through the Spirit of Christ. Through mankind, God desires to reveal His character, nature, principles, precepts, and righteousness to the world. This is an *eternal* plan that applies to our present lives on earth and will apply throughout eternity.

God intended man to live and work on earth. Yet, because of the fall, our spirits will separate from our bodies when we die; the spirits of the redeemed will join God in heaven. Yet God promised that when we come to heaven, we will stay only until the day when our bodies will be resurrected to rejoin our spirits. Then we will continue to rule in the new earth God will create. (See 1 Corinthians 15:42–44, 51–53; Isaiah 65:17.)

God will not raise you from the dead just to live with Him forever. He will raise you so you can get on with your work—your calling and vocation. Today, as we live and work in this fallen world, and in the future, when we will live and reign with Jesus (see Revelation 5:10; 20:4, 6; 22:5), God's commission for us is unchanging: *"Let them rule...over all the earth"* (Genesis 1:26).

Prayer: Father, the authority Jesus won has been
restored to mankind according to Your will. I desire to share
in that authority and see Your will carried out on the earth.
Use me for Your purposes.
In Jesus' name, amen.

Thought: Because of Christ, we can live as true sons
and daughters of God.

Reading: **Exodus 12–13; Matthew 16**

Accept Your Authority in Christ

M any believers do not advance God's kingdom on earth, often because they do not recognize or accept the calling and authority they received in Christ. They do not know their rights based on the *"new covenant"*:

> *Not that we are competent in ourselves to claim anything for ourselves, but our competence comes from God. He has made us competent as ministers of a new covenant—not of the letter but of the Spirit; for the letter kills, but the Spirit gives life.* (2 Corinthians 3:5–6)

I believe our fear of being proud or presumptuous, along with our failure to accept our worth in Christ, have robbed us of the reality of His finished work on our behalf. How slow we are to act on what we are in Christ!

For years, the church has not understood the true nature of humility. We have been taught about our weaknesses and unworthiness in such a way that we scarcely dare to affirm what God says we are: *"a new creation"* (2 Corinthians 5:17). Yet *"if anyone is in Christ, he is a new creation; the old has gone, the new has come! All this is from God"* (vv. 17–18). This is not something we made up. It is from God.

Ephesians 1:7 says, *"In him we have redemption through his blood, the forgiveness of sins, in accordance with the riches of God's grace."* Who are we in Christ? We are the redeemed! The Second Adam redeemed mankind. Therefore, not only are we new creations, but we also have redemption that is literal and absolute.

Prayer: Father God, I am a new creation in Christ.
How amazing are those words!
Enable me to live as the new creation that You have made me.
In Jesus' name, amen.

Thought: What does Christ's redemption mean to you today?

Reading: **Exodus 14–15; Matthew 17**

JANUARY 27

Delivered from Darkness

Satan became the god of this world when he successfully tempted Adam and Eve to reject God's ways. Yet Christ delivered us from Satan's dominion. Even though we live in a fallen world, we do not belong to it, but to God's kingdom: *"He has rescued us from the dominion of darkness and brought us into the kingdom of the Son he loves"* (Colossians 1:13). *"But you are a chosen people, a royal priesthood, a holy nation, a people belonging to God, that you may declare the praises of him who called you out of darkness into his wonderful light"* (1 Peter 2:9). Satan no longer has authority over us; rather, we have authority over him in the name of Jesus.

Christ also delivered us from the power of sin. *"Sin shall not be your master, because you are not under law, but under grace"* (Romans 6:14). When we repent of our sins and believe in Jesus as our Savior, we are *"in Christ"* (2 Corinthians 5:17) and are *"the righteousness of God"* in Him (v. 21). Since He is sinless, we, too, are free from sin. *"Where sin increased, grace increased all the more, so that, just as sin reigned in death, so also grace might reign through righteousness to bring eternal life through Jesus Christ our Lord"* (Romans 5:20-21). Because of redemption, sin no longer reigns in our lives—grace does.

Our right to *"approach the throne of grace with confidence"* (Hebrews 4:16) through Christ brings us the delight of a restored relationship with God. This enables us to pray in agreement with the Father and to ask Him to meet our needs and the needs of others.

Prayer: Father, thank You that we can approach Your throne of grace with confidence. Please enable me to walk in the boldness You have given me. In Jesus' name, amen.

Thought: *"You are a chosen people, a royal priesthood."*

Reading: **Exodus 16–18; Matthew 18:1–20**

Jesus Is Our Model of Authority

J esus reclaimed our dominion authority and modeled how to exercise it. His prayer life exemplified the prayer life we are to have. You may say, "Yes, but Jesus was different from us. He was divine, and so He had an advantage over us."

When Jesus was on earth, was He in a better position than we are? No. What He accomplished on earth, He accomplished in His humanity, not His divinity. Otherwise, He could not have been man's Representative and Substitute. Jesus kept a close relationship with the Father through prayer. He did what God directed Him to, relying on the Spirit of God. We can do the same.

God loved Jesus because He lived to fulfill God's purposes. *"The reason my Father loves me is that I lay down my life—only to take it up again"* (John 10:17). God revealed to Jesus His plans and how Jesus' ministry related to His overall purpose. I believe God will do the same for us as we live and work in the Spirit of Christ.

Jesus' prayers were effective because He had a relationship with God, knew His purposes, and prayed according to God's will. We are to imitate Him, letting His Spirit rule in our lives. *"Let this mind be in you which was also in Christ Jesus"* (Philippians 2:5 NKJV). We are to live in the new covenant that God grants us in Christ, which restores our unity with God's will:

> *"This is the covenant I will make with the house of Israel after that time," declares the LORD. "I will put my law in their minds and write it on their hearts. I will be their God, and they will be my people."*
>
> (Jeremiah 31:33)

Prayer: Father, I pray that I may
follow Jesus' example of a life of obedience.
In Jesus' name, amen.

Thought: God will reveal His plans to us as we live
in the Spirit of Christ.

Reading: **Exodus 19–20; Matthew 18:21–35**

JANUARY 29

Are You Willing?

I n a previous devotional, I asked, "What gives you the right to pray?" It is not only your calling in creation, but also your redemption in Christ that gives you this right. This is a solid truth that dispels doubt, fear, uncertainty, and timidity in regard to prayer.

Because of Christ, you can have a relationship of love with God the Father, the certainty of your redemption, an understanding of your calling and authority in Christ, and a clear idea of God's purpose for your life. God wants you to live confidently in the authority He has given you. Christ says,

> I tell you the truth, whatever you bind on earth will be bound in heaven, and whatever you loose on earth will be loosed in heaven. Again, I tell you that if two of you on earth agree about anything you ask for, it will be done for you by my Father in heaven.

(Matthew 18:18–19)

Do you want God to bring about His purposes for your life and for our fallen world? Invite Him to do so through prayer.

From Genesis to Revelation, God always found a human being to help Him accomplish His purposes. He comes to you now and asks, in effect, "Are you willing? Will you help Me fulfill My purposes for your life and for the earth? Or are you content to live an unfulfilled existence and to let the influences of sin and Satan encroach upon your world? 'Who is he who will devote himself to be close to me?' (Jeremiah 30:21)."

Prayer: Father, I pray that my desire to be close to You
will increase. Help me to live in oneness with You
and Your purposes, through the Spirit of Christ.
In Jesus' name, amen.

Thought: *"Who is he who will devote himself to be close to me?"*

Reading: **Exodus 21–22; Matthew 19**

Putting Prayer into Practice

For several days, we have talked about our redemption in Christ. Now, ask yourself these questions: Do I ever feel isolated from God, unsure of where I stand with Him, or unclear about how to pray? Am I praying based on the effects of the fall or the effects of Christ's redemptive work on my behalf?

Take some action steps in the coming days in regard to your redemption. Begin today to apply the redemption of Christ to your prayer life by acknowledging Jesus' restoration of your relationship with the Father and your purpose of dominion. Remind yourself daily that your redemption means that Satan and sin no longer have authority over you, that you have access to the Father and authority through Jesus' name, and that you have authority through the Word of God.

Start approaching God based on this promise: *"Let us then approach the throne of grace with confidence, so that we may receive mercy and find grace to help us in our time of need"* (Hebrews 4:16).

Now let us pray together:

Prayer: Heavenly Father, thank You for never giving up on us but for redeeming us for Yourself and Your purposes through Jesus Christ, the Second Adam. Paul prayed for the Thessalonians that You would count them worthy of Your calling, and that by Your power You would fulfill every good purpose of theirs and every act prompted by their faith. We ask You to count us worthy of our calling and to enable us to fulfill Your purposes, through the grace, faith, and authority we have in Christ. We pray these things in the name of Jesus, our Redeemer and King. Amen.

Thought: Am I praying based on the effects of the fall or the effects of Christ's redemptive work on my behalf?

Reading: **Exodus 23–24; Matthew 20:1–16**

Principles of Authority in Prayer

Today, reflect on these principles of authority in prayer:

1. God's plan of redemption is consistent with His character and purposes. He redeemed man while keeping man's free will and earthly authority intact.

2. Through Christ we are restored to our purpose, and through Him we have a right to pray with authority.

3. As the Second Adam, Christ is the image of God, exhibits a relationship of love with God, lives to do God's will, and reigns as King of the earth and Judge of mankind.

4. Christ reclaimed our earthly authority in these ways:

   • Jesus came as a man. Thus He was a qualified Representative of earthly authority.

   • Jesus was perfectly obedient and sinless. As the Son of God, He restored man's relationship with the Father by overcoming sin and death through His sacrifice on the cross.

   • Jesus rose victoriously. He was qualified to defeat sin and Satan, regain authority over the earth, and be its rightful King.

5. The position and authority that Jesus won have been returned to mankind through spiritual rebirth in Christ. (See John 3:5.)

6. When we do not live in our position of authority, it is because we do not recognize or accept our calling in Christ, because we do not know our covenant rights.

7. Man's redemption allows him to have dominion. This means that Satan and sin have no authority over us; we have access to the Father and authority through Jesus' name, and we have authority through the Word of God.

8. Jesus is our model of dominion authority. What He accomplished on earth, He accomplished in His humanity, even though He was also divine. He relied on the grace and Spirit of God, as we can.

9. Our right to pray comes from both our calling in creation and our redemption in Christ.

Reading: **Exodus 25–26; Matthew 20:17–34**

How to Enter God's Presence

To pray, we must enter into God's presence with the right spirit, approach, and preparation. The term "entering into God's presence" is frequently used in the church today to refer to worship and prayer. However, in casual, twenty-first century Christianity, few really understand this concept. We often fall short of entering into God's presence because we lack a genuine reverence for Him.

When I was growing up in the Bahamas, a man would remove his hat when he walked past a church in order to show respect for the place in which God was worshipped. Today, we say, "That's unnecessary. It's the attitude of the heart that counts." Yet I think we have lost the attitude with the custom. We need to be spiritually sensitive to God's holiness, might, and worthiness of reverence.

We must also enter God's presence with a heart of love. Jesus said the greatest commandment of all is to *"love the Lord your God with all your heart and with all your soul and with all your mind"* (Matthew 22:37). God is saying to the church, in essence, "Don't obey Me because of the things you want from Me. Obey Me because you love Me. *'If you love me, you will obey what I command'* (John 14:15). If you love Me, you won't need chastisement and discipline to do what I ask of you."

God doesn't want us to use Him merely as safety insurance from hell. He wants a relationship, not a religion. He wants to be our Father. He wants communion with us—an atmosphere of intimacy in which we express our love, discover His will, and then pursue it. Communion is entering into the mind and heart of God to become one with Him and His purposes.

Prayer: Father, please show me how to have oneness of heart with You. I want to give You the reverence and love that You deserve. In Jesus' name, amen.

Thought: Enter God's presence with the right spirit, approach, and preparation.

Reading: **Exodus 27–28; Matthew 21:1–22**

Enter with a Pure Heart

To seek God, we need holiness, for *"without holiness no one will see the Lord"* (Hebrews 12:14). As Jesus said, *"Blessed are the pure in heart, for they will see God"* (Matthew 5:8). I don't believe these verses refer to seeing God in heaven after we die, but rather to seeing God now, in the sense of entering into His presence in a relationship of intimacy so we can know His heart and mind.

What does it mean to be pure in heart? *Pure* means holy. Therefore, Jesus was saying, in effect, "Blessed are the holy in heart, for they will see God." The word *holy* means to "sanctify, or set apart," or "to be set." *"Blessed are the* [set] *in heart, for they will see God."* When you are pure in heart, your mind is set on God and His ways.

"I am the LORD your God; consecrate yourselves [set yourselves apart] *and be holy, because I am holy"* (Leviticus 11:44). *"I am the LORD, who makes you holy"* (Leviticus 20:8). Perhaps no word describes God better than *holiness.* God is saying, "Set yourself in the same way that I set myself; be holy, just as I am holy." To consecrate yourself means to position yourself in such a way that you say, "I'm not going to stop until I get what I'm going after."

Leviticus 20:26 says, *"You are to be holy to me because I, the LORD, am holy, and I have set you apart from the nations to be my own."* Holiness always involves separation. It has to do with fixing yourself on God and not being influenced by people whose minds are not centered on Him and who do not believe His Word.

Prayer: Father, I desire to be holy as You are holy.
Show me how to consecrate myself unto You and Your Word.
In Jesus' name, amen.

Thought: Holiness is critical to prayer because
"without holiness no one will see the Lord."

Reading: **Exodus 29–30; Matthew 21:23–46**

Holiness and Integrity

Holiness means "one"—not the numeric value, but one in the sense of "complete." Holiness connotes the concept of integrity, a quality God has because *what He says, what He does, and who He is are the same.* God always does what He says He will because He is one with Himself.

God's presence cannot abide anything that isn't holy. In the Old Testament, anyone who entered His presence without being holy died. God warned the priests, in effect, "Do not come into My presence unless you are holy, because I am holy. Coming without being holy will destroy you." Those who perished in this way died because holiness and impurity cannot coexist. The pure alone will see God. (See Matthew 5:8.)

When we pray, we must have integrity. God says, *"You will seek me and find me when you seek me with all your heart"* (Jeremiah 29:13). We can't just *say* we seek God; we must *really seek Him* if we want to find Him. We must determine, like Jacob, "God, I'm not going to let You go until I see you." (See Genesis 32:24–30.)

What does it mean to "see" God in relation to prayer? The Scriptures say, *"Stand still, and see the salvation of the LORD"* (Exodus 14:13; 2 Chronicles 20:17 NKJV). In essence, God says, "If you are holy, then I will manifest Myself to you. You will see My salvation in your life." If you are convinced that He will do what He has promised, then you will see Him answer prayer. In this sense, holiness is being convinced that what God says and what He does are equivalent.

Prayer: Father God, You are holy because
Your words, actions, and identity are one.
Help me to be holy as You are holy.
In Jesus' name, amen.

Thought: If you are holy, what you believe, say, and do
will be the same.

Reading: **Exodus 31–33; Matthew 22:1–22**

A Double-Minded Man

*If any of you lacks wisdom, he should ask God, who gives generously to all without finding fault, and it will be given to him. But when he asks, he must believe and not doubt, because he who doubts is like a wave of the sea, blown and tossed by the wind. That man should not think he will receive anything from the Lord; he is a **double-minded man, unstable in all he does.*** (James 1:5–8, emphasis added)

A person who is *"double-minded"* and *"unstable in all he does"* demonstrates unholiness by the inconsistency between what he says and what he actually believes and does. God says to us, in effect, "If you ask Me for something and then doubt that I will give it, don't even think you will receive it."

If God were not true to His Word, He would be acting in an unholy way. Because we know God is holy, we can believe He will fulfill what He has promised. Since God is holy, we, too, must be holy to receive answers to prayer. Note that only when the followers of Jesus were of one accord was the Holy Spirit given to them. (See Acts 2:1 NKJV.)

Double-mindedness is the opposite of holiness and integrity. Again, if you have integrity, then your words, actions, and beliefs are consistent. If you tell God you believe Him, but act in the opposite way, you lack integrity, purity, and holiness. You are double-minded. *"That man should not think he will receive anything from the Lord"* (James 1:7).

Prayer: Father, I do not want to be a double-minded believer. I will stay in Your Word and believe it. You are faithful and true, and You will fulfill what You have promised. Thank you, Lord. In Jesus' name, amen.

Thought: If you seek God with all your heart, mind, and conscience, He promises that you will find Him.

Reading: **Exodus 34–35; Matthew 22:23–46**

A Kingdom of Priests

When God told Moses, *"Go and tell the Israelites, 'You will be for me a **kingdom of priests** and a holy nation'"* (Exodus 19:6, emphasis added), He was reflecting His purposes for mankind from Adam to Abraham to Jacob to the children of Israel, to the church. God's plan is that we be His representatives or "priests" on earth. In God's perspective, the priesthood is not just for a special group of people, but for all who belong to Him. God's purposes are eternal, and His original plan for mankind, which began with Adam, was passed on to succeeding generations.

The first man was created as a priest—one who served as God's intermediary for the earth. We know that God wanted Adam to spread His will and His nature throughout the earth, to administer His kingdom by filling the world with a single "nation" of Spirit-led people. Adam failed, and the earth became populated with many nations who did not know God. God created a nation—Israel—to serve as priest before the other nations. All the people of this nation were to be priests, as we saw in Exodus 19:6. Israel also failed to fulfill God's calling, so God chose a small group from that nation, a tribe called the Levites, to serve as priests. God instructed the Levites to mediate for the nation of Israel. This would enable Israel to fulfill its calling as God's representative to the other nations so that, ultimately, all nations would return to Him. That was the purpose of the Levitical priesthood: to restore the purpose of God to Israel so Israel could help restore God's purpose for the world.

Prayer: Father, thank You for desiring a priesthood of believers.
I belong to You; teach me how to serve You as You desire.
In Jesus' name, amen.

Thought: God wants to win the world through a priesthood of
believers.

Reading: **Exodus 36–38; Matthew 23:1–22**

 DAILY POWER & PRAYER DEVOTIONAL

A Faithful Priest Forever

Yesterday, we saw that the Levitical priests were intercessors or mediators between God and the people of Israel. In the book of Leviticus, we find God's commandments to the priests. The Levitical priesthood was to restore the purpose of God to Israel.

However, just as Adam and the entire nation of Israel had, this Levitical priesthood failed to follow God and became corrupted. God then sent the prophets to tell the priests to return to Him, but Israel killed or ignored the prophets. Finally, God had to come personally. He raised up a Priest—not only from the line of Abraham, but also from His own house, One who would be faithful—Jesus, the Son of God, our High Priest. *"God said to him, 'You are my Son; today I have become your Father.' And he says in another place, 'You are a priest forever, in the order of Melchizedek'"* (Hebrews 5:5-6).

This Priest served God perfectly. He knew how to enter God's presence and how to represent man to God and God to man. He created a new nation of people—the church—to be God's priests to the world. God told the church the same thing He had said to Israel, because God's purposes are eternal. The apostle Peter wrote,

> *You also, like living stones, are being built into a spiritual house to be* **a holy priesthood,** *offering spiritual sacrifices acceptable to God through Jesus Christ....But you are a chosen people,* **a royal priesthood,** *a holy nation, a people belonging to God, that you may declare the praises of him who called you out of darkness into his wonderful light.*
>
> (1 Peter 2:5, 9, emphasis added)

Prayer: Father, You have sent a true and faithful Priest to us.
Please show me how to follow His example.
In Jesus' name, amen.

Thought: Jesus is our true and faithful High Priest.

Reading: **Exodus 39–40; Matthew 23:23–29**

A New Nation of Priests

W hen God told Abraham He would create a great nation from Abraham's lineage and that through him all nations of the world would be blessed, His intent was to redeem the whole world. Keeping His Word, God created a new nation from Abraham's descendant, Jesus of Nazareth, and his spiritual offspring who believe in Jesus—*"those who are of the faith of Abraham"* (Romans 4:16, emphasis added).

This new nation comprises both Israelites (Jews) and Gentiles (non-Jews) who have placed their faith in Christ. It is the single nation of Spirit-led people that was God's original purpose: *"There is neither Jew nor Greek, slave nor free, male nor female, for you are all one in Christ Jesus"* (Galatians 3:28).

When the Lord Himself came to earth as God the Son, His intent was to create a new nation in which all would receive the Holy Spirit, through whom they could be His intermediaries for the world. In the Old Testament, Joel prophesied,

> *And afterward, I will pour out my Spirit on all people. Your sons and daughters will prophesy, your old men will dream dreams, your young men will see visions. Even on my servants, both men and women, I will pour out my Spirit in those days.* (Joel 2:28–29)

In this new nation of believers, people are no longer separated and categorized. If anyone—male or female, young or old—repents of sin and receives Christ, God fills that person with His Spirit and makes him His priest. As believers, you and I are priests before God. The Bible calls the priesthood an eternal ordinance. (See Numbers 18:8 NKJV.) It is forever!

Prayer: Father, thank You for pouring out Your Holy Spirit on Your people so that we may serve You and help reconcile the world to You. You have enabled us to serve You as priests forever!
I thank you in Jesus' precious name, amen.

Thought: God created a new nation of Spirit-filled intercessors.

Reading: **Leviticus 1–3; Matthew 24:1–28**

Entering His Presence as Priests

A aron, the first high priest, is a model for us as the priesthood of believers who serve God in Christ. God's commandments to Aaron help us understand our New Testament role as *"a royal priesthood"* (1 Peter 2:9). From God's instructions to Aaron on how to enter His presence on the Day of Atonement, we may understand how to come into His presence today.

For the next week or so, we will study Leviticus 16 to discover ten ways to enter and remain in God's presence, where we can commune with Him, offer effectual prayer, and mediate on the world's behalf.

First, we need a clear appropriation of *God's grace* in our lives. Leviticus 16:3 says, *"This is how Aaron is to enter the sanctuary area: with a young bull for a sin offering and a ram for a burnt offering."* God told Aaron to offer animal sacrifices to atone for the sins of Israel. Aaron could not enter the sanctuary area without the sin offering and burnt offering. Similarly, God says to us, "If you desire to enter My presence, your sin has to be dealt with." Therefore, the first step in prayer is not to present our petitions, but to examine our life for sins.

Sometimes sins are not glaring; they may be more subtle. They may relate to our families, the church, our finances, or our jobs. When we go to God in prayer, He may say, "I have a problem with this area. You want Me to cooperate with you, but you have disobeyed Me. If I answer your prayer, I am condoning disobedience." God wants to answer our prayers. That's why He wants us to confess our sins and appropriate His grace.

Prayer: Father, reveal to me the sins, both subtle and glaring, that keep me from You. I want to walk in Your grace and holiness. In Jesus' name, amen.

Thought: Do I examine my life as I come before God in prayer?

Reading: **Leviticus 4–5; Matthew 24:29–51**

He Is Faithful and Just to Forgive

First John 1:9 says, *"If we confess our sins, he is faithful and just and will forgive us our sins and purify us from all unrighteousness."* This promise applies to Christian believers who have a relationship with Christ. God wants to bless us and answer our prayers, so He tells us to deal with our sins.

We need to accept Christ's sacrifice and repent from wrongdoing. We need to uproot the secret sin and disobedience within us so we can pray effectively. Our sins are forgiven when we go to Christ, who covers us with His blood and cleanses us. We need continual cleansing so we can live before God in holiness—the holiness Christ died to provide.

God essentially says, "If you want Me to do business with you, you have to get rid of sin, disobedience, and neglect." *"But your iniquities have separated you from your God; your sins have hidden his face from you, so that he will not hear"* (Isaiah 59:2). The point is not to feel guilty about these sins, but rather to ask for forgiveness and receive cleansing. God is gracious, and we can even ask Him to forgive the sins we don't realize we have committed. King David prayed, *"Who can discern his errors? Forgive my hidden faults"* (Psalm 19:12). We also have this promise from God's Word:

> *For as high as the heavens are above the earth, so great is his love for those who fear him; as far as the east is from the west, so far has he removed our transgressions from us.* (Psalm 103:11–12)

Prayer: Father, You are a God of forgiveness. As I walk with You, please reveal the secret sins of my heart so that I might forsake them. Please forgive my sins and cleanse me from unrighteousness. In Jesus' name, amen.

Thought: God has promised throughout His Word to forgive; our part is to repent.

Reading: **Leviticus 6–7; Matthew 25:1–30**

Receiving Forgiveness

To receive forgiveness, we don't bring animal sacrifices as the Israelites did, but our sins must still be atoned for by blood. The *principles* of the Old Testament still apply in the New Testament, which reveals their significance. For example, *"the* [Old Testament] *law requires that nearly everything be cleansed with blood, and without the shedding of blood there is no forgiveness"* (Hebrews 9:22). The difference in the New Testament is that the sacrifice was fulfilled once and for all in Christ, the Lamb of God. *"He sacrificed for their sins once for all when he offered himself"* (Hebrews 7:27).

First John 1:7 says, *"But if we walk in the light, as he is in the light, we have fellowship with one another, and the blood of Jesus, his Son, purifies us from all sin."* When you are cleansed with the blood of Jesus, nothing separates you from God. You can have genuine fellowship with Him and with other believers, which brings the power of agreement in prayer.

God is serious about holiness and obedience. We can't live in sin and unbelief if we want our prayers answered. If you struggle with a particular sin, surrender it to God, ask Him to purify you (see 1 John 1:9), and seek the counsel of mature believers so this sin will not block your relationship with God. Take your sins to His throne of grace, where He waits to forgive you. *"To the Lord our God belong mercy and forgiveness"* (Daniel 9:9 NKJV). *"In* [Christ] *we have redemption through his blood, the forgiveness of sins"* (Ephesians 1:7).

Prayer: Father, thank You that You are a God of mercy and
forgiveness. May I never take for granted the reality
that my sins are covered by Jesus' redeeming blood.
In Jesus' name, amen.

Thought: Forgiveness of our sins brings power in prayer.

Reading: **Leviticus 8–10; Matthew 25:31–46**

Putting on Righteousness

Aaron's priestly preparation for entering the presence of God also included what I call "putting on righteousness." *"He is to put on the sacred linen tunic, with linen undergarments next to his body"* (Leviticus 16:4). This second preparation corresponds to the New Testament admonition, *"Put on the new self, created to be like God in true righteousness and holiness"* (Ephesians 4:24). God tells us to be clothed with our new righteousness and holiness in Him.

In Ephesians 6:11–20, Paul talked about putting on the *"full armor of God"* (vv. 11, 13). I believe this analogy presents the believer preparing for prayer. (See verses 18–20.) Before we pray, we need to be wearing *"the helmet of salvation"* (v. 17). This refers to our atonement: being saved by the blood of Christ and being cleansed from our sins.

We are also to put on *"the breastplate of righteousness"* (v. 14). A breastplate protects the heart and other precious organs. With this analogy, God is saying, "I want you to be pure in the most vital areas of your life." We can do that only by appropriating the righteousness of Christ through faith: *"God made him who had no sin to be sin for us, so that in him we might become the righteousness of God"* (2 Corinthians 5:21). We also need to live in that righteousness, doing what is right by keeping in step with the Spirit. (See Galatians 5:25.)

When we put on God's righteousness, we can rejoice before the Lord:

> I delight greatly in the LORD; my soul rejoices in my God. For he has clothed me with garments of salvation and arrayed me in a robe of righteousness, as a bridegroom adorns his head like a priest, and as a bride adorns herself with her jewels. (Isaiah 61:10)

Prayer: Father, thank You for clothing me in the righteousness of Your Son. I rejoice in the priestly clothing You have given me. In Jesus' name, amen.

Thought: We come into God's presence only through the righteousness of Christ.

Reading: **Leviticus 11–12; Matthew 26:1–25**

Putting on Truth and Honesty

L et us look again at how Aaron was to enter God's holy place, as described in Leviticus:

> *He is to put on the sacred linen tunic, with linen undergarments next to his body; he is to tie the linen sash around him and put on the linen turban. These are sacred garments; so he must bathe himself with water before he puts them on.* (Leviticus 16:4)

In the analogy of the armor of God, the linen sash corresponds to the *"belt of truth"*: *"Stand therefore, having your loins girt about with truth* [*"with the belt of truth buckled around your waist"* NIV]" (Ephesians 6:14 KJV). The sash covers the secret areas of your life. David said, *"Surely you desire truth in the inner parts; you teach me wisdom in the inmost place"* (Psalm 51:6). The third preparation for entering God's presence, therefore, is to practice truth and honesty.

Do we fear the Lord, desiring to be people of truth? We are to gird ourselves with the sash of truth by being transparent and clean before the Lord. Is this your desire? The high priest had to come before God in truth and purity, and as His *"royal priesthood"* (1 Peter 2:9), we are to come before Him in the same way.

"Who may ascend the hill of the LORD? *Who may stand in his holy place? He who has clean hands and a pure heart"* (Psalm 24:3–4). We can be pure before God by turning from our sinful ways, receiving forgiveness through Christ, and walking in the Spirit. (See Romans 8:3–4.)

Prayer: Father, I desire a heart of honesty. I will put on
Your Word as the belt of truth. Help me to walk always
in that truth, through Your Spirit.
In Jesus' name, amen.

Thought: Be transparent and clean before the Lord.

Reading: **Leviticus 13; Matthew 26:26–50**

Cleansed by God's Word

These are sacred garments; so he must bathe himself with water before
he puts them on. (Leviticus 16:4)

B efore Aaron put on the sacred garments of the priesthood, he had
to cleanse himself. Likewise, before we enter God's presence, we
must be cleansed; this is the fourth preparation.

In the Old Testament, Aaron had to wash his entire body with water
and put on linen in order to be clean when he entered the holiest places
of the tabernacle. With the fulfillment of the law in the New Testament,
we no longer need to wash with actual water. In John 15:3, Christ told
His disciples, *"You are already clean because of the word I have spoken to you."*
Ephesians 5:25–26 says, *"Christ loved the church and gave himself up for her*
to make her holy, cleansing her by the washing with water through the word."

Christ said we are clean through the words He has spoken. The
Word of God is our water for spiritual cleansing; therefore, we need to
meditate continually on the Scriptures. David emphasized this truth:

How can a young man keep his way pure? By living according to
your word. I seek you with all my heart; do not let me stray from your
commands. I have hidden your word in my heart that I might not sin
against you. (Psalm 119:9–11)

When we come before God, we need to make sure that we've read
the Word and that we are obeying it. Otherwise, we will enter God's presence with our own ideas and attitudes. The Word washes us completely,
cleansing our hearts and minds, purifying our attitudes and actions.

Prayer: Father, thank You for cleansing me
through Your Word. Help me to remain in Your Word
so I may enter into Your presence with a clean heart.
In Jesus' name, amen.

Thought: The cleansing of the Word will change your heart
and transform your life.

Reading: **Leviticus 14; Matthew 26:51–75**

Worship Rises Like Incense

[Aaron] is to take a censer full of burning coals from the altar before the LORD and two handfuls of finely ground fragrant incense and take them behind the curtain. He is to put the incense on the fire before the LORD, and the smoke of the incense will conceal the atonement cover above the Testimony, so that he will not die.

(Leviticus 16:12–13)

In the Bible, incense symbolizes *worship*. Jesus told the woman at the well, in effect, "The Samaritans seek God on the mountain; the Jews seek God in the temple in Jerusalem. Yet, if you really want to come into God's presence, you must worship Him in spirit and in honest motivation—in truth." (See John 4:19–24.)

Our fifth preparation for coming into God's presence includes worship. God has told us we need to worship, but sometimes we try to bypass this step and jump right into prayer. God tells us, "Honor My name first. Worship Me." He wants us to put some incense on the fire!

Worship leaders are very important in the body of Christ because they prepare the way for the congregation to enter into the Lord's presence. Problems can result when the worship leaders' hearts aren't right. If our corporate worship is not as it should be, our worship leaders should examine their hearts. Are they putting incense on the fire, or are they jumping over the fire, trying to enter God's presence without paying the price of purity?

Prayer: Father God, thank You for receiving my
praise and worship. Your Word says that You inhabit
the praises of Your people. Show me how to
worship You from a pure heart.
In Jesus' name, amen.

Thought: Worship is a choice of the heart.

Reading: **Leviticus 15–16; Matthew 27:1–26**

Separate Yourself to the Lord

No one is to be in the Tent of Meeting from the time Aaron goes in to make atonement in the Most Holy Place until he comes out, having made atonement for himself, his household and the whole community of Israel. (Leviticus 16:17)

Aaron was *separated* from the rest of the people when he entered God's presence. A sixth way we prepare for prayer is by separating ourselves from our normal environment and activities. When you seek God, you can't be listening to the radio, watching television, or listening to other people talk. You can't be distracted. If you plan to seek God, you must be serious about it. God says, "If you want to find Me, you will do so only if you seek Me with all your heart." (See Jeremiah 29:13.)

God told Aaron, in effect, "The Tent is where I will meet you." He didn't meet Aaron just anywhere. Aaron had to enter the Tent of Meeting to be in God's presence.

As with Aaron, God doesn't meet you just anywhere, in any way. In the Old Testament, there was an actual tent, a physical place. Yet remember that the New Testament fulfills the Old Testament. This means that there is still a place where God meets you in prayer, but it's not a building. It's not even your body. It's a place *in God!* God has prepared a place in Him *just for you*, and you need to enter that place. If your heart, your attitude, or your motives aren't right, God says, "You aren't yet in the place where I want you to be."

Prayer: Father, thank You for loving me so much
that You have given me a special place of prayer in You.
Help me to find that special place You have prepared for me.
In Jesus' name, amen.

Thought: God has prepared a place in Him just for you.

Reading: **Leviticus 17–18; Matthew 27:27–50**

Faith in God's Power

Then [Aaron] shall come out to the altar that is before the LORD and make atonement for it. He shall take some of the bull's blood and some of the goat's blood and put it on all the horns of the altar. He shall sprinkle some of the blood on it with his finger seven times to cleanse it and to consecrate it from the uncleanness of the Israelites.

(Leviticus 16:18–19)

In the Old Testament, the blood of animal sacrifices had atoning power. Yet when the high priest put the blood on the horns of the altar, he had to *believe* that God's power was great enough to atone for sin. After the sacrifices were offered on the people's behalf and the scapegoat was sent out into the desert, the people had to *believe* that the sacrificial offerings cleansed them from their sins. They needed faith in God's power to fulfill His promise. In requiring the high priest to sprinkle blood on the horns of the altar, I believe God was telling us, "I want you to confess that I have power to do anything I have promised you."

In the Old Testament, the power of atoning blood lasted only one year; the high priest returned each year on the Day of Atonement to sacrifice. Christ's death on the cross made these animal sacrifices obsolete because He sacrificed Himself once—for all people and for all time: *"Unlike the other high priests, he does not need to offer sacrifices day after day, first for his own sins, and then for the sins of the people. He sacrificed for their sins once for all when he offered himself"* (Hebrews 7:27). It is now up to us to believe in the power of His sacrifice on our behalf. This then, is our seventh preparation: to believe.

Prayer: Father, thank You for sending Jesus to atone for my sins once and for all. I believe You have forgiven my sins. Help me not to take Your power and love for granted. In Jesus' name, amen.

Thought: God has the power to do what He has promised.

Reading: **Leviticus 19–20; Matthew 27:51–66**

The Power of Jesus' Blood

R omans 3:25 says, "*God presented him as a sacrifice of atonement, through faith in his blood.*" I wasn't around when Adam sinned. I wasn't there when Jesus died. How can blood shed two thousand years ago cleanse me today? Because *the blood still has power.* God says, in effect, "I received the animal sacrifices that the high priests brought to Me. When My power connected with them, it was so potent that it atoned for the sins of three million Israelites. How much more will the *'precious blood of Christ, a lamb without blemish or defect'* (1 Peter 1:18) atone for your sins?"

> When Christ came as high priest of the good things that are already here, he went through the greater and more perfect tabernacle that is not man-made, that is to say, not a part of this creation. He did not enter by means of the blood 'of goats and calves; but he entered the Most Holy Place once for all by his own blood, having obtained eternal redemption...How much more, then, will the blood of Christ, who through the eternal Spirit offered himself unblemished to God, cleanse our consciences from acts that lead to death, so that we may serve the living God! (Hebrews 9:11–12, 14)

Christ is the atoning Sacrifice for the sins of the world. (See 1 John 2:2.) When Jesus came to John to be baptized, John said, "Look—God has provided His own Lamb." (See John 1:29.) God provided this Lamb as the Sacrifice for our sins so we can enter the Holy of Holies where He dwells (see Hebrews 4:16), trembling because we fear God, but confident because we know Jesus' blood has completely cleansed us.

Prayer: Father God, I am in awe of Your love and power.
Thank You for sending Jesus as the Sacrifice for my sins.
Thank You that His blood has the power to cleanse me forever.
In Jesus' name, amen.

Thought: Christ's blood has the power to cleanse us from all sin.

Reading: **Leviticus 21–22; Matthew 28**

Give God the Glory

Aaron *"shall also burn the fat of the sin offering on the altar"* (Leviticus 16:25). After we enter God's presence through the blood of Jesus, believing in His power to cleanse us, the eighth preparation is to *give God the glory.*

God instructed the Israelites not to eat the fat of the sacrifices, but to collect it and burn it to Him on the altar. Fat is a symbol of glory because fat is excess. *"I am the LORD; that is my name! I will not give my glory to another or my praise to idols"* (Isaiah 42:8). *"How can I let myself be defamed? I will not yield my glory to another"* (Isaiah 48:11). God deserves all the glory for giving us the riches of redemption. We give God the glory by acknowledging and thanking Him for the abundance of His grace—for receiving, forgiving, and redeeming us so we can enter His glorious presence. God also desires the excess or glory of the material provision He's given us. We honor Him by giving to others out of the abundance of His blessings to us.

Our ninth preparation is to wash in the Word. In Leviticus 16:26, God instructed Aaron, *"The man who releases the goat as a scapegoat must wash his clothes and bathe himself with water; afterward, he may come into the camp."* The Word's first function is cleansing. Its second use is for appropriating God's promises. God is saying, in effect, "You have done all that you are supposed to do, and you have given Me the glory. I am pleased. Tell Me what you want." Since everything is clear between you and God, you can now *"present your requests to God"* (Philippians 4:6). Ask Him to fulfill His purposes based on His will and promises.

Prayer: Father, thank You for cleansing and redeeming me, and receiving me into Your presence. Thank You for the promises of Your Word. Please help me to glorify You in my words and actions. In Jesus' name, amen.

Thought: Are you giving God the glory and appropriating His promises?

Reading: **Leviticus 23–24; Mark 1:1–22**

Remain in the Anointing

*The priest who is anointed and ordained to succeed his father as high priest is to make atonement. He is to put on the sacred linen garments and make atonement for the Most Holy Place, for the Tent of Meeting and the altar, and for the priests and all the people of the community. **This is to be a lasting ordinance for you** [My people].*

(Leviticus 16:32–34, emphasis added)

O ur final instruction for entering God's presence is to remain in *the anointing.* We must maintain a right relationship with God so we may dwell continually in our meeting place with Him.

We can live in continual unity with God because of Christ's atonement for our sins. When Jesus Christ came, He was anointed and ordained as High Priest by God. The high priests who preceded Him were only types of Him. His atonement is eternal—an everlasting ordinance. *"When this priest had offered for all time one sacrifice for sins, he sat down at the right hand of God"* (Hebrews 10:12).

To be in God's presence, we must remain in a state of preparedness for prayer; we must not approach God in a careless way. It is important to learn what it means to honor the Lord and reflect His holy nature in our lives.

All these steps of preparation we have looked at are important to God because Jesus Christ came to make them possible. It is because of Christ alone that we can enter the presence of an almighty and holy God and call Him Father.

Prayer: Father, I can enter Your presence because Your Son Jesus opened the way by His sacrifice. May I always maintain a right relationship with you, through Christ. In Jesus' name, amen.

Thought: We must follow God's instructions and ways if we want to remain in His presence.

Reading: **Leviticus 25; Mark 1:23–45**

Putting Prayer into Practice

Today, let's take time to think about how we currently enter into prayer. We should ask ourselves some heartfelt questions: In what attitude or manner do I approach God in prayer? Am I being casual about the sin in my life, without regard for God's holiness? Do I think I can get God to hear my prayers by doing good deeds—or do I come to Him through Christ alone? What does it mean to be a member of the priesthood of believers? Do I rejoice that I can enter God's presence because of Christ's sacrifice?

I encourage you to practice what you have learned about how to come into God's presence. Before you pray, review the ten steps for entering and remaining in the presence of God. See what steps you may be omitting and which areas you need to correct. Finally, consider your special God-given role as priest, or intercessor, before God on behalf of the world. Let that knowledge guide how you pray.

Now, let's pray together:

Prayer: Heavenly Father, Your Word says that the pure in heart are truly blessed, because they will see You. We want to enter into Your presence. We want to be in the place where You meet us. Guide us to that place. Forgive us for being careless and unthinking in the way we approach You. We acknowledge that You are a holy and righteous God. We receive the cleansing of our sins through the blood of Jesus. We worship You in humility and love. Thank you for the privilege of entering confidently into the place where You dwell, because of the atonement Your Son made on our behalf. We pray this in the name of Jesus, the Lamb of God who takes away all our sin. Amen.

Thought: *"You...are being built into a spiritual house to be a holy priesthood."*

Reading: **Leviticus 26–27; Mark 2**

Principles for the Priesthood of Believers

R eflect on these principles today:

1. As believers, we are *"a chosen people, a royal priesthood, a holy nation, a people belonging to God"* (1 Peter 2:9).
2. As God's priests, we are to intercede for others so they will return to God and be coworkers in His purposes.
3. Ten steps of preparedness for entering God's presence in prayer are:

   - *Appropriate God's Grace:* Acknowledge God's holiness, turn from your sins, and be cleansed through the blood of Christ.
   - *Put on Righteousness:* Appropriate the righteousness of Christ through faith. Live in that righteousness, doing what is right by keeping in step with the Spirit.
   - *Put on Truth and Honesty:* Be transparent and clean before the Lord, desiring truth in the innermost parts and living with integrity.
   - *Cleanse Yourself with the Word:* Before you come before God, make sure that you've *read* the Word and that you are *obeying* the Word.
   - *Worship and Praise God:* Honor and worship God in spirit and in truth (see John 4:24–24), acknowledging Him as your all in all.
   - *Separate Yourself:* Leave your normal environment, activities, and distractions. Find the place in God where He meets you, coming to Him with the right heart, attitude, and motives.
   - *Believe:* Have faith in God's power to keep His promises and in the effectiveness of Christ's sacrifice.
   - *Give God the Glory:* Acknowledge that God provided for your atonement and reconciliation, and is worthy to be praised.
   - *Wash in the Word:* Ask God to fulfill His purposes based on His will and promises.
   - *Remain in the Anointing:* Remain in a state of preparedness for prayer. Honor the Lord by reflecting His nature in your life.

Reading: **Numbers 1–2; Mark 3:1–19**

A Lifestyle of Prayer

O f all the things Jesus' disciples observed Him say and do, the Bible records only one thing they asked Him to teach them—how to pray as He prayed. (See Luke 11:1.) We might wonder, "Why would the disciples ask to learn to pray instead of how to do 'big things,' like feeding multitudes, calming storms, casting out demons, healing the sick, raising the dead, or walking on water?" *It is because they saw Jesus pray more than anything else.*

The disciples lived with Jesus. They went everywhere He went and observed Him for three and a half years. The Scriptures suggest that Christ prayed for hours every morning. Mark 1:35 says, *"Very early in the morning, while it was still dark ["rising up a great while before day" KJV], Jesus got up, left the house and went off to a solitary place, where he prayed."* Jesus would get up while the disciples were still snoring and slip off by Himself to pray for hours. The disciples would wake up and ask, "Where's the Master?" When they found Him, they would see Him praying.

Jesus would spend five hours with God His Father, then travel somewhere to spend a few minutes healing a blind man or casting out a demon. Note the ratio: He spent hours praying and a few minutes ministering. The disciples probably said, "That's impressive. This must mean that what Jesus does in the morning in prayer is even more important than everything else He does during the day!"

What is the most important thing you will do today? Will it be spending time in prayer before the Lord? Shouldn't it be?

Prayer: Father, please forgive me for not placing the right priority on prayer. Thank You for Jesus' example that prayer is the primary thing, and that we can walk in a lifestyle of prayer. In Jesus' name, amen.

Thought: The secret to Jesus' success in ministry was a lifestyle of prayer.

Reading: **Numbers 3–4; Mark 3:20–35**

Too Busy to Pray?

The great Reformation leader Martin Luther said something like this: "When I have a lot to do in a day, I spend more time in prayer, because more work is done by prayer than by work itself." He was right. If you are to busy to pray, you are too busy.

We can never be too busy to pray because prayer makes our lives much more focused, efficient, and peaceful. Learning this principle has been essential to me. When I have many things on my heart and mind, or when I face overwhelming circumstances, I don't try tackling these problems myself. I go to God in prayer, and He gives me the wisdom and guidance I need. The church today doesn't yet understand this truth. We spend just a few minutes with God, and then we try to do many hours of work in His name.

We often sing, "This is the day that the Lord has made." God is asking us, "If this is My day, then why don't you come and talk to Me about it?" We do many things in God's day that He didn't plan for us, so we must ask Him for His agenda. One hour with God in prayer can accomplish ten hours of work because it eliminates trial and error. God will tell you what is really important, and He will give you wisdom for the circumstances in your life.

Prayer enables you to think clearly and wisely. It gives you spiritual discernment that you would otherwise lack. Jesus knew what was important because He spent time with the Father. Hours with God make minutes with men effective.

Prayer: Father, help me to realize that my own efforts can be wasted if I haven't heard from You. Give me Your agenda for my day as I come to You in prayer.
In Jesus' name, amen.

Thought: "More work is done by prayer than by work itself."
—Martin Luther

Reading: **Numbers 5–6; Mark 4:1–20**

Prayer Saves Time

*P*rayer saves you time. Many of us say we believe this principle, but our lives suggest otherwise. We put off praying because we think it is a waste of time—or at least less important than other activities. Moreover, we think the length of time we pray is unimportant.

Why did Jesus spend hours in prayer? Because He had a genuine relationship with the Father, and any relationship takes time to build and maintain. God says to us, in effect, "You will get more done in My presence than you accomplish in the presence of other people. You spend all day talking foolishness with others, and in the end, nothing is solved, nothing has changed, and you're depressed. You could have spent those hours praying for the government, the gangs, and other situations."

When we spend time in prayer, God often uses *us* to change circumstances. Instead of having this powerful role in God's plan, we spend most of our time trying to figure out what God wants us to do, and we waste the whole day. Christ is saying to us, "I go to the Father first; I see what He's already done, and I do it." (See John 5:19–20.) This is the pattern He wants us to follow. Through prayer, man discovers what God has already done in the unseen, and in faith he sees it manifested on earth. (See Matthew 18:18.)

As you spend time with God, He will show you what you should do next. The time you save can be used in effectively serving His kingdom.

Prayer: Father, thank You for caring about me so much that You want to share Your plans with me. Show me what to do today as I seek Your direction. In Jesus' name, amen.

Thought: When you spend time with God, He reveals what He wants you to do next.

Reading: **Numbers 7–8; Mark 4:21–41**

My Father Is Always at Work

One day, Jesus healed a man who had been sick for thirty-eight years. People reacted in various ways: some were deeply impressed, some were angry, and some wanted answers. *"So, because Jesus was doing these things on the Sabbath, the Jews persecuted him. Jesus said to them, 'My Father is always at his work to this very day, and I, too, am working'"* (John 5:16–17). The *New King James Version* reads, *"My Father has been working until now, and I have been working."*

When I discovered what Jesus was teaching here, my perspective of myself and my relationship to the Father changed. In effect, Christ was saying to those who questioned His healing, "I spent time with My Father this morning. I already had my whole day worked out for Me because I had fellowship with the One who made days. My Father has already healed the people I'm touching. Their healing is the result of My knowing what My Father is doing. I'm just manifesting it. My Father works; therefore, I work." What we do should manifest what God the Father has already done!

I tell you the truth, the Son can do nothing by himself; he can do only what he sees his Father doing, because whatever the Father does the Son also does. For the Father loves the Son and shows him all he does. (John 5:19–20)

Prayer: Father, help me realize that I can do nothing by myself, and that I need to seek Your will and Your purpose in prayer each day. Show me what You want me to do today. In Jesus' name, amen.

Thought: Jesus' ministry was to manifest the desires and works of the Father.

Reading: **Numbers 9–11; Mark 5:1–20**

Manifesting God's Thoughts

Words are an extension of our thoughts, but we *are* what we think. Proverbs 23:7 says, *"As [a man] thinks in his heart, so is he"* (NKJV). God desires not just to talk to you, but to "think" to you. When Jesus said, "I do what I see My Father doing" (see John 5:19), He meant, "I do what I mentally see My Father thinking." God showed Jesus everything He was thinking and said to His Son, "Manifest that for Me."

When asked why He healed the sick man, Jesus said, in essence, "I am the Word. I manifest the thoughts of God. I have to heal this man because that is what I saw My Father doing." *"The Son can do nothing by himself; he can do only what he sees his Father doing, because whatever the Father does the Son also does"* (John 5:19). In prayer, Jesus saw His Father heal, so Jesus healed. The Father wants to reveal His thoughts to us in prayer as well.

"For the Father loves the Son and shows him all he does" (John 5:20). Every time Jesus talked about His work, He mentioned the love of His Father. Jesus was saying, "My Father loves Me so much that He does not just talk to Me, because talking isn't intimate enough. He loves Me so much that He speaks to My Spirit and mind." The Father will share His thoughts with us in prayer because He has the same love for us. (See John 17:23.)

Commune with the Lord in prayer. He wants to share His thoughts with you.

Prayer: Father, I come to Your throne in the name of Jesus, Your Son. I want to commune with You and hear Your heart and thoughts toward me. Please help me to spend my early morning time with You.
In Jesus' name, amen.

Thought: Spend time with the Lord to find out what is on His mind.

Reading: **Numbers 12–14; Mark 5:21–43**

Jesus Was Naturally Supernatural

When God speaks to us, He usually speaks to our minds through our spirits. Many people are waiting for a burning bush or an angel. They miss God because they're waiting in the wrong way. God doesn't generally speak audibly—that's not intimate enough. He speaks directly to our spirits. For example, you may say, "I think I should call and encourage Brother Smith." That's God, saying He wants you to encourage Brother Smith. How do you know? It's when an idea keeps coming back to you. If you don't make the call, two hours later the thought will return. You might dismiss it, only to learn that Brother Smith really needed encouragement. Yet you didn't respond to God's prompting because you wanted something more "profound." You wanted a prophet to appear and say, "Thus saith the Lord: 'Call Brother Smith.'"

Jesus was naturally supernatural. He would ask a man who was an invalid, "How long have you been sick?" "Thirty-eight years." "Fine. Take up your bed and walk." To a woman who was bent over, He would say, "Straighten up," and she would straighten up. To another, He'd ask, "Are you blind?" "Yes." He would touch the person's eyes, and the person would see. The religious people said, "Wait a minute. You're not being spiritual enough. You're supposed to say, 'Stand back, everybody. I'm getting ready to perform a miracle.'" Religious people prepare a long time when they attempt to do miracles. Christ just walked around, spoke, touched—and things happened. People criticized Jesus because they thought He was not spiritual enough, but He was spiritual long before they knew. As we have seen, He was spiritual in prayer for five hours so He could be natural for one minute.

Prayer: Father, please show me how to walk in the
supernatural in a way that is natural. Speak to
my spirit, Lord, and give me ears to hear You.
In Jesus' name, amen.

Thought: God will speak to Your spirit; just turn your
heart toward Him.

Reading: **Numbers 15–16; Mark 6:1–29**

Common-Union with the Father

J esus wants us to spend much time in loving communion with the Father and to accomplish much for the kingdom. He prayed,

That all of them may be one, Father, just as you are in me and I am in you. May they also be in us so that the world may believe that you have sent me. I have given them the glory that you gave me, that they may be one as we are one. (John 17:21–22)

Jesus was referring not only to unity in the church, but also to the intimate union of believers with the Father and Son. He was saying, "Make My disciples one, the way You and I are one with each other. Make them one with You in the same way that I am." The Father loves you and wants the same communion or "common-union" with you that He had with Jesus. Your prayer life can make you so intimate with God that you will naturally manifest His works, just as Jesus did.

Most people didn't know how Jesus spoke with such wisdom and did such miracles. The disciples knew Jesus' secret because they observed His lifestyle of prayer. They knew He had a special communion with the Father, so they said, in effect, "Lord, don't teach us to do miracles; teach us to pray." If we learn what they learned, we will do the things Jesus did. "Lord, teach us to pray!"

Prayer: Father, it is exciting that You desire
to have communion with me, as You had with Jesus.
Help me to develop an intimate relationship
with You and to manifest Your works.
In Jesus' name, amen.

Thought: The Father wants the same communion with you
that He had with Jesus.

Reading: **Numbers 17–19; Mark 6:30–56**

Prayer Does Not Come Automatically

For the next several days, we will study the model prayer that Jesus taught His disciples. Luke 11:1 says, *"One day Jesus was praying in a certain place. When he finished, one of his disciples said to him, 'Lord, teach us to pray, just as John taught his disciples.'"* The Scripture says, *"One day Jesus was praying."* The disciples were present, but they were not involved. While Jesus prayed, they observed Him.

Whenever the Bible mentions Jesus praying, it tells specific things about His actions. For example: *"After he had dismissed them, he went up on a mountainside by himself to pray. When evening came, he was there alone"* (Matthew 14:23). *"One of those days Jesus went out to a mountainside to pray, and spent the night praying to God"* (Luke 6:12). *"Very early in the morning, while it was still dark, Jesus got up, left the house and went off to a solitary place, where he prayed"* (Mark 1:35). Christ never seemed to pray with the disciples. What was the reason for this? I believe He wanted them to ask Him about this most important aspect of His ministry, and He also wanted to teach them that prayer is a personal relationship and responsibility. Corporate prayer should never be a substitute for private time with the Father.

Next, the disciples said, *"Lord, teach us to pray."* This implies that knowing how to pray is not automatic, or something they could do without His instruction. As young Jewish men, the disciples had been brought up in the synagogue, where they had been taught to pray. They daily read and repeated prayers in the synagogue. However, Jesus' prayers differed from what they had been taught. They prayed; He *prayed.* They spoke words; He secured *results.*

Prayer: Father, show me through Your Word all that
You wanted the disciples to know about prayer.
I want to pray as Christ did.
In Jesus' name, amen.

Thought: Prayer is a personal relationship and responsibility.

Reading: **Numbers 20–22; Mark 7:1–13**

When You Pray…

I n Luke 11:2, Jesus began to teach His disciples to pray. This means Jesus agreed that the disciples *needed to learn how to pray.* He confirmed that prayer is not automatic; it must be learned. When a person becomes a believer, he is usually told, "Read the Word, go to church, and pray." Yet many people don't realize that these things don't necessarily come naturally. We must learn how to study the Word, how to function in the body of Christ, and how to pray. A new believer who has never prayed may be told, "Just talk to God and tell Him how you feel." That sounds good—but that's not what Jesus taught His disciples.

Prayer is not just "talking to God." I used to teach that, and I used to pray that way, but nothing happened! I had to learn what Jesus taught His disciples before I could pray effectively.

If you have difficulty praying, don't be discouraged. Many people don't really understand prayer. They may whoop and holler when they pray, or they may use fancy words, but that doesn't mean they are praying correctly. Remember that Jesus said, *"And when you pray, do not keep on babbling like pagans, for they think they will be heard because of their many words ["much speaking" KJV]. Do not be like them, for your Father knows what you need before you ask him"* (Matthew 6:7–8). Many churches and religious groups have *"much speaking."* However, it is not noise that gets God's attention, nor is it how loudly we pray or even the big words we use. There is a way we are to pray, and it has to be learned.

Prayer: Father, I don't want to use meaningless words
to speak with You. Teach me how to pray
as You taught the disciples.
In Jesus' name, amen.

Thought: Jesus modeled a lifestyle of prayer.

Reading: **Numbers 23–25; Mark 7:14–37**

Our Model for Prayer

Jesus taught His disciples a sample prayer. We may call it the "Lord's Prayer," but, it is really a *model* for prayer. In other words, we don't need to repeat the words verbatim, but should use them as a pattern.

Our Father in heaven, hallowed be Your name. Your kingdom come. Your will be done on earth as it is in heaven. Give us day by day our daily bread. And forgive us our sins, for we also forgive everyone who is indebted to us. And do not lead us into temptation, but deliver us from the evil one. (Luke 11:2–4 NKJV)

Let's look together at this model prayer. Jesus began, "**Our** Father." The first thing we learn is that we never come alone to prayer. God is **our** Father. When we approach God, we are to bring other people's concerns with us, as well. Most of us go to prayer with our own shopping lists: our financial needs, our career needs, and so forth. We say, "Lord, please do these things for me." Our prayers are selfish if they don't include the concerns of others. God will ask, "Where is everybody else? All men are my concern." Therefore, we are to begin prayer by thinking of others as well as ourselves.

"Our **Father**." Second, we address God as "*Father*." We identify who He is. One definition of the word *father* is "source." We must confess that He is the Source who can provide for the needs of everyone. Whatever your problem, the Father has the answer. He is "*Abba*" (Mark 14:36), the Source.

Prayer: Lord, You are the Source of my life. I thank You that I can come before You in full assurance that You are my Father and that You want to hear from me.
In Jesus' name, amen.

Thought: Draw near to God, for He is your Father.

Reading: **Numbers 26–27; Mark 8:1–21**

Our Father in Heaven

O ur *Father in heaven*" (Luke 11:2 NKJV, emphasis added). In His model prayer, Jesus specifically mentioned heaven, the Father's dwelling, to remind us, "When you pray, remember that you're not praying to someone on earth."

Why is it important to be reminded of this? Because earth is where the problem is, and we need external help. When you pray, "*Our Father in heaven*" you are saying to God, "I recognize that I need help from outside my realm." It is a confession of submission. "You're greater than all of us, O Lord. We need *Your* help from heaven." This prayer also reminds us that if the Father is not on earth, we need an intermediary. We must depend on Jesus and the Holy Spirit to be our intermediaries with God, who is in heaven.

"**Hallowed** be *Your name.*" The word *hallowed* means reverenced, set apart, or sanctified. We are to worship the Father as the Holy One. Later on, we can make our requests, but we begin our prayer with worship.

When you pray, honor all the attributes of God's holiness, such as His love, faithfulness, integrity, and grace. Worship Him. Adore Him. Exalt Him. Magnify Him. Glorify Him. After you pray, keep honoring Him in your life and all your relationships.

Have you ever wondered how people can pray for long periods of time without running out of words? Christ says, "Begin by acknowledging that the Father is your all in all, and worship Him." We will never run out of reasons to worship God. Hallowed be His name!

Prayer: Father, You are greatly to be praised.
Help me never to forget the holiness of Your name.
In Jesus' precious name, amen.

Thought: "*Let the name of the LORD be praised, both now and forevermore*" (Psalm 113:2).

Reading: Numbers 28–30; Mark 8:22–38

It's Your Kingdom, Lord

Your kingdom come. Your will be done on earth as it is in heaven" (Luke 11:2). A true person of prayer is committed to God's kingdom and what He wants to accomplish. We should always ask God to fulfill His desires before our own.

We are to ask, "Father, what do You want to happen on earth?" God is delighted when we are excited about the things He's excited about. He will bless us in the course of accomplishing His work on earth. We don't have to worry about our own needs if we pray for God's will to be done in other people's lives.

God is pleased when we bring other people's requests to Him and ask Him to meet their needs. Remember, that is why we are to pray, "*Our Father*...." When you pray for other people, God will bless you. He will see that you have aligned your will with His will, that you are reaching out to others in love and compassion. He will answer your own requests because you are obeying Him.

James 5:16 emphasizes this truth: *"Pray for each other so that you may be healed."* When you minister to someone else, God ministers to your needs. Isn't that just like God? *"Give, and it will be given to you"* (Luke 6:38). Therefore, if you have problems, find someone else who has problems and start helping to solve them. If you need someone to pray for you, pray for someone else. If you need financial help, give to someone who has less than you do. In prayer, and in everything we do, we are to *think about God's kingdom first.*

Prayer: Father, may Your kingdom be revealed in my life.
Please help me to choose Your will over my own,
Your kingdom over having my own way.
In Jesus' name, amen.

Thought: God will bless you in the course of accomplishing His work on earth.

Reading: **Numbers 31–33; Mark 9:1–29**

The Lord's Provision Is Daily

G ive **us** *day by day our daily bread"* (Luke 11:3, emphasis added). The plural tense used in this statement is tied to the *"Our"* in *"Our Father"* (v. 2). If you tell God that you are bringing Him the concerns of other people, then, when you request bread, you have to request bread for everybody. We often pray, "Lord, provide for me," without thinking of anyone else. Yet Jesus tells us again, "Ask for others as well as for yourself. Pray for others."

In Jesus' day, the term "daily bread" was a cultural idiom that referred to everything necessary to make bread. When you pray, *"Give us day by day our daily bread,"* you ask not only for food, but also for the whole process that makes food possible. To make bread, you need sunshine, seed, soil, nitrogen, oxygen, nutrients, minerals, time, harvesting, grinding, ingredients, mixing, kneading, and baking. Implied in those steps are strength for the farmer to sow and harvest the grain and strength for the one mixing and kneading the bread. In other words, you are praying for healthy bodies and a healthy environment in which food can grow.

"Give us day by day our daily bread" is a loaded statement. It teaches us to thank God for His provision in every part of the process. We need to be praying specifically in this way. We take too much for granted and fail to ask God to protect and bless what we need for daily living—not only for our own sake, but also for the sake of others.

Prayer: Father, thank You for providing all of our needs according to Your glorious riches in Christ Jesus. In Jesus' name, amen.

Thought: Jehovah-Jireh is the Lord our Provider!

Reading: **Numbers 34–36; Mark 9:30–50**

Please Forgive Me, Lord

A nd *forgive us our sins, for we also forgive everyone who is indebted to us"* (Luke 11:4). There are a number of deep truths about kingdom living in Jesus' model prayer. Here, He was saying, "When you pray, consider those with whom you are in relationship." Check to see if anyone has anything against you or if you are holding anything against anyone. Don't expect answers to prayer if you ask God to forgive you but refuse to forgive others.

Jesus made this sobering statement: *"For if you forgive men when they sin against you, your heavenly Father will also forgive you. But if you do not forgive men their sins, your Father will not forgive your sins"* (Matthew 6:14–15). If God doesn't forgive you, He won't answer your prayer.

We often overlook the importance of our relationships and how they affect our prayers. For example, we go to church and sing a few worship songs, quickly forgetting our anger at others and subsequently neglecting to resolve to make things right. We let the songs cover up our anger, but it remains. Later, we remember what made us angry, and we allow it to fester into bitterness. Yet having good relationships is one of the keys to answered prayer:

> *Therefore, if you are offering your gift at the altar and there remember that your brother has something against you, leave your gift there in front of the altar. First go and be reconciled to your brother; then come and offer your gift.* (Matthew 5:23–24)

Prayer: Father, I ask for Your forgiveness. Help me to remember to forgive others as soon as I am injured, so that I can be free in my relationship with You. In Jesus' name, amen.

Thought: Having good relationships is one of the keys to answered prayer.

Reading: **Deuteronomy 1–2; Mark 10:1–31**

Choose to Forgive Others

J esus made it clear that we can't bring an unforgiving heart to a holy altar. We are to forgive freely.

Peter came to Jesus and asked, "Lord, how many times shall I for-give my brother when he sins against me? Up to seven times?" Jesus answered, "I tell you, not seven times, but seventy-seven times."
(Matthew 18:21-22)

When you pray, God will reveal your bitterness toward others. He will convict you of broken relationships you have forgotten. Once the Lord reveals them to you, He can talk to you about them. He can finally get through to you because you're listening.

You may have faith that God will answer your prayers, but your refusal to forgive renders your faith ineffectual. Galatians 5:6 says, *"The only thing that counts is faith expressing itself through love."* So God will say to you, "Yes, but faith works when love is in order, and you are not living in forgiveness." You need faith to please God (see Hebrews 11:6), but you also need love, for *"God is love"* (1 John 4:8, 16). Forgiveness frees your prayers to receive answers.

Assess your relationships. Have you sinned against anyone? Are you holding on to a grudge? Do you have any broken relationships? God looks for clean hands and a pure heart. (See Psalm 24:3-4.) A broken and a contrite heart the Lord will not ignore or despise. (See Psalm 51:17.) If we regard iniquity in our hearts, the Lord will not hear us. (See Psalm 66:18 KJV.) However, when we forgive others, God will also forgive us, opening a channel for Him to hear and answer our prayers.

Prayer: Father, please search my heart
to see if there is any wicked way in me.
If I am withholding forgiveness, reveal it to me.
In Jesus' name, amen.

Thought: We can't do business at a holy altar
when we have a bitter heart.

Reading: **Deuteronomy 3–4; Mark 10:32–52**

Keep Me Far from Temptation

A nd do not lead us into temptation, but deliver us from the evil one" (Luke 11:4). Does this verse mean God might steer us into temptation against our wills? Absolutely not! It means we are to ask God for wisdom so we won't put ourselves into situations that cause us to compromise our relationship with Him. Some of us set ourselves up for trouble, then ask God to deliver us. God is saying, "When you come before Me, pray for strength and wisdom to make good decisions and to avoid bad decisions and places that tempt you to sin."

Before His arrest and crucifixion, Jesus asked Peter, James, and John to stay with Him while He prayed in the garden of Gethsemane. But the disciples fell asleep. "'Could you men not keep watch with me for one hour?' [Jesus] asked Peter. 'Watch and pray so that you will not fall into temptation. The spirit is willing, but the body is weak'" (Matthew 26:40–41). Jesus knew that although he claimed he would die with Jesus, Peter was about to deny Him. He told Peter to remain alert and pray.

Jesus encouraged this same watchfulness and prayer when He taught us to pray, "Do not lead us into temptation." We must be alert to the temptations and weaknesses that threaten our relationship with God and our testimony for Him—things Satan will exploit to cause us to stumble. Then we need to pray that God will keep us from succumbing to them.

Prayer: Father, please keep me far from temptation.
Show me how to put on Your armor so I can stand against
all the devil's schemes. I want to stand strong in You.
In Jesus' name, amen.

Thought: Are you watching and praying as you go about your day?

Reading: **Deuteronomy 5–7; Mark 11:1–18**

The Kingdom, Power, and Glory

S ome biblical manuscripts include this benediction at the end of Jesus' teaching on prayer in Matthew's gospel: *"For Yours is the kingdom and the power and the glory forever. Amen"* (Matthew 6:13 NKJV).

This is a perfect ending to Jesus' model prayer. After we have prayed, we worship the Father again. In doing so, we're saying to God, "I know You're going to answer this prayer; therefore, I'm going to thank You ahead of time. I'm going to give You all the glory for the outcome. When the answer to my prayer is manifested, I'm going to tell everybody that it is because of You."

All power and glory belong to God forever—for who He is and what He does because of His relationship with us. Let us spend time giving Him glory today:

> *Give thanks to the Lord, call on his name; make known among the nations what he has done. Sing to him, sing praise to him; tell of all his wonderful acts. Glory in his holy name; let the hearts of those who seek the Lord rejoice. Look to the Lord and his strength; seek his face always. Remember the wonders he has done, his miracles, and the judgments he pronounced....Sing to the Lord, all the earth; proclaim his salvation day after day. Declare his glory among the nations, his marvelous deeds among all peoples. For great is the Lord and most worthy of praise.* (1 Chronicles 16:8–12, 23–25)

Prayer: Father God, the kingdom, the power, and the glory belong to You, Your Son Jesus, and the Holy Spirit!
Thank You for receiving my praises.
In Jesus' name, amen.

Thought: Give God the glory in advance for answered prayer!

Reading: **Deuteronomy 8–10; Mark 11:19–33**

Did the Disciples Learn the Secret?

Jesus' disciples observed His lifestyle of prayer and asked Him to teach them to pray. Is there any evidence they learned His secret?

In Acts 1:14, we read that after Jesus was resurrected and had ascended to heaven, the disciples and other followers of Jesus *"all continued with one accord in prayer and supplication."* They were waiting for the *"power from on high"* (Luke 24:49) that Jesus had promised them—and they were "watching and praying," just as He had taught them. On the day of Pentecost, God filled the disciples with His Holy Spirit. At the outpouring of the Spirit, three thousand people were converted and *"everyone was filled with awe, and many wonders and miraculous signs were done by the apostles"* (Acts 2:42). The disciples' prayers resulted in their receiving the baptism of the Holy Spirit and working wonders and signs to God's glory, just as Jesus had done.

The disciples maintained the lifestyle of prayer Jesus had demonstrated for them. In Acts 6:3–4, they declared, *"We...will give our attention to prayer and the ministry of the word."* The entire book of Acts describes how the disciples continued the ministry of Jesus through prayer and the power of the Holy Spirit. They had learned the secret to Jesus' effectiveness in ministry.

Now that you have learned the same secret, what will you do with it?

Prayer: Father God, thank You that I can live in the book of Acts today, praying effective prayers as Your disciples did. Help me to walk in this truth. In Jesus' name, amen.

Thought: Is there evidence of prayer in your life?

Reading: **Deuteronomy 11–13; Mark 12:1–27**

Putting Prayer into Practice

Today, let's review Jesus' teachings on effective prayer. Ask yourself a few questions: Do I seek an intimate relationship with the Father on a daily basis? Are my prayers heartfelt expressions of communion with God or more like a shopping list or rote repetition? Are my life and ministry effective, bringing about God's will and kingdom on earth?

The following are some action steps for putting prayer into practice in your life. During the next few weeks, increase the time you spend with God in prayer each day in order to build a relationship of intimacy with Him. Use Jesus' model prayer to guide your prayers. Take each step and personalize it as a heartfelt expression of your growing relationship with God. I challenge to you to set a goal to spend an hour in prayer each day. As you follow Jesus' model prayer, you will find that the hour in His presence passes quickly.

Let's pray together:

Prayer: Heavenly Father, like Jesus' disciples, we, too, need to learn to pray. Thank You for giving us this model prayer so we can know how to pray as Jesus did and be effective in ministry as He was. Your Word says that You who call us to prayer and ministry are faithful and You will do it. You have called us to a lifestyle of prayer, and we ask You to fulfill that calling in us. Give us a heart to seek an intimate relationship with You every day and to follow Your thoughts and ways rather than our own thoughts and ways—or others' opinions. We pray this in the name of Jesus, our Great Intercessor. Amen.

Thought: What will your prayer time be like this week?

Reading: **Deuteronomy 14–16; Mark 12:28–44**

Principles of Prayer from Jesus

R eflect on these principles today:

1. Prayer is more important than all other activities. Through prayer, God gives guidance, wisdom, and discernment for fulfilling His will and purposes.
2. Through His intimacy with the Father, Jesus knew God's thoughts and heart, and manifested in His ministry what God was doing in the world. God wants the same communion with us that He had with Jesus so that we will naturally manifest His works.
4. Prayer does not come automatically. It must be learned.
5. Prayer is asking God to accomplish His will in the earth. Christ taught His disciples a model prayer by which to fulfill this purpose.
6. The elements of Jesus' model prayer are the following:
   - *"Our Father"*: We acknowledge God as our Source, presenting Him with the concerns of others, as well as ourselves.
   - *"In heaven"*: We admit we need help from outside our earthly realm. We depend on Jesus and the Spirit as our intermediaries with God.
   - *"Hallowed be Your Name"*: We worship the Father as the Holy One, glorifying all His attributes. We honor Him in our actions and inter- actions with others.
   - *"Your kingdom come. Your will be done on earth as it is in heaven"*: We express interest in God's kingdom and put His priorities first.
   - *"Give us day by day our daily bread"*: We ask God to supply daily needs for ourselves and others and to provide for all aspects of this process.
   - *"And forgive us our sins, for we also forgive everyone who is indebted to us"*: We forgive others so that God will forgive us and will hear and answer our prayers.
   - *"And do not lead us into temptation, but deliver us from the evil one"*: We ask God to keep us from succumbing to our personal weaknesses and Satan's schemes.
   - *"For Yours is the kingdom and the power and the glory forever. Amen"*: We worship the Father again, giving Him all the glory in advance for answered prayer.

Reading: **Deuteronomy 17–19; Mark 13:1–20**

Have You Found a Quiet Place?

Upon evaluating the prayer lives of Jesus, Abraham, Moses, David, Ezekiel, and other biblical figures, I saw that they used a similar pattern in prayer. Their prayers received God's attention and produced powerful results. *"The prayer of a righteous man is powerful and effective"* (James 5:16). I call their prayer pattern the "Twelve Action Steps to Prayer." We will look at each of these powerful steps in the next two weeks.

First, prayer should begin with silence. We don't normally make a practice of this, but it's a very important aspect of prayer. To be silent means to gather oneself, to be still.

In Matthew 6:6, Jesus said, *"When you pray, go into your room, close the door and pray to your Father, who is unseen. Then your Father, who sees what is done in secret, will reward you."* Jesus was telling us to go to a quiet, private place where we will not be disturbed. In New Testament times, most housetops were flat, and people often prayed on the roof. That was their quiet place.

You need a place of silence or isolation where you can pull your entire self together. Have you found your quiet place? For some people, it is in the living room or a chair in the corner of the bedroom. For others, it is outside, where they sense God's presence in nature. If you haven't found a quiet place where you can commune with the Lord, take time to find it today. In the coming days, you can meet your Father there in prayer.

Prayer: Father, I desire to begin my prayer times with you in contemplative silence. Help me to lay aside the distractions of this world to meet You in a quiet place. In Jesus' name, amen.

Thought: Prayer necessitates collecting yourself by coming into a quiet place before God.

Reading: **Deuteronomy 20–22; Mark 13:21–37**

Be Still and Know...

Yesterday, we talked about the first step in prayer, silence before the Lord. When you enter into prayer, you need to eliminate distractions and become quiet. You can't pray effectively when all around you the children are playing, music is blaring, the television is on, and people are asking you questions. Does this sound familiar?

Prayer necessitates collecting yourself—your thoughts, your attention, your concentration. We are usually distracted by many things when we come to prayer. Our bodies are there, but our minds are somewhere else. We might be experiencing all kinds of emotions. Therefore, you need to put yourself in a position where you can become quiet. Let the Lord calm your heart. *"You will keep in perfect peace him whose mind is steadfast, because he trusts in you"* (Isaiah 26:3). The word for *"peace"* in Hebrew is *shalom*, which means "more than enough." God provides everything you need, so you don't have to be distracted by worry when you pray.

When you come before the Lord in your private place, be quiet and listen to nothing but Him. The Lord says, *"Be still and know that I am God"* (Psalm 46:10). In relation to this command, we can say, "Prayer is the expression of man's dependency upon God for all things."

I encourage you to spend time in quiet contemplation before the Lord. Don't worry about speaking. It's all right to say nothing. Just be quiet and bring your whole self to God in prayer. Calm your heart and come into the quiet place where you can hear Him. That's when you are really praying.

Prayer: Father, I long to be still and know You. I want to commune with You in the quiet of my heart. Help me find that place in You. In Jesus' name, amen.

Thought: Silence helps bring you into a unity of heart and purpose with yourself and God.

Reading: **Deuteronomy 23–25; Mark 14:1–29**

Come Let Us Adore Him

T he second step in our pattern of prayer is adoration. Adoring the Lord is not just something we sing about during the Christmas season—"O come, let us adore Him...." Rather, this step corresponds to hallowing God's name, as in Jesus' model prayer: *"Our Father which art in heaven, hallowed be thy name"* (Luke 11:2 KJV). Adoration means worshipping God. When you adore someone, you express how precious that person is to you.

In the Psalms, King David gave countless examples of how we can give adoration to God. Each morning, you can begin your day with adoration from the Scriptures, expressing to the Lord your love for Him. The first part of Psalm 25 is a good example. It makes a great worship song:

> *Come, let us sing for joy to the* LORD; *let us shout aloud to the Rock of our salvation. Let us come before him with thanksgiving and extol him with music and song. For the* LORD *is the great God, the great King above all gods....Come, let us bow down in worship, let us kneel before the* LORD *our Maker; for he is our God and we are the people of his pasture, the flock under his care.* (Psalm 95:1-3, 6-7)

What a song of adoration! *"Come, let us bow down in worship."* You can match these words with your own melody and sing them to the Lord throughout the day.

Another example is Psalm 147:1: *"Praise the* LORD*. How good it is to sing praises to our God, how pleasant and fitting to praise him!"* Go through the Psalms, offering praise to the Lord. He alone is worthy!

Prayer: Father God, I adore You. Lord Jesus, I worship You. Holy Spirit, I love You. Please meet with me in prayer today. In Jesus' name, amen.

Thought: God is saying to us, "Honor My name first. Worship Me."

Reading: **Deuteronomy 26–27; Mark 14:27–53**

Adoration from Your Heart

T he psalms teach us much about giving God adoration. In Psalm 98:1, David wrote, *"Sing unto the LORD a new song, for he has done marvelous things."* You can worship the Lord with David's words from the Bible, or you can express your love for the Lord with a "new song" from your heart.

A new song can proclaim the words of adoration, praise, and thanksgiving that flow from your inmost being as you think about God. We are to worship God for who He is: King of all the earth, our Creator, our Savior, our All in All.

Worship, adore, and bless Him; tell Him how you see Him. Praise Him from your heart with words such as these:

Lord, You are powerful, great, awesome, omnipotent, matchless. You are God above everyone and everything. You are merciful and wonderful. You are my Counselor. You are perfect. You are abiding. You are eternal. You are above all things and in all things. Everything receives its meaning in You, Lord. You are powerful. There is nothing besides You; no one can compare with You. You alone are God. You are the only wise God: no one is as wise as You. You are all-knowing: You know everything about me and everyone else. You understand things we don't understand. You are all in all and through all. There is no one like You.

There is no one like our God; no words can adequately describe His awesome magnificence and His love for us. For thousands of years, men and women of God have composed and sung songs of adoration to Him. Sing a new song to Him today!

Prayer: Father, there is no one like You. You alone are worthy of all of our praise. Show me how to express my heart of love for You. In Jesus' name, amen.

Thought: No one and nothing compares with our God.

Reading: **Deuteronomy 28–29; Mark 14:54–72**

The True Heart of Confession

I taught a course on prayer for Christ For The Nations ministry every semester for about three years at Oral Roberts University. I shared with the students the Twelve Action Steps to Prayer, and when we discussed step three—confession—most of them would ask, "Shouldn't we *start* with confession?" I would answer, "If you did, you wouldn't know what you should confess."

Most of us have been taught that confession means bringing up our past sins and feeling remorse. The heart of confession, however, is agreeing with God about what He says *to* you and *about* you. When you enter God's presence with adoration, He shines His light on places in your life you thought He knew nothing about, bringing things into the open. God says to us, in effect, "I don't want you to condemn yourself; I want you to tell Me I'm right. Am I right? Is it sin? If it is, then you must agree with Me that it is wrong and stop doing it."

Confession takes place when God points out something in your life and says, "Get rid of that," or "You know you shouldn't have done that," or "That's sin," and you say, "Yes, God, You're right. I won't do that any longer." Then you put your trust in Him to forgive you and enable you to walk by the Spirit. *"Live by the Spirit, and you will not gratify the desires of the sinful nature"* (Galatians 5:16).

When the Holy Spirit shows you something in your life that is not right, you are to agree with Him. That is the heart of confession.

Prayer: Father, I want to see myself as You see me.
Please reveal where I have sinned against You so that
I can make true confession before You.
In Jesus' name, amen.

Thought: Confession means agreeing with God about what
He says *to* you and *about* you.

Reading: **Deuteronomy 30–31; Mark 15:1–25**

David's Agreement with God

When you are quiet before God and worship Him, His holiness surrounds you, and He reveals areas in your life you need to change.

When God reveals your sin, don't deny it. He will respond, in effect, "I can't do business with you unless you agree with Me. You are holding iniquity in your heart, and I want you to do something about it. This is blocking your prayer life."

David was one of the worst sinners in the Bible. He committed adultery, fathered a child out of wedlock, and killed a man. Yet God called him "a man after My own heart." (See 1 Samuel 13:14.) Why? If anybody confessed quickly after having his sin pointed out to him, David did. He didn't make excuses. His honest confession of sin brought him forgiveness and made his prayer life powerful. Here is an example of his agreement with God:

> *Have mercy on me, O God, according to your unfailing love; according to your great compassion blot out my transgressions. Wash away all my iniquity and cleanse me from my sin. For I know my transgressions, and my sin is always before me. Against you, you only, have I sinned and done what is evil in your sight, so that you are proved right when you speak and justified when you judge.* (Psalm 51:1–4)

When David confessed, he said, *"Against you, you only, have I sinned and done what is evil in your sight"* (v. 4). Sin opposes God's nature, character, purity, righteousness, love, and grace. David confessed, "You call it sin, O God, and You are right." David agreed with God. Have you?

Prayer: Father, I confess my sin before You. Cleanse me; make me *"whiter than snow."* Thank you for Your unfailing love. In Jesus' name, amen.

Thought: You have to admit your sin and turn from it to receive cleansing.

Reading: **Deuteronomy 32–34; Mark 15:26–47**

Confess It Quickly

Unconfessed sin will hinder your life. If you persist in sinning, God cannot cleanse you. What you desire for your life will never happen, for you undermine your own prayers. If you have done something wrong, confess it quickly.

I was a chaplain at Oral Roberts University for several years. One day, the senior chaplain and the dean of the School of Theology called me to a meeting to discuss something I had done that was not right in order to try to help someone. As I was trying to justify my actions, the dean stopped me and said, "Hold it. Don't ever do that if you want God to bless you." "Do what?" I asked. He replied, "Whatever you justify, you have not repented of. Whatever you explain, you are not sorry for. Just say, 'I was wrong; forgive me,' and ask God to forgive you. This meeting should have been over in two minutes. You're making this a long meeting and messing up your life. Don't carry this habit out of this office."

If you sin, just confess, agree, ask for forgiveness, and go on with your life. Whatever you justify, you cannot repent of. Instead of making excuses, say, "God, forgive me. I was wrong." God asks, "Is it sin?" "Yes." "Good. You agree with Me that it's sin; now, I will forgive you. Let Me clean you up." God is faithful. Once He cleanses you, no one can condemn you. *"Who will bring any charge against those whom God has chosen? It is God who justifies. Who is he that condemns?"* (Romans 8:33–34).

Prayer: Father, thank You that if we confess our sins,
You are faithful and just to forgive us and cleanse us
from all unrighteousness. I desire to be free
from sin and cleansed in Your sight.
In Jesus' name, amen.

Thought: Once God cleanses you, no one can condemn you.

Reading: **Joshua 1–3; Mark 16**

Give Thanks with a Grateful Heart

After confession comes thanksgiving. *"Be joyful always; pray continually; give thanks in all circumstances, for this is God's will for you in Christ Jesus"* (1 Thessalonians 5:16–18). Thanksgiving is God's will for us.

Once you have confessed, you can give thanks abundantly because your heart is free. God not only gives you freedom, but He also gives you something to be thankful for. He just forgave you. Your gratitude should last for hours.

David was thankful even as he confessed his terrible sins to the Lord. He recognized that God alone could save him from the punishment he deserved. *"Save me from bloodguilt, O God, the God who saves me, and my tongue will sing of your righteousness. O Lord, open my lips, and my mouth will declare your praise"* (Psalm 51:14–15). Confession, forgiveness, praise—these are all joined together in one thankful prayer to God the Savior.

As a matter of fact, this confession psalm ends in worship. *"The sacrifices of God are a broken spirit; a broken and contrite heart, O God, you will not despise....Then there will be righteous sacrifices, whole burnt offerings to delight you; then bulls will be offered on your altar"* (vv. 17, 19). Offering sacrifices and burnt offerings was an Old Testament method of worship. If you have confessed before God, your heart is right and you can offer sacrifices of praise to Him. *"Through Jesus, therefore, let us continually offer to God a sacrifice of praise—the fruit of lips that confess his name"* (Hebrews 13:15).

Prayer: Father, I thank You for freedom from sin. I thank You for a heart that is cleansed to serve You. I thank You with a grateful heart. And I thank You for receiving my praise. In Jesus' name, amen.

Thought: The Lord's praise will always be on my lips.

Reading: **Joshua 4–6; Luke 1:1–20**

A Deep Passion in Prayer

I n Philippians 4:6, Paul encouraged us, *"Do not be anxious about any-thing, but in everything, by prayer and petition* ["supplication" NKJV], *with thanksgiving, present your requests to God."* The fifth step to a life of confident and successful prayer is to make supplication.

Merriam-Webster's *11th Collegiate Dictionary* defines supplication as "to ask for earnestly and humbly." *Supplication* implies three more things to me: to intercede, to petition, and to brood. By brooding, I mean a deep passion. When you offer supplication, you feel the heart of God and greatly desire His will. This often involves weeping in prayer or praying more fervently. God shows you some of what He's feeling and unites you with His purposes and desires. Supplication is a natural outgrowth of thanksgiving. When you give thanks, you usually move into supplication because thanksgiving pleases God, and He reveals to you what is in His heart.

The Bible gives many examples of earnest supplication to the Lord. On Mt. Carmel, while confronting the prophets of Baal, Elijah cried out, *"Answer me, O LORD, answer me, so these people will know that you, O LORD, are God, and that you are turning their hearts back again"* (1 Kings 18:37). When King Jehoshaphat and the people of Judah were surrounded by three enemy armies, the king cried out, *"O LORD, God of our fathers, are you not the God who is in heaven? You rule over all the kingdoms of the nations. Power and might are in your hand, and no one can withstand you....We do not know what to do, but our eyes are upon you"* (2 Chronicles 20:6, 12). Cry out to the Lord with a heart of passion.

Prayer: Father God, I desire to bring my petitions to You
in earnest prayer. Please hear my heart as I approach
Your throne of grace in my time of need.
In Jesus' name, amen.

Thought: Come before the Lord in earnest prayer.

Reading: **Joshua 7–9; Luke 1:21–38**

Be Specific in Your Prayers

P rayer is not mumbo jumbo. It is an articulate, intentional form of communication. Step six in our prayer pattern is to *pray specifically* according to God's Word for what you need.

Before he presents his case in court, a lawyer performs research so he can provide information pertinent to the case; otherwise, a prosecutor or defense lawyer may object, "Irrelevant!" Similarly, when you bring your petitions before God, provide relevant evidence from God's Word—His promises to us—and from His very nature.

God has many names in Scripture, and you can address Him accordingly for your particular petitions. If you want peace, you appeal to Him as Jehovah-Shalom, "The Lord our Peace," rather than Jehovah-Jireh, "The Lord our Provider." If you need healing, He is Jehovah-Rapha, "The Lord our Healer." You can say, "Lord, I need You to be Jehovah-Rapha specifically in this case. I need to be healed. Your Word says that if I love You and follow Your commands, 'the LORD *will take away from* [me] *all sickness'* (Deuteronomy 7:15 NKJV)."

Therefore, specify your petitions by acknowledging God's name and His Word. Write down your prayer requests, listing next to each item the Scriptures you will use when you pray. Prayer needs to be intentional and practical. It's not something you throw together. When you present your list of petitions, God will know the thought and purpose behind them and will respond. *"This is the confidence we have in approaching God: that if we ask anything **according to his will**, he hears us. And if we know that he hears us—whatever we ask—we know that we have what we asked of him"* (1 John 5:14–15, emphasis added).

Prayer: Father, I pray today for the specific petitions on
my heart. I thank You that You hear and answer
my prayers according to Your Word.
In Jesus' name, amen.

Thought: Prayer needs to be intentional and practical.

Reading: **Joshua 10–12; Luke 1:39–56**

Secure the Promises of God

The seventh action step in prayer is related to the previous one: *Secure your promises from God's Word.* You must hold on to God's promises as you take His Word before Him, applying it to your specific requests.

When Jesus ministered to people, He never assumed what they needed. He asked them, *"What do you want me to do for you?"* (Matthew 20:32). God answers specific requests based on His promises. Bartimaeus was blind, begging by the side of the road. When he heard Jesus was coming, he said, *"Jesus, Son of David, have mercy on me!"* (Mark 10:47). Jesus answered, *"What do you want me to do for you?"* (v. 51). Jesus asked people what they specifically wanted. *"The blind man said, 'Rabbi, I want to see.' 'Go,' said Jesus, 'your faith has healed you.' Immediately he received his sight and followed Jesus along the road"* (v. 52).

Bartimaeus was healed because he asked for healing based on his legal rights. He cried, *"Son of David."* That's a legal statement. Abraham's covenant came through David. The Scripture says the Messiah will come through David's line and that David's throne will last forever. (See Isaiah 9:6–7.) Bartimaeus reasoned, "If Jesus is the Messiah, He must be the Son of David. If He is the Son of David, then every covenant promise God made to Abraham, Moses, and David can come to me through Jesus." So he said, *'Son of David, have mercy on me!'...'Go,'* said Jesus, *'your faith has healed you.'"* The man was healed because he petitioned according to God's promises. Likewise, we can secure God's promises when we pray.

Prayer: Father, please remind me that I can secure
Your promises because of my rights in Jesus.
In His precious name, amen.

Thought: Jesus asks, "What do you want Me to do for you?"

Reading: **Joshua 13–15; Luke 1:57–80**

A Daughter of Abraham

One Sabbath day, Jesus entered a synagogue where a woman was sitting hunched over with a back problem. Jesus stood and read the Scriptures. Then He looked at the crowd, setting His eyes on the woman. He called her to Him, put His hands on her, and healed her. The Bible says, *"Immediately she straightened up and praised God"* (Luke 13:13). The religious leaders murmured among themselves, in effect, "How dare He heal her on the Sabbath day!" Jesus turned to them and said, *"Should not this woman, **a daughter of Abraham**, whom Satan has kept bound for eighteen long years, be set free on the Sabbath day from what bound her?"* (Luke 13:16, emphasis added).

Even though this woman hadn't asked Jesus for healing, He gave evidence of her rights according to God's promises. This woman had been sick for years, but she wasn't healed until the legal action was in place. Jesus didn't heal her just because it was the Sabbath; He healed her according to the contract God had made with His chosen people on behalf of Abraham, in which He said, *"The LORD will take away from you all sickness"* (Deuteronomy 7:15). As a daughter of Abraham, she had the right to the healing God had promised His people.

We usually ask the Lord to heal us because we're hurting, and He does heal us with compassion. (See Matthew 14:14.) However, the primary reason He heals us is that we give Him evidence it is our legal right through Christ. Again, we pray specifically, according to God's Word, and we secure the promises!

Prayer: Father, thank You for fulfilling your promises in Christ. Thank You that I have the legal right to answered prayer. In Jesus' name, amen.

Thought: God answers prayer when we give Him legal evidence that it is our right.

Reading: **Joshua 16–18; Luke 2:1–24**

Can You Plead Your Case?

*P*leading *your case* is the eighth action step in prayer. Pleading does not mean begging or becoming emotional. That neither impresses God nor elicits answers. In teaching the parable of the widow and the judge, Jesus said to His disciples, in effect, "Let Me show you not only how to pray, but also how to get answers." He revealed how to plead one's case before God. (See Luke 18:1.)

Jesus began, *"In a certain town there was a judge who neither feared God nor cared about men"* (v. 2). Jesus used an example of the worst person to receive petitions. I believe He did this to emphasize that it is our legal rights that enable us to receive answers. We'll talk more about this concept tomorrow.

Jesus continued, *"And there was a widow in that town who kept coming to him with the plea, 'Grant me justice against my adversary'"* (v. 3). In Jesus' day, a widow was often without hope. If a married man died, his brother had to marry the man's widow and care for her. If the second brother died, the third one had to marry her, and so on. Thus, a woman became a widow when no relatives remained to help her.

The widow's helplessness is significant. God wants you to pray with this attitude: "You're the only One who can help me." Often, we pray for God's help, but we have a backup plan, just in case. God says, in essence, "I will not answer until you have no other place to turn. Then you will know that I am your Provider." God doesn't want to be treated as a "spare tire." This woman had no option, no alternative. As we come to God with our petitions, we must depend completely on Him.

Prayer: Father, thank You for letting me come before You with my petitions to plead my case. I acknowledge that You are the only One whom I can depend on to hear and answer my prayers.
In Jesus' name, amen.

Thought: The Lord fulfills all your petitions.

Reading: **Joshua 19–21; Luke 2:25–52**

Persistence with the Judge

Today we continue looking at the parable of the widow and the judge, in which Jesus taught His disciples to pray without giving up. *"For some time [the judge] refused"* (Luke 18:4) the woman's plea. Even though the answers to our prayers are not always immediate, that doesn't mean they are never coming.

Jesus concluded His story, *"Finally [the judge] said to himself, 'Even though I don't fear God or care about men, yet because this widow keeps bothering me, I will see that she gets justice, so that she won't eventually wear me out with her coming!'"* (vv. 4–5). The judge did not cut her a break, but used a legal word: *"I will see that she gets **justice** [what is rightfully hers]."*

God's promises must come to pass. The integrity of His name and His Word calls us to be persistent in prayer. *"God is not a man, that he should lie, nor a son of man, that he should change his mind. Does he speak and then not act? Does he promise and not fulfill?"* (Numbers 23:19).

Jesus explained, *"Listen to what the unjust judge says. And will not God bring about justice for his **chosen ones**, who cry out to him day and night? Will he keep putting them off? I tell you, he will see that they get justice, and quickly"* (Luke 18:6–8, emphasis added). Jesus said, in effect, "If a man who doesn't acknowledge God gives a woman he doesn't like the justice she deserves, how much more will God, who loves you, see to it that you get justice—and quickly!" God will not hesitate to give justice to His chosen ones, those who have received His promises as a spiritual inheritance.

Prayer: Father, help me to be persistent in prayer. I know that You are a faithful God who desires to answer my petitions. In Jesus' name, amen.

Thought: Plead your case based on God's Word and His integrity.

Reading: **Joshua 22–24; Luke 3**

Whatever You Ask for in Prayer...Believe

*B*elieve—this is difficult for many of us. As in the parable of the unjust judge, God says that after we plead our case, we are to believe. This is step nine in our action steps for prayer. Asking, in itself, doesn't cause you to receive. Read carefully Christ's words in this passage; this is another mini-seminar on prayer:

> *"Have faith in God," Jesus answered. "I tell you the truth, if anyone says to this mountain, 'Go, throw yourself into the sea,' and does not doubt in his heart but believes that what he says will happen, it will be done for him. Therefore I tell you, whatever you ask for in prayer, believe...."* (Mark 11:22–24)

What's the next phrase? *"...that you have received it"* (v. 24). When you ask for something, believe then and there that you have already received it. It is possible to ask for something in prayer and not believe. We do it all the time. We usually give up too soon.

Do you believe that what you prayed last night is going to happen? Then confess, "Lord, I believe." Maybe you tend to doubt. You might not be a believer all the way. When you start doubting, be honest, like the father of the demon-possessed boy, and say, *"Lord, I believe; help my unbelief!"* (Mark 9:24 NKJV). We can't let doubt enter into our prayers. It will short-circuit them.

When you pray according to God's Word and believe that you *have received* what you asked, it will be yours. That is God's promise to you.

Prayer: Father, my heart's desire is to believe You.
When doubts rise up, help me to turn to You. Lead me to Your
Word so that my faith will grow. I believe that You will
help my unbelief and answer my prayers.
In Jesus' name, amen.

Thought: Faith is believing the promises.

Reading: **Judges 1–3; Luke 4:1–30**

Living in Thankful Expectation

After you have believed God, step ten is to offer *thanksgiving* again. Recall that step four was also to give thanks. The first time, giving thanks expressed your appreciation for God's forgiveness and mercy. This step of thanksgiving is the highest form of faith. You thank God for what you don't yet see because you believe it is already done. *"Now faith is being sure of what we hope for and certain of what we do not see"* (Hebrews 11:1).

If you truly believe you have already received your request, you will thank God. We are not to wait until we see the manifestation of our answer before expressing gratitude. You don't show God your belief until you thank Him. Suppose you request a loan from a banker, who approves the loan and says, "Consider it done. The money will be deposited to your account." You don't see the money, so you don't know if he did it, but you thank him and do business based on his word. God wants us to do the same with Him and give thanks even before we see the answer manifested. If we will believe God, the answer will come.

Step eleven is to *live in expectation.* After you pray, continue in a spirit of thanksgiving—living in anticipation of the answer to your prayer. Ephesians 3:20 says, *"Now to him who is able to do immeasurably more than all we ask or imagine, according to his power that is at work within us."*

Live in expectation. Our Lord is powerful!

Prayer: Father, thank You for hearing and answering
my prayer. Thank You for Your faithfulness to answer
my petition even before I see the manifestation.
In You I can live a life of expectation.
In Jesus' name, amen.

Thought: Close all your prayer times with thanksgiving because
what you have asked for has already been received.

Reading: **Judges 4–6; Luke 4:31–44**

Practicing Active Belief

The last step in our twelve action steps to prayer is to *practice active belief*—prove you're living in expectation. It is what Jesus meant by "seeking and knocking." In Luke 11:1, when the disciples said, *"Lord, teach us to pray,"* Jesus taught them a model prayer. Luke 11:9 is part of that lesson: *"So I say to you: Ask and it will be given to you; seek and you will find; knock and the door will be opened to you."*

Jesus tells us, in essence, "Don't stop after you pray. Get up and look for what you asked for. You will find it if you seek it. It may be behind some closed doors. If that's the case, then knock." No door or barrier can stop what God has for you if you believe it's yours. When the devil tries to hold back your answer, just persist in knocking until the door falls down. This is the meaning of active prayer. Practice active belief and continue to live before God in holiness and truth. God will bless you as you ask, seek, and knock.

Use these twelve action steps as a guide to prayer, and make sure your life aligns with God's will and purposes. As you learn to pray according to biblical principles, you will become a powerfully effective believer.

Prayer: Father, thank You for Your wonderful
words of encouragement to me.
If I ask, seek, and knock, You will open the doors.
My expectations are settled in You.
In Jesus' name, amen.

Thought: No door or barrier can stop what God has for you when
you believe and act accordingly!

Reading: **Judges 7–8; Luke 5:1–16**

Putting Prayer into Practice

Take some time today to review your prayer habits. Ask yourself these questions: Do I quiet myself before the Lord prior to prayer, or do I usually pray hurriedly, just to get through one more task in my day? Do I pray sporadically and haphazardly, or do I pray purposefully according to God's Word? Is there any sin in my life that I am trying to justify?

This week, gradually incorporate the twelve action steps into your prayers. If you have been justifying wrongdoing in your life, agree with God that it is sin and truly repent by turning from it and asking God to cleanse you from all unrighteousness. (See 1 John 1:9.) Take one of your prayer requests and start living in expectation of it, practicing active belief. Anticipate that what you pray for according to God's Word will happen, and make preparation for the answer.

Now, let's pray together:

Prayer: Heavenly Father, thank You for giving us principles for prayer in Your Word. Help us to continually meditate on Your precepts and contemplate Your ways. Don't allow us to walk away from Your truths and forget them. Help us to study these principles and consider carefully Your desires as revealed in Your Word. Then encourage us to step out in faith to put these principles into practice in our lives. As we do, we thank You for answering our prayers and doing immeasurably more than all we ask or imagine, according to Your power that is at work within us. We pray this in the name of Jesus, the Mediator of the new covenant. Amen.

Thought: Pray, believe, expect!

Reading: **Judges 9–10; Luke 5:17–39**

Principles for Effective Prayer

Today, reflect on the twelve action steps to prayer:

1. *Become Silent:* Be still, and gather yourself. If your spirit, body, mind, and emotions are separated, then you will be unable to pray God's will with singleness of purpose. Silence helps bring you into unity with God.

2. *Give Adoration:* Worship God for who He is: King of all the earth, your Creator, your Savior, your All in All.

3. *Make Confession:* Agree with God about what He says to you and about you. Don't dwell on past sins, but obey God immediately when He shows you that you are wrong.

4. *Give Thanks:* Offer sacrifices of praise to God for all that He has done for you.

5. *Make Supplication:* As God shows you what He desires, agree wholeheartedly with Him in prayer to fulfill His will.

6. *Specify Petitions and Requests:* When you ask God to do something for you, bring evidence relevant to the case—in the form of God's will and Word—through specific, intentional communication.

7. *Secure the Promises:* When you petition the Lord, take God's promises before Him, applying them to the specific request you are making. Then hold onto God's promises.

8. *Plead the Case:* Don't beg or moan before God, but pray intelligently because you rightfully deserve the answer based on God's promises.

9. *Believe:* Believe right at the time you are asking that you have the answer to your request, and you will receive it.

10. *Give Thanks:* Thank God for what you don't yet see because you believe it is already done.

11. *Live in Expectation:* Anticipate the answers to your prayers and prepare the way for them.

12. *Practice Active Belief:* Don't stop after you have prayed. Get up and look for what you asked for. If you seek and knock, it will come to pass.

Reading: **Judges 11–12; Luke 6:1–26**

Learning about Prayer versus Practicing It

Prayer is the greatest privilege offered to a person in Christ. Satan knows that an individual is only as powerful as his or her prayer life. Therefore, he uses misconceptions about prayer to thwart our prayer potential. These misconceptions are hurdles we must overcome in order to receive answers to prayer.

The first hurdle is the desire to read *about* the Bible and prayer rather than *to study* the Word itself and equip oneself for prayer. We gain a false sense of satisfaction when we learn *about* something but don't actually *do* it. We may think it's part of our lives, but it really hasn't moved from our heads to our hearts, from theory to practice. Satan loves it when we read about what we should be doing but never do it; when we buy books on prayer and the Bible but never follow what they say. It's like buying a cookbook but never making the recipes. Many Christians read in the Bible about believers receiving answers to their prayers, and they feel inspired. They may say, "Daniel prayed, Joseph prayed, and look at the results they had. *'The prayer of a righteous man is powerful and effective'* (James 5:16). I should pray, too." However, they never commit to prayer.

We often have the false idea that if we *know* a great deal about prayer, somehow we *have* prayed. You may say, "This is powerful. This can change my life." However, if you don't apply these principles to your life, you will not grow spiritually. *A major cause of unanswered prayer is becoming an expert in the knowledge of prayer but not a master in the practice of praying.*

Prayer: Father, I don't want to be a hearer of the Word
only, but also a doer. As I learn about the principles
of prayer, help me to apply them in my prayer life.
In Jesus' name, amen.

Thought: The best approach to prayer is *to pray.*

Reading: **Judges 13–15; Luke 6:27–49**

Mental Assent versus Faith

M ental assent looks so much like faith that many people cannot distinguish one from the other. Mental assent *agrees* with God but doesn't *believe* God. When we have mental assent, we merely accept the Word as truth but do not allow it to have an impact on us. This is the third hurdle to answered prayer we must overcome.

The mental assentor affirms that the entire Bible is God's infallible revelation. In crises, however, he says, "I believe the Bible is true, but it doesn't work for *me*." He often quotes Scriptures he doesn't really believe. He might affirm, *"God will supply all my needs according to His riches in glory by Christ Jesus"* (Philippians 4:19 NKJV), without truly trusting God to do so.

A mental assentor says, "Lord, what You said is wonderful!"—and leaves it at that. He may know much about the Word, but he has failed in his spiritual life. The true believer is a doer of the Word, not a hearer only. (See James 1:22.)

A variation of mental assent is "sense knowledge." This attitude says, "I'll believe it when I see it." The Bible tells us, *"We walk by faith, not by sight"* (2 Corinthians 5:7 KJV). Faith and sense knowledge are not compatible. Faith is the substance and evidence of things that your sense knowledge cannot see. (See Hebrews 11:1.)

Many of us have been educated to live by our five senses alone. If we cannot analyze something and draw empirical conclusions, we don't believe it's real. However, God says that what He has promised is already a reality. Yet it will become a *manifested* reality only when we believe it is real *before* we see it—by trusting God and His Word. That's how faith operates.

Prayer: Father, I thank You that Your promises are
true. Help me to act on Your truth.
In Jesus' name, amen.

Thought: Mental assent agrees with God but does not believe God.

Reading: **Judges 16–18; Luke 7:1–30**

Evidence of Things Not Seen

Hebrews 11:1 says, *"Faith is the substance of things hoped for, the evidence of things not seen"* (KJV). Note that this verse does *not* say faith is the evidence of things that *do not exist.* Faith is the evidence of things *you cannot see.* These things already exist in God, but you can't see them yet. Live by faith. God says, "I will supply all your needs. Trust Me to do it." Trusting God's Word is faith in action.

If you have been mentally assenting to the truth but not acting on it, you have been living below your privilege. Again, James 1:22 says, *"Do not merely listen to the word, and so deceive yourselves. Do what it says."* This verse separates mental assent from faith. If you think just listening to the Word makes a difference, you deceive yourself. You must apply what you hear by believing and acting on it. Jesus said to the chief priests and elders,

> *"There was a man who had two sons. He went to the first and said, 'Son, go and work today in the vineyard.' 'I will not,' he answered, but later he changed his mind and went. Then the father went to the other son and said the same thing. He answered, 'I will, sir,' but he did not go. Which of the two did what his father wanted?" "The first,"* they *answered.* (Matthew 21:28–31)

The second son assented to obey, but never took action. The first son, though initially rebellious, later met his father's request. We can't just say we believe; we have to live out our faith by doing what God asks.

Prayer: Father, You have promised to meet the needs
of Your children. Help me to trust You and to act in faith
even when what You've promised isn't visible.
In Jesus' name, amen.

Thought: If you have been only mentally assenting to the truth,
you have been waiving your privilege.

Reading: **Judges 19–21; Luke 7:31–50**

Hearing the Word but Not Absorbing It

A nother major hurdle to answered prayer is hearing the Word without absorbing it into one's life. When we don't absorb the Word, Satan steals it away. In the parable of the sower, Jesus said, "*When anyone hears the message about the kingdom and does not understand it, the evil one comes and snatches away what was sown in his heart*" (Matthew 13:19). In this parable, seed represents the Word of God, while different types of soil represent human attitudes. When the seed is sown along the path—when the Word is not central to a person's life—the enemy steals it.

The enemy attacks the Word because it is the source of our spiritual life. Even as you read the Bible, your adversary tries to rob you of God's truth. If you don't consciously apply God's Word to your life, the enemy will try to make you forget what you've just read.

Jesus often ended His lessons by saying, "*He who has ears to hear, let him hear!*" (See, for example, Matthew 13:9 NKJV.) There is physical hearing, and there is spiritual hearing. Jesus knew the people heard His words, but He told them, in essence, "My words need to be established in your hearts."

> *Anyone who listens to the word but does not do what it says is like a man who looks at his face in a mirror and, after looking at himself, goes away and immediately forgets what he looks like. But the man who looks intently into the perfect law that gives freedom, and continues to do this, not forgetting what he has heard, but doing it—he will be blessed in what he does.* (James 1:23–25)

Prayer: Father, please give me ears to hear You in Your Word and in those You have called to teach Your Word.
In Jesus' name, amen.

Thought: *"He who has ears to hear, let him hear!"*

Reading: Ruth; Luke 8:1–25

Growing Your Faith

The only way God's promises will become a reality in your life is if you act on them—and you can't act on them without faith. The very word *promise* requires faith. If I promise you something, then you don't have it yet; you must believe I will give it to you. God tells us, "I promise to do this for you, but it's actually already done. I want you to believe that what I promise is real. It is already accomplished."

Start living by the faith God gave you so that His Word can come to pass in your life. People say, "I need more faith." Faith is easy to obtain: it comes by hearing the Word of God. *"So then faith comes by hearing, and hearing by the word of God"* (Romans 10:17 NKJV). When you receive the Word, your faith grows. Every time you hear or read the Word and apply it, your spiritual life is strengthened. You don't receive the Word of God without being changed for the better.

Remember the promise regarding the seed that fell on good soil in Jesus' parable of the sower:

> But the one who received the seed that fell on good soil is the man who hears the word and understands it. He produces a crop, yielding a hundred, sixty or thirty times what was sown. (Matthew 13:23)

Planted in good soil, a seed will grow because the power is in the seed. Let the Word of God be planted in you and "grow" your faith in the love and power of God our Father.

Prayer: Father, Your Word is the seed of faith in the
soil of my heart. Let my heart be "good soil," watered by
Your Holy Spirit, so that I will reap a harvest for You.
In Jesus' name, amen.

Thought: You don't receive the Word of God without
being changed for the better.

Reading: **1 Samuel 1–3; Luke 8:26–56**

Let the Message Sink in

I like how *The Living Bible* paraphrases Jesus' command in Revelation 2:7: *"Let this message sink into the ears of anyone who listens to what the Spirit is saying to the churches."* Let the message sink in. Stay focused after you've heard or read the Word, and let it truly sink into your spirit through the process of meditation.

Meditation was an important spiritual exercise in both the Old and New Testaments. Many believers don't practice meditation because they misunderstand the word. Biblical meditation differs greatly from transcendental meditation, a practice of eastern religions involving chants and incantations. Biblical meditation focuses on God's Word. The psalmist wrote, *"I mediate on your precepts and consider your ways"* (Psalm 119:15).

When Joshua became leader of the Israelites, God said to him, *"Do not let this Book of the Law depart from your mouth; meditate on it day and night, so that you may be careful to do everything written in it."* He added, *"Then you will be prosperous and successful"* (Joshua 1:8). This would happen when Joshua meditated on the Word to make it part of his life.

After the apostle Paul instructed Timothy in God's ways, he said, *"Meditate on these things; give yourself entirely to them, that your progress may be evident to all"* (1 Timothy 4:15). The Greek word for *"meditate"* in this verse is *meletao*, which means to "revolve in the mind." Rather than mindless chanting, biblical mediation involves using your mind—reflecting on something to understand all its truths and implications, then applying them to your life.

Prayer: Father, teach me how to mediate on Your Word daily.
I want Your precepts to sink into my heart so that
my thoughts and actions reflect You.
In Jesus' name, amen.

Thought: Meditation means letting the Word truly
sink into your spirit.

Reading: **1 Samuel 4–6; Luke 9:1–17**

Meditation: A Twofold Process

Meditation has been compared to rumination, the process by which a cow chews its cud. A cow has two stomachs. The first takes in the food as the cow eats it. When the cow is full, it ruminates, bringing the food back up into its mouth to chew again. Rumination digests the food, putting it into a form easily assimilated into the cow's system through its second stomach. Thus the food becomes strength and life to the animal.

The Bible says we also must undergo a twofold process to absorb the Word of God. The first step is receiving the Word. When you read the Bible or hear a biblical teaching, the Word enters your "first stomach"—your heart. (See Matthew 13:19.) To receive spiritual strength and life, however, you must meditate on that Word, "digesting" it so it can permeate your entire being. The psalmist said, *"Oh, how I love your law* [Word]! *I meditate on it **all day long**. Your commands make me wiser than my enemies, for **they are ever with me**"* (Psalm 119:97–98, emphasis added).

Satan never wants you to reach the meditation stage because that's when the Word of God can become the means for answered prayer. Just hearing a good Sunday morning sermon is not enough; rather, you must absorb the Word that is preached. Remember, *"when anyone hears the message about the kingdom and does not understand it, the evil one comes and snatches away what was sown in his heart"* (Matthew 13:19). Meditate on God's Word after hearing a message; absorb it into your life. The devil won't be able to stop the Word because God will use it to accomplish His purposes.

Prayer: Father, Your Word says that meditating on You
will be sweet. Help me to absorb whatever I hear
from You, in the Bible or in a sermon.
In Jesus' name, amen.

Thought: Meditation on God's Word can be strength
and life to you.

Reading: **1 Samuel 7–9; Luke 9:18–36**

Hope Is Not Faith

People often mistake hope for faith, but these concepts are distinct. The Bible says, *"And now these three remain: faith, hope and love. But the greatest of these is love"* (1 Corinthians 13:13). The Greek word for *"faith"* is *pistis*, meaning "belief" or "confidence." It can also mean "conviction" or "assurance." The word for *"hope"* is *elpis*, meaning "expectation" or "anticipation." Biblical hope is based on faith because it anticipates the ultimate fulfillment of that faith.

Hope is necessary for anticipating heaven, the second coming of Christ, and everything God has promised us in the future—the culmination of our salvation, the resurrection of our bodies, the new heaven and earth, and our eternal reign with Jesus. Biblical hope looks to future blessings: *"We have this hope as an anchor for the soul, firm and secure"* (Hebrews 6:19). *"May the God of hope fill you with all joy and peace as you trust in him, so that you may overflow with hope by the power of the Holy Spirit"* (Romans 15:13).

When hope is misapplied, however, it is a hurdle to answered prayer. God wants to bless us in this life. If we think blessings are for the future only, we will fail to exercise faith to see their fulfillment *now*. Where faith is not applied, fulfillment cannot come. Believers with this perspective will receive the future blessings for which they have hope and faith, but they will miss the blessings God wants to give them today.

Prayer: Father, thank You for the hope of salvation.
I look forward to an eternity with You. Help me to understand
the difference between biblical hope and faith so I can walk
according to Your purpose for my life.
In Jesus' name, amen.

Thought: The expectation of future blessings is what
biblical hope is all about.

Reading: 1 Samuel 10–12; Luke 9:37–62

When Hope Is Wishful Thinking

S ometimes people talk about hope, but they're really talking about
wishful thinking. Biblical hope is based on faith, while wishful
thinking is based on uncertainty or doubt. The first is hope; the second
is "hoping." Hoping says, "I *hope* this happens; I *hope* this works; I *hope*
God hears my prayers."

Wishful thinking is destructive to the practice of prayer. Hebrews
11:1 says, *"Now faith is being **sure** of what we hope for and **certain** of what we
do not see"* (emphasis added). We receive what God has promised *when*
we pray. Having faith means affirming this fact until the answer manifests itself. Hoping is dangerous because it can cancel our prayers. For
example, suppose you ask God for something according to His Word,
saying, "Lord, I believe." If you finish your prayer time and say, "I sure
hope it happens," you have just nullified your prayer.

When you pray for a present-day blessing, hope plays a part only
in your confidence that your answer is on its way. When Daniel per-
severed in prayer for three weeks, he was not hoping for an answer; he
was waiting for an answer. There's a difference. Suppose you call a friend
and say, "I'm making a cake, and I ran out of butter. Would you bring some
over?" Your friend says, "I'm on the way." Are you hoping to receive butter?
No. You continue preparing the cake because you believe the butter is
coming. You expect it because your friend promised to bring it.

How much more you can rely on God to do what He has promised!
The Bible says, "If God said it, He will do it. If He promised it, He will
bring it to pass." (See Numbers 23:19.)

Prayer: Father, I don't have to just *hope* You will be there for me;
You have promised it in Your Word. Help me to walk in faith.
In Jesus' name, amen.

Thought: Wishful thinking is destructive to prayer.

Reading: **1 Samuel 13–14; Luke 10:1–24**

Are You on "Someday Island"?

Hoping doesn't accomplish anything. Faith makes you work; hoping doesn't. Hoping says, "Someday...." How long have you been on "Someday Island"?

God's blessings have already been accomplished in the spiritual realm; He waits for people of faith on whom to release them. If you want to go to college but have no money, pray, "God, You said the righteous will be *'like a tree planted by streams of water, which yields its fruit in season and whose leaf does not wither. Whatever he does prospers'* (Psalm 1:3). I'm obeying Your Word. I expect to prosper. I'm going to college because I am the righteous, and my fruit shall come in season." After praying, fill out applications and make other preparations as you await the manifestation of your request. Otherwise, college will remain merely a dream.

When we engage in wishful thinking and doubt, we reveal our lack of trust in God's character and integrity. Doubt is an insult to God. No wonder James said that if a person doubts, *"that man should not think he will receive anything from the Lord"* (James 1:7).

Many of us wish and wait. When we don't receive what we asked for, we wonder if God's Word is true. The problem is not with God's Word, but with us. He has already accomplished our request, but we aren't expecting it. We don't act as if we have it, so God can't give it. We're holding Him up. He promises, *"The Lord bestows favor and honor; no good thing does he withhold from those whose walk is blameless"* (Psalm 84:11).

Prayer: Father, I would never want to insult You with my unbelief. As I read Your Word and pray, please help me change my doubt to a firm and steadfast faith in You.
In Jesus' name, amen.

Thought: Doubt is really an insult to God.

Reading: 1 Samuel 15–16; Luke 10:25–42

The Size of Your God

L uke 17:5 says, *"The apostles said to the Lord, 'Increase our faith!'"* If you have prayed like that, you are in good company. The disciples lived with Jesus for more than three years. They saw Him cast out demons, heal the sick, and raise the dead, yet they still asked Him to increase their faith. *"He replied, 'If you have faith as small as a mustard seed, you can say to this mulberry tree, "Be uprooted and planted in the sea," and it will obey you'"* (Luke 17:6).

Praying for faith is another hurdle to answered prayer. Jesus was telling His disciples, "You don't need any more faith; just a small amount will move mountains. The little you have can do much, but you aren't using it."

It is not the size of your faith that counts—it is the size of your God. If you believe, you activate heaven. Perhaps you are thinking, "I'm not sure I have faith." *"Faith comes from hearing the message, and the message is heard through the word of Christ"* (Romans 10:17). If you want to increase your faith, increase your intake of the Word of God. What you know of the Word becomes the limit of your faith because you can believe only what you know. It is essential to belong to a local body of believers where spiritually grounded teaching addresses all aspects of the Christian life. We need to understand how God operates in every area of life because we want to have faith in all those areas. Jesus said, *"According to your faith will it be done to you"* (Matthew 9:29).

Prayer: Father, please strengthen me to spend
more time in Your Word. I want my faith
in You and in Your Word to grow larger and deeper.
Thank You for being all that I need.
In Jesus' name, amen.

Thought: It's not the size of your faith that
counts—it's the size of your God.

Reading: 1 Samuel 17–18; Luke 11:1–28

Neglecting Prayer Altogether

A final hurdle to answered prayer is *neglecting prayer altogether.* Laziness and distractibility are the worst reasons for not praying. None of us wants to be called a *"wicked, lazy servant"* (Matthew 25:26) by God.

In the parable of the sower, Jesus said, *"The one who received the seed that fell among the thorns is the man who hears the word, but the **worries of this life** and the **deceitfulness of wealth** choke it, making it unfruitful"* (Matthew 13:22, emphasis added). When a person doesn't bother to pray because he feels he has more important things to do, or is too involved with the cares and concerns of this life, even what he knows about prayer will bear no fruit for him.

When we neglect prayer, we ignore exhortations from God's Word: *"And pray in the Spirit on all occasions with all kinds of prayers and requests. With this in mind, be alert and always keep on praying for all the saints. Pray also for me..."* (Ephesians 6:18–19). *"Devote yourselves to prayer, being watchful and thankful"* (Colossians 4:2). Failing to pray is neglecting the Word of God.

Matthew 3:10 says, *"The ax is already at the root of the trees, and every tree that does not produce good fruit will be cut down and thrown into the fire."* We must avoid becoming complacent in our knowledge of the Word and neglecting to nurture it. However, when we hear, absorb, and apply the Word, we will bear the fruit of spiritual growth and answered prayer. We will see the fulfillment of God's original purposes for blessing the earth.

Prayer: Father, I do not want to neglect Your Word.
Help me to pray for myself and others and not succumb
to laziness or life's distractions.
In Jesus' name, amen.

Thought: None of us wants to be called a wicked and lazy servant!

Reading: 1 Samuel 19–21; Luke 11:29–54

Putting Prayer into Practice

We have examined six hurdles to answered prayer over the last several days. Now, ask yourself the following questions: Which of these hurdles best describes my practice of prayer and reading the Word? Is it a lack of application, mental assent, not allowing the message to sink in, or laziness? What attitude or outlook do I need to repent of in order to surmount this obstacle through God's grace?

After answering these questions, choose one hurdle that characterizes your current practice of prayer. Take conscious steps to overcome it by applying the truth of God's Word. Each day, as you read the Bible, ask God to open the eyes of your heart to see what He is saying to you in His Word. Practice meditation by thinking about the implications and applications of what you have read. After church this week, spend at least five minutes sitting quietly, reflecting on the message and what God is saying to you through it.

Let's pray together:

Prayer: Heavenly Father, Your Word cautions us to be
self-controlled and alert because our enemy the devil is
prowling around like a roaring lion, looking for someone to devour,
and that we need to resist him as we stand firm in the faith.
We ask You to help us remain alert to the hurdles in our lives
that the enemy wants to use to destroy our prayer potential.
Help us to resist him as we stand firm in our faith. Let
Your Holy Spirit show us where we are being deceived
in our attitudes toward prayer and the Word so that
we can understand and practice true and effective prayer.
We ask these things in the name of Jesus, who resisted
the enemy through the power of Your Word. Amen.

Thought: Have I identified a hurdle to prayer in my life,
and am I committed to overcoming it through God's grace?

Reading: **1 Samuel 22–24; Luke 12:1–31**

Principles for Overcoming Hurdles to Prayer

T oday, reflect on the six hurdles to answered prayer:

1. *Learning about prayer but not practicing it:* We gain a false sense of satisfaction when we learn about prayer but fail to apply it. No amount of knowledge will help us spiritually unless we put it into practice. The best approach to prayer is to pray.

2. *Mental assent rather than action:* Mental assent agrees with God but does not believe God. A variation of mental assent is "sense knowledge," which says, "I'll believe it when I see it." Faith is believing before we see the manifestation of our prayers. If we think just listening to the Word is enough, we are deceived. We must believe the Word and act on it.

3. *Hearing the Word but not absorbing it:* When we don't absorb the Word, Satan steals it away to keep it from having an impact on our relationship with God. We absorb the Word by meditating on it.

4. *Hoping rather than having faith:* Hope can interfere with what God wants to accomplish through prayer when we misapply the biblical definition of hope (future fulfillment) to present-day situations and when our hope is not the biblical kind, but is really just wishful thinking.

5. *Praying for faith:* When we pray for faith, we pray to believe. Either we believe or we don't. Such a prayer is really based on unbelief; therefore, it will not be answered. Faith comes and increases as we hear, believe, and obey the Word.

6. *Laziness and/or the cares of the world:* If we are too lazy to pray, we risk being called a *"wicked, lazy servant"* (Matthew 25:26) by God in regard to this crucial purpose for our lives. When we allow the concerns of this life to crowd out the practice of prayer, even what we know about prayer will bear no fruit in our lives.

Reading: **1 Samuel 25–26; Luke 12:32–59**

Everyone Lives by Faith

When we read, *"The just shall live by faith"* (Romans 1:17 NKJV; Galatians 3:11 NKJV), we must define what the Bible means by this statement, because everyone lives by faith. Faith of some kind works in all our lives, whether or not we are aware of it.

To do any kind of business with God, we need the faith the Bible speaks of. *"Without faith it is impossible to please God"* (Hebrews 11:6). Many of us were taught that faith is necessary, but we weren't usually taught how to obtain the faith that pleases God.

How do we define faith in general terms? Remember that the New Testament word *"faith"* comes from the Greek word *pistis*, meaning "belief" or "confidence." Faith means belief and confidence in the words you hear. It is believing in something unseen as if it were already a reality—and then speaking it and expecting it until it manifests itself. Again, everyone lives by this definition of faith, and people usually receive exactly what they have faith for. Why? Human beings were created in God's image to operate in the way He does—through words of faith. *"For he spoke, and it came to be; he commanded, and it stood firm"* (Psalm 33:9).

People live either by positive faith—based on the Bible—or negative faith. Both come by the same means: what we listen to and believe. Sometimes our prayers fail because we have the wrong kind of faith. It is not that we *lack* faith; we have the wrong *kind* of faith. Understanding the different kinds of faith and how faith functions are key preparations for prayer.

Prayer: Father, thank You for giving me positive faith.
Teach me to always pray in faith according to Your Word.
In Jesus' name, amen.

Thought: Everyone lives by some kind of faith.

Reading: 1 Samuel 27–29; Luke 13:1–22

Created to Walk in Faith

People were created in God's image to operate as He does—*through words of faith.* This truth is vital to our prayer lives.

God created the heavens and the earth by believing in the reality of what He would create before He saw its manifestation. *"By faith we understand that the universe was formed at God's command, so that what is seen was not made out of what was visible"* (Hebrews 11:3). Nothing was visible until God spoke the universe into being.

God not only spoke words to create things, but He *continues* using words to keep the universe running! Hebrews 1:3 says, *"The Son is the radiance of God's glory and the exact representation of His being, **sustaining all things by His powerful word**"* (emphasis added). God sustains everything by the power of His Word. He spoke, and the universe came into being. He *keeps on speaking,* and this keeps the universe going.

When you ask for something in prayer according to God's will, you should speak in faith as if it already exists. Moreover, you must *keep* speaking in faith to see its manifestation. When it comes, it's not enough to receive it from God; you must maintain God's blessing by continuing to speak it in faith. When God fulfills a promise and gives you something, you obtain the "title deed" to it. If Satan *steals* what you have received from God, you still have the title deed; you own the property even if Satan possesses it. If you have lost something God gave you, appropriate His promise of restoration (see Joel 2:25–27) and expect its return in faith.

Prayer: Father God, the power of Your words of faith stir my spirit to have faith as well. Show me how the power of my words enable me to receive and guard Your promises. In Jesus' name, amen.

Thought: God sustains the entire universe by the power of His words!

Reading: **1 Samuel 30–31; Luke 13:23–35**

The Word Is Near You

The apostle Paul wrote, *"But the righteousness that is by faith says:...'The word is near you; it is in your mouth and in your heart'"* (Romans 10:6, 8). This passage refers to *"the word of faith"* (v. 8, emphasis added). Where is that word? It *"is near you; it is in your mouth and in your heart."* The word of faith is close to us; it dwells in our hearts, and we speak it from our mouths.

The word *"near"* also has to do with what we listen to. When you turn on the television, words of faith—that is, words that create the raw material for your belief—are near you. The same thing is true when people talk to you. What they say goes into your ears, which are the gateway to your heart, and *"out of the overflow of the heart the mouth speaks"* (Matthew 12:34).

Your words reflect what is in your heart, what you believe. Again, you will likely receive what you say because God has given you the same ability He possesses—creative expression through your words. Just as God created His world with His words, you create your world with your words. Every word is a word of faith.

This is a crucial truth for us to remember. *Faith is active belief.* It is belief combined with expectation and action.

Prayer: Father God, please open my heart to Your Word.
I want the word that is near me to be from You,
a word full of faith and truth.
Help me to hear and act on Your Word.
In Jesus' name, amen.

Thought: Faith is belief in action!

Reading: **2 Samuel 1–2; Luke 14:1–24**

The God Kind of Faith

I n Romans 10:8, Paul gave a qualification: *"'The word is near you; it is in your mouth and in your heart,' **that is, the word of faith we are proclaiming"*** (emphasis added). The word he wanted to plant in believers' hearts was the word of faith he was preaching, the one given by God.

One of the most important illustrations in the Bible concerning faith and prayer is found in Mark 11:12–14:

> *The next day as they were leaving Bethany, Jesus was hungry. Seeing in the distance a fig tree in leaf, he went to find out if it had any fruit. When he reached it, he found nothing but leaves, because it was not the season for figs. Then he said to the tree, "May no one ever eat fruit from you again." And his disciples heard him say it.*

What did Jesus do? He used words. What kind of words? Words of faith. Remember that faith is active belief. When He spoke to the tree, He actively believed the tree would die.

What happened to the tree Jesus addressed? *"In the morning, as they went along, they saw the fig tree withered from the roots. Peter remembered and said to Jesus, 'Rabbi, look! The fig tree you cursed has withered!'"* (Mark 11:20–21). Most translations give Jesus' reply as, *"Have faith in God"* (v. 22). Yet this is not the way it was written in the original Greek. Its literal translation is, "Have the God kind of faith."

Prayer: Father, I want the God kind of faith. I want to walk in faith as Jesus did, to speak words of faith and believe in my heart. Please show me the way.
In Jesus' name, amen.

Thought: The Lord wants to plant His Word of faith in each believer's heart.

Reading: **2 Samuel 3–5; Luke 14:25–35**

Faith Comes by Hearing

I tell you the truth, if anyone says to this mountain, "Go, throw yourself into the sea," and does not doubt in his heart but believes that what he says will happen, it will be done for him. Therefore I tell you, whatever you ask for in prayer, believe that you have received it, and it will be yours. (Mark 11:23–24)

The Bible says, *"Faith comes by hearing"* (Romans 10:17 NKJV). Faith doesn't just come the first time we hear. *It continues to come by continual hearing.* If you listen to one hour of solid teaching followed by two hours of negative talk, you will have faith for the negative. Faith comes from the word that is near you, which is why I'm careful about the company I keep. I want to be around people who speak words that produce *the faith of God*, because this is the kind of faith we are to have.

Be aware that other kinds of faith surround you, not just the "God kind of faith." I encourage you to check the company you keep, the books you read, the music you listen to, the movies and videos you watch, even the church you attend—you will become what you listen to and speak what you hear.

What you hear creates faith for what you are hearing. The more you hear it, the more you believe it. You speak it, and it happens to you. That is why Jesus said that if we want to operate as He does, we have to have the God kind of faith.

Prayer: Father, I desire to guard my ears and heart.
Help me to listen to Your Word and to those who believe
Your Word so I may be encouraged in my faith.
In Jesus' name, amen.

Thought: Faith continues to come by continual hearing.

Reading: **2 Samuel 6–8; Luke 15:1–10**

Faith Comes by His Word

How do you obtain the "God kind of faith"? Remember that Romans 10:8 says, *"The word is near you; it is in your mouth and in your heart."* Again, whatever is in your heart comes out of your mouth. We could define *"heart"* in this instance as the subconscious mind. It's where you store everything you have been listening to. As we have learned, what comes out of our mouths helps create our world because we are just like God in the way we function. Whatever we speak has the power to happen.

I want you to remember this truth because it will be the biggest test of your faith. What do you say in the midst of trouble? What do you say when faced with adversity? What do you say when things are not going your way? What you have been listening to will proceed from your mouth, because that is what is in your heart.

It is vital to have a constant diet of the Word of God so that it will be in your heart. It will nourish your heart so that, when you experience troubles, the Word is what will come out of your mouth, and you will create what the Word says.

May my lips overflow with praise, for you teach me your decrees. May my tongue sing of your word, for all of your commands are righteous.
(Psalm 119:171–172)

May the words of my mouth and the meditation of my heart be pleasing in your sight, O LORD, my Rock and My Redeemer.
(Psalm 19:14)

Prayer: Father, may my words reveal that Your Word
is fixed in my heart. Then my heart and my words
will be truly pleasing in Your sight.
In Jesus' name, amen.

Thought: When you experience troubles, the Word
should proceed from your mouth.

Reading: **2 Samuel 9–11; Luke 15:11–32**

The Word of Faith for Salvation

A person is saved by confessing with his mouth and believing in his heart. In Romans 10:8–9, the word that is near us is *"the word of faith we are proclaiming: that if you confess with your mouth, 'Jesus is Lord,' and believe in your heart that God raised him from the dead, you will be saved."* Being born again is difficult for some people to understand because they expect a feeling to accompany the supernatural activity of God. They err, saying, "I prayed this prayer, but I don't feel anything." The Bible says anyone who wants to be saved must believe and speak—not feel.

To be saved, a person must say with his mouth, *"Jesus is Lord."* We say, "God, can't I do something more exciting than that? How about having a light shine down from heaven? How about having me fall down and shake or something? Don't tell me to just talk!" Yet God says, "That's how faith works." When you confess with your mouth and believe in your heart, salvation comes.

This truth is crucial to your life and prayers. *Your **salvation** came by the confession of your mouth and the belief in your heart.* When you confessed your faith in the Lord Jesus, He actually became your Lord. In light of this truth, consider the following: If you are born again by your words, if you can be saved from hell and go to heaven by your words, if there is that much power in what you say, *what effect are the other words you speak having on your life?* Spend some time with the Lord considering this truth today.

Prayer: Father, I desire to speak words of faith that will have a positive, powerful, eternal effect on my life.
Help me to speak Your words of truth.
In Jesus' name, amen.

Thought: You can be positively or negatively affected by what you say and believe.

Reading: **2 Samuel 12–13; Luke 16**

APRIL 22

Jesus, You Are My Owner

*J*esus is Lord" (Romans 10:9). The word *lord* means "proprietor" or "owner." We can substitute the word *owner* for "*Lord*" to say we are saved by confessing, "Jesus is my Owner! He owns my life: body, mind, and spirit; past, present, and future. He owns my body; I can't go just anywhere I want. He owns my mind; I can't fill it with just anything. He owns my spirit; there's no room for the devil there. He owns my house; I can't do anything immoral in it." If Jesus is truly your Lord, this will be manifested in your attitude and actions.

We read in 1 Corinthians 12:3, "*No one who is speaking by the Spirit of God says, 'Jesus be cursed,' and no one can say, 'Jesus is Lord,' except by the Holy Spirit.*" You are saved by confessing that "*Jesus is Lord,*" and you can't say this unless the Holy Spirit enables you. You can't fake this confession, saying Jesus is your Lord but doing whatever you want. If you call Jesus your Lord but fail to live as if He owns your life, you insult Him. You probably know people who claim to have accepted Christ as Lord but have not changed their lifestyles. They say Jesus is their Lord, but they do not live by the Spirit of Christ.

When you truly believe and confess, "Jesus is my Lord," heaven goes into action to make sure you receive the Holy Spirit because heaven recognizes the word of faith.

Prayer: Father, thank You for Your Son, Jesus, who is the Lord of my life. Thank You for Your Holy Spirit, who enables me to make this confession of faith! In Jesus' name, amen.

Thought: Jesus is my owner; He owns all of my life.

Reading: **2 Samuel 14–15; Luke 17:1–19**

You Will Not Be Ashamed

*F*or it is with your heart that you believe and are justified, and it is with your mouth that you confess and are saved. As the Scripture says, 'Anyone who trusts in him **will never be put to shame**'" (Romans 10:10–11, emphasis added). When you say that Jesus is your Lord, you have to trust that He truly is. If you keep believing and saying that, the Bible says you will not be made ashamed.

If you tell people, "I have confessed Jesus as my Lord, and I am a child of God," they may ask, "How do we know that? You're still the same person we always knew." Yet, if you keep confessing and believing it, you will not be made ashamed. People will see a difference in you. If you keep studying and practicing God's Word, He will truly become Lord of all areas of your life.

Likewise, if you believe what you pray, if you confess and hold on to God's truth concerning your situation, you will not be made ashamed. God promised that if we live righteously and delight in His Word, we will be *"like a tree planted by streams of water, which yields its fruit in season and whose leaf does not wither,"* and whatever we do will prosper. (See Psalm 1:1–3.) You can claim that truth for yourself in prayer, and if you keep saying and believing it, God says, "You won't be made ashamed concerning it." God is faithful, so keep on praying and believing according to the word of faith.

Prayer: Father, You are faithful to Your Word.
Thank You for revealing to me Your faithfulness.
I believe that I can pray in faith and not be ashamed.
In Jesus' name, amen.

Thought: If you keep confessing and believing, you will
not be made ashamed.

Reading: **2 Samuel 16–18; Luke 17:20–37**

Are You Planted by the Stream?

P aul wrote in Ephesians 5:25-26, "*Christ loved the church and gave himself up for her to make her holy, cleansing her by the washing with water through the word.*" In the Bible, water is a symbol of the Word of God. The tree mentioned in Psalm 1:3 is "planted by streams of water." It is healthy and fruitful because it is near the streams and can draw water with its roots. Similarly, you must be connected to the Word of God so it can flow continuously into your life; then you will bear your fruit in its season. You might not receive an immediate answer to prayer, but the season will come because the Word is flowing into your life. Everyone who has questioned your trust in God will see your fruit. You can say, "I haven't seen any results yet, but there's fruit in the tree."

How do you keep believing? You must be planted in a place where the Word is prevalent and the people around you are continually speaking and living it. Spending time in the Word will transform your mind. When you hear something continually, it becomes a part of your heart. You start believing it, and you reflect your belief by what you say. Then the fruit starts to appear.

> *Blessed is the man...[whose] delight is in the law [Word] of the LORD, and on his law [Word] he meditates day and night. He is like a tree planted by streams of water, which yields its fruit in season and whose leaf does not wither. Whatever he does prospers.* (Psalm 1:1-3)

Prayer: Father, please forgive me for not remaining planted beside the water of Your Word every day. Allow my roots to go down deep into the Word so I can bear much fruit. In Jesus' name, amen.

Thought: When you stay connected to the Word of God, you will bear fruit in season.

Reading: **2 Samuel 19–20; Luke 18:1–23**

Dwelling on the Riverbank

H ave you been waiting for an answer to prayer? Some of your prayer requests have not yet been manifested because their season has not come. Therefore, between the seed prayer (your prayer in faith) and the manifestation of the fruit, you must dwell on the riverbank, reading, meditating on, speaking, living, and breathing the Word of God.

To sustain belief, you must keep taking in the Word. In fact, believers should be as riverbanks to one another, building up each other with the Word. We can *"speak to one another with psalms, hymns and spiritual songs"* (Ephesians 5:19). We also must remind others to keep believing as they await their seasons' arrival. *"Encourage one another daily, as long as it is called Today, so that none of you may be hardened by sin's deceitfulness"* (Hebrews 3:13).

*"'Anyone who trusts in him will never be put to shame.' For there is no dif-ference between Jew and Gentile–the same Lord is Lord of all and richly blesses **all** who call on him"* (Romans 10:11, emphasis added). God blesses *"all who call on Him"* because of their faith. When you trust God and believe what He has promised you, He says He will vindicate you in the end. He will make you such a blessing that people will wonder and say, "Tell me about your God." Then you can pass along the word of faith to others. Faith is a ministry God releases. He sends the word of faith, using us to deliver it to others.

Prayer: Father, give me strength to dwell along the
riverbank, drawing from Your Word and encouraging
my brothers and sisters in Christ. Together, we will
see You bring fruit in our lives.
In Jesus' name, amen.

Thought: A constant diet of the Word of God will
nourish your heart.

Reading: **2 Samuel 21–22; Luke 18:24–43**

Are You Living in Reality?

J esus told His disciples to *"be of good cheer"* in the midst of a bad storm at sea. (See Matthew 14:22–33 NKJV.) Most people would respond, "You can't be serious. There's nothing to be cheerful about. There's a storm, the boat's breaking apart, we're sinking, and you say, 'Be of good cheer'? You can't see reality, can you?"

When you express faith, some people say, "You're not facing reality." We've been trained to think that reality is what we can see. Actually, the person who is not living in faith is the one who is not living in reality. *"Faith is being sure of what we hope for and certain of what we do not see"* (Hebrews 11:1). Faith is your title deed, the proof of your legal ownership of what you are praying for. Faith is your reality!

Again, make sure you exercise the "God kind of faith." Jesus said, "If you remain in me and my words remain in you, ask whatever you wish, and it will be given you" (John 15:7). In effect, He said, "Tell Me what I tell you." The God kind of faith puts complete trust in God's Word.

Keep believing and speaking of God's goodness and the "impossible" things He can bring to pass. Romans 4:17 says God fulfills His Word and *"calls things that are not as though they were."* Affirm in your heart, "This is the beginning of a new lifestyle of faith for me—the God kind of faith." Remember, all prayers must be prayers of faith!

Prayer: Father, I believe that if I pray according to
Your Word, You will be faithful to answer me. Continue
to lead me into this exciting life of prayer.
In Jesus' name, amen.

Thought: Faith, active belief, and expectation all come by
what we hear.

Reading: **2 Samuel 23–24; Luke 19:1–27**

Putting Prayer into Practice

A sk yourself some tough questions: How much time do I spend absorbing God's Word compared to taking other viewpoints from television, movies, books, magazines, and the Internet? Which influences me most—God's Word or what others say? If faith is belief in action, what do my actions say about what I believe? What negative ideas have I allowed to permeate my life?

Take steps today to change your way of thinking to God's way. First, list any negative thoughts you think or hear during the day. In the evening, review and counteract them with truths found in God's Word. Start developing the "God kind of faith" by applying God's Word to a specific situation in your life. State your findings, pray about the situation, and hold fast to the Word whenever you are tempted to doubt! Spend less time with negative people and more time with those who read and live out the Word. If your spouse and children are negative, live in a way that expresses your own faith and speak the Word of God to them as you have opportunity. Finally, I challenge you to spend at least as much time in the Word this week as you do watching television. Then, watch the power and presence of God change your life!

Let's pray together:

Prayer: Heavenly Father, the Bible says that the word
of faith is near us, that it is in our mouths and in our hearts.
We pray that we will place our trust in You and Your Word
rather than in the words of faith all around us that are contrary
to Your truth. Forgive us for spending more time dwelling on
our own plans, ideas, scenarios, analyses, and schemes
than on taking Your Word into our hearts and living by it.
Open the truths of Your Word to us and let us rely on You alone.
We pray this in the name of Jesus,
who is the Living Word. Amen.

Thought: What do my actions say about what I believe?

Reading: **1 Kings 1–2; Luke 19:28–48**

Principles for Cultivating
the God Kind of Faith

Today, reflect on these principles:

1. Unanswered prayer has more to do with our having the wrong kind of faith than a lack of faith.

2. Men and women were created in God's image to operate in the same way He does—through words of faith.

3. Faith is active belief. It is a point of action or belief combined with expectation.

4. "'The word is near you; it is in your mouth and in your heart'" (Romans 10:8). Positive faith and negative faith come by the same means: what we listen to and believe.

5. Sometimes God doesn't answer our prayers because He knows what we're asking for wouldn't be good for us.

6. What you say reflects what is in your heart—what you believe. What you keep saying is what you will receive.

7. Paul said that the word of faith he wanted to plant in believers' hearts was the one he was preaching—the one given by God. (See Romans 10:8.)

8. The literal translation of Jesus' statement, "Have faith in God" (Mark 11:22), is, "Have the God kind of faith."

9. The God kind of faith comes from hearing His Word.

10. A constant diet of God's Word will nourish your heart. When you experience troubles, the Word will proceed from your mouth, and you will create what the Word says.

11. If you confess and hold on to God's truth, you will not be made ashamed. He will answer. (See Romans 10:10–11.) Stay connected to the Word of God to bear fruit in season. (See Psalm 1:1–3.)

12. To keep believing, you must plant yourself in a place where the Word is prevalent and the people around you are continually speaking and living it.

Reading: **1 Kings 3–5; Luke 20:1–26**

The Power behind Prayer

I t is vital to understand the power behind prayer. We need to recognize three areas of power: God's Word and Spirit, the Christian life and fasting, and the name of Jesus. We will explore these themes in the coming days, beginning with the power of God's Word.

To understand the power of the Word, we first need to understand the heart of prayer. The heart of prayer is asking God to intervene in the world to fulfill His eternal purposes for mankind. We are to pray to God on the basis of His Word—the revelation of His identity, His will, and His promises. God gave man dominion over the earth, but this doesn't mean he should do anything he wants with his life or the resources of the world. Outside of God's will, man and the world will not function properly because they were designed to function according to God's purposes. Just as an inventor knows how he designed his product to function, our Creator knows how we function best and has provided this knowledge in His Word.

Therefore, the key to effective prayer is understanding God's purpose for your life—as a human being in general, and as an individual specifically. In this way, God's will can become the authority of your prayers. True prayer calls forth what God has already purposed and predestined—the establishment of His plans for the earth. Whatever we ask God to do in our lives, in the lives of others, or in the world must be based on His will. God's purpose should be the motivation for and the subject of our prayers.

Prayer: Father, please help me to see Your plan for my life.
I want to have an active part in Your purpose on this earth.
In Jesus' name, amen.

Thought: God's purpose is the raw material of prayer.

Reading: **1 Kings 6–7; Luke 20:27–47**

Handling the Word of God

O ur power in prayer is the Word of God. Through God's Word, we can know, believe, and agree in faith with God's will. Without His Word, our prayers lack a solid foundation; they rest on a flimsy base of opinions, desires, and feelings rather than on *"the living and enduring word of God"* (1 Peter 1:23). Such prayers are powerless to effect change, but all the power of God is available to true prayer.

Prayer is very simple—it's speaking the Word to God exactly as He gave it to us. Since we receive the same raw material for prayer as other believers, our effectiveness in prayer often depends on how we handle God's Word. This can make the difference between answered and unanswered prayer. We must handle the Word properly and responsibly. (See 2 Timothy 2:15.)

First, we must understand that God Himself is speaking in the Word, because the Word is who He is: *"In the beginning was the Word, and the Word was with God, and the Word was God"* (John 1:1, emphasis added). God's presence becomes part of our prayers when we speak His Word in faith. In 1 Kings 19, Elijah did not find God in the wind, earthquake, or fire, but in *"a still small voice"* (v. 12 NKJV). Many people want a manifestation of God's power, but they don't realize His Word is the foundation of that power—*that the power is only a reflection of the greatness of God Himself.* God's Word is so powerful that faith the size of a mustard seed can move mountains. (See Matthew 17:20.)

Prayer: Father, without Your Word, our prayers have no foundation. Please help me grow in Your Word so my communion with You will be true and my prayers will be effective. In Jesus' name, amen.

Thought: God Himself is speaking in the Word.

Reading: **1 Kings 8–9; Luke 21:1–19**

Revealing God's Nature

T he Word reveals God's nature, and His nature reflects His will. Everything God says reveals His character and purposes. Remember, God and His Word are inseparable. Because of His integrity, God fulfills His Word.

How will we respond to what the Word reveals about God's character? Numbers 23:19 says, *"God is not a man, that he should lie, nor a son of man, that he should change his mind. Does he speak and then not act? Does he promise and not fulfill?"* Do we believe that God will keep His Word? A cardinal principle of answered prayer is belief in the trustworthiness of the One to whom you pray. The power of your prayers depends on it. The Word will work in your life only as you believe it:

> And we also thank God continually because, when you received the word of God, which you heard from us, you accepted it not as the word of men, but as it actually is, the word of God, **which is at work in you who believe.**   (1 Thessalonians 2:13, emphasis added)

Placing confidence in someone's word and character demonstrates that you believe him. The same thing applies to your relationship with God. What do you demonstrate about your belief (or disbelief) in God? Your belief is evidence that you trust Him. He is not impressed by how many Scriptures you quote or how long you pray. He is moved and convinced when you believe what He has told you and when you prove it by acting on it.

Prayer: Father, I believe that You are honorable and true
to Your Word. Help me to grow in my faith, to learn
to trust You more and more each day.
In Jesus' name, amen.

Thought: Belief is trust in action!

Reading: 1 Kings 10–11; Luke 21:20–38

The Word Is Alive

There is power in the Word because it is more than knowledge and facts; *it is life itself.* Take time today to meditate on these powerful passages of Scripture:

*Take to heart all the words I have solemnly declared to you this day, so that you may command your children to obey carefully all the words of this law. They are not just idle words for you—**they are your life.***
(Deuteronomy 32:46–47, emphasis added)

*The Spirit gives life; the flesh counts for nothing. The words I have spoken to you are spirit and **they are life.***
(John 6:63, emphasis added)

*You have been born again, not of perishable seed, but of imperishable, through **the living and enduring word of God**. For, "All men are like grass, and all their glory is like the flowers of the field; the grass withers and the flowers fall, but the word of the Lord stands forever." And this is the word that was preached to you.*
(1 Peter 1:23–25, emphasis added)

***The word of God is living and active.** Sharper than any double-edged sword, it penetrates even to dividing soul and spirit, joints and marrow; it judges the thoughts and attitudes of the heart.*
(Hebrews 4:12, emphasis added)

The Word is alive—that's how powerful it is! Embrace this truth from God's Word today.

Prayer: Father, Your Word is alive and active in my life.
I surrender to the living and enduring Word of God.
Help me to embrace the truth of Your Word.
In Jesus' name, amen.

Thought: The backbone of prayer is our agreement
with God's Word.

Reading: **1 Kings 12–13; Luke 22:1–20**

The Power of the Word

What did God use to create the world? *"The Word...was with God in the beginning. Through him all things were made; without him nothing was made that has been made"* (John 1:1-3). What did God give Abraham that caused him to believe? *"Abram fell facedown, and **God said to him,** 'As for me, this is my covenant with you: You will be the father of many nations'"* (Genesis 17:3-4, emphasis added).

What was the source of Moses' success? *"**God called to him** from within the bush, 'Moses! Moses!' And Moses said, 'Here I am'"* (Exodus 3:4, emphasis added; see also verses 5-10). Why was Ezekiel a powerful prophet? In the book of Ezekiel, the prophet reported fifty times, *"**The word of the Lord** came to me"* (emphasis added).

How did God redeem the world? *"**The Word became flesh and made his dwelling among us**"* (John 1:14, emphasis added).

What did Jesus give His disciples for salvation and sanctification? *"Whoever **hears my word** and believes him who sent me has eternal life and will not be condemned; he has crossed over from death to life"* (John 5:24, emphasis added). *"You are already clean because of **the word** I have spoken to you"* (John 15:3, emphasis added). *"Sanctify them by the truth; **your word is truth**"* (John 17:17, emphasis added).

What did the disciples use to continue Jesus' ministry on earth?

*"Now, LORD, consider their threats and **enable your servants to speak your word** with great boldness."...And they were all filled with the Holy Spirit and **spoke the word of God boldly**.*

(Acts 4: 29, 31, emphasis added)

In every situation, the answer is the same: the powerful Word of God!

Prayer: Father, thank You for the presence and power
of Your Word, which transforms my life.
In Jesus' name, amen.

Thought: God's Word is the source of all creation.

Reading: **1 Kings 14–15; Luke 22:21–46**

If…You Abide in Me

It is likely that no one quoted Scripture more than Jesus. When He was tempted by Satan in the wilderness, He responded with God's Word alone. (See Matthew 4:4, 7, 10.) Jesus was so familiar with the Word that He wasn't fooled when the enemy distorted it. (See verse 6.) When Jesus spoke the Word in faith, God fulfilled it, and Christ overcame temptation.

God says, "[My Word] *will not return to me empty, but will accomplish what I desire and achieve the purpose for which I sent it*" (Isaiah 55:11). If the church would believe this Scripture, it could shake the world. No word of God is empty of power.

If we want the Word to work powerfully in our lives, we must make sure it's inside us. Jesus said, "*If you abide in Me, and My words abide in you, you will ask what you desire, and it shall be done for you*" (John 15:7 NKJV). Perhaps you've read this verse and tried it, but felt it didn't work. Yet Christ was giving us the key to success.

Two conditions for answered prayer are "*If you abide in Me*" and "*If…My words abide in you.*" *Abiding in Jesus* means continual spiritual communion with Him by fellowship, worship, prayer, and fasting.

To test whether God's Word is *abiding* or *living* in you, assess the first thing that comes out of your mouth when you're under pressure. Is it an affirmation of faith, or is it fear, confusion, doubt, or anger? The Word is truly inside us when it directs our thoughts and actions, even under pressure.

Prayer: Father God, Jesus quoted Your Word when He faced temptation, and I want to do the same. Help me to know Your Word so I can defeat the devil with it as Your Son did. In Jesus' name, amen.

Thought: The Word is working mightily in me.

Reading: 1 Kings 16–18; Luke 22:47–71

If...My Words Abide in You

J esus said, *"If you abide in Me, and My words abide in you, you will ask what you desire, and it shall be done for you"* (John 15:7 NKJV).

You can't get the Word inside you by keeping your Bible on a shelf, putting it under your pillow at night, or even by hearing someone preach it to you. Preaching only stirs up faith; you have to have the Word in you beforehand through regular reading and meditation.

Jesus gave us the condition, *"If...My words abide in you,"* so the last part of the verse could be fulfilled in us: *"Ask what you desire, and it shall be done for you."* If His words are in you, your desires and requests will reflect those words. If you are filled with the Word, you won't ask for just anything. You will ask on the basis of *His Word*, which He fulfills.

Remember that many of our prayers aren't being answered because we pray for things He never asked us to pray for. When we pray according to His Word, however, we know we are praying the will of God. God performs His Word and nothing else—neither your suggestions nor your feelings. Therefore, if you don't bring Him His Word, you won't experience the promise *"it shall be done for you."* Too often we think the phrase *"ask what you desire"* means we can ask for anything. Yet Christ says, in effect, "If My Word is abiding in you, then you can ask for what's abiding in you, and it will be done." That is the power of the Word.

Prayer: Father, may Your Word abide in me so that it
can flow out of my heart and mouth in prayer.
In Jesus' name, amen.

Thought: God fulfills His Word—not your
suggestions or feelings.

Reading: 1 Kings 19–20; Luke 23:1–25

The Word Builds Faith

T he Word of God is powerful because it produces in us what pleases God and causes Him to respond to our requests: faith. *"Faith comes from hearing the message, and the message is heard through the word of Christ"* (Romans 10:17). *"By faith we understand that the universe was formed at God's command, so that what is seen was not made out of what was visible"* (Hebrews 11:3). Faith is the result of dwelling in the Word of God. When we practice the Word of God, it becomes power to us.

It should be your goal throughout life to build your faith because the Bible makes it clear that faith is how we live: *"The righteous will live by his faith"* (Habakkuk 2:4; see also Romans 1:17; Galatians 3:11; Hebrews 10:38). We live by faith, not by sight. (See 2 Corinthians 5:7.)

> I have been crucified with Christ and I no longer live, but Christ lives in me. The life I live in the body, I **live by faith** in the Son of God, who loved me and gave himself for me.
> (Galatians 2:20, emphasis added)

You have to work on having faith in God and His Word. Jesus said, *"It is written: 'Man does not live on bread alone, but on every word that comes from the mouth of God'"* (Matthew 4:4). Your faith needs nourishment from the Word if you are to be spiritually sustained. Feed your faith by filling it with God's Word and acting on that Word. The word of man is what man is; the Word of God is what God is. To live as a child of God, you must believe His Word.

Prayer: Father, As I read and meditate on Your Word, I believe that my faith will grow. Thank You for giving me the faith I need to walk with You through this life.
In Jesus' name, amen.

Thought: Faith is simply taking God at His Word.

Reading: **1 Kings 21–22; Luke 23:26–56**

Are You Living by Doubt?

It is safer and healthier to live by faith than to live by doubt and wishful thinking. Those things produce only tension and high blood pressure and make people angry at the world because they can't see past their weak hope. Those who live by faith confound the world's understanding with their peace and joy in the midst of difficulty. Like Jesus, they can rest during storms.

God says, "You aren't supposed to live by what you see, but by what I told you." (See 2 Corinthians 5:7.) That means *what you know is more important than what you see.* Much of what you see contradicts what you know from God's Word, but what you know can supersede what you see. If you know that God will deliver you from every tribulation (see 2 Timothy 4:18), your "problems" are no more than temporary discomforts.

I don't use the word *problems* anymore because I understand that everything is under God's command. The Bible says, "*We know that in all things God works for the good of those who love him, who have been called according to his purpose*" (Romans 8:28). Everything, without exception, works for my good because I'm called according to God's purpose and will. I am confident in the knowledge that He "*calls things that are not as though they were*" (Romans 4:17). If I live only by what I see, I live in sin. "*Everything that does not come from faith is sin*" (Romans 14:23). There are many such sinners in the church who rebel against God's will by living according to what they see rather than by what God says.

Prayer: Father, thank You that all things work to my good because I love you and am called according to Your purpose. As I abide in Your Word, I believe my faith will grow so I can live by what I know about You, and not only by what I see in this world.
In Jesus' name, amen.

Thought: Faith grows out of one thing—the Word of God.

Reading: **2 Kings 1–3; Luke 24:1–35**

God's Promises Are "Yes"

S ome of the promises in the Bible were spoken to specific people or groups, yet Jesus made these promises accessible to everybody. *"No matter how many promises God has made, they are 'Yes' in Christ"* (2 Corinthians 1:20). However, you have to qualify in the same way they had to qualify—by faith. Once you know the promise, you don't have to say, "If it is God's will." A person says that only when he's unsure. God doesn't go against His promises. That's why praying the Word is so important.

Sometimes God will back you into a corner and remove all your alternatives to show you His miracle-working power. If God's Word is all you have to go on, you're about to receive a miracle! As long as you have a scheme to fall back on, you won't see the miracle. However, when you say, "I can't do anything else. If God doesn't come through, I'm finished," then God gets involved because He loves to do the impossible!

If you have faith in His Word, God will take what seems impossible and accomplish it like an everyday task. He enabled Sarah in the Old Testament and Elizabeth in the New Testament to bear sons when they were barren and past childbearing age. He enabled Mary to become the mother of Jesus when she was an unwed virgin. I like Mary's response to the angel who told her God had chosen her for this honor: *"I am the Lord's servant....May it be to me as you have said"* (Luke 1:38). In other words, "Lord, do whatever You want to do."

Prayer: Father, you have so many wonderful promises
in Your Word, and they are "yes" for me in Christ Jesus.
Please help me to surrender the "impossible" to You
and watch for miracles in my life.
In Jesus' name, amen.

Thought: God gives you the promise ahead of the blessing so that
when it comes, you'll know it came from Him.

Reading: **2 Kings 4–6; Luke 24:36–53**

Faith for Difficult Circumstances

When we pray God's Word in faith, things that have been bound up will suddenly be released. You will say, "But I have been trying to accomplish that for ten years!" Yes, but you hadn't prayed according to God's Word and trusted God's faithfulness until now. Belief will open doors that hard work can't unlock.

God says if you believe Him, He will give you the best. (See Genesis 45:18.) At your workplace, God may first put you in a lesser position to check your attitude. He may keep you there to develop your character until you qualify, when God will say, "It's time to move up!" Even if people try to thwart you, prayer will foil their plans. Expect God to act and look for the fulfillment of the promise—or it may pass you by.

The local church in Jerusalem met and prayed for Peter when he was imprisoned for preaching the gospel, and an angel delivered him from prison. Peter knocked on the door of a house where many of the believers were praying. When they saw Peter, they were astonished, even though they had been praying for his release. (See Acts 12:1-16.)

I believe they were astonished because they didn't really believe in the power of prayer, they didn't believe God could deliver Peter from his very difficult circumstances, and they didn't believe God could answer prayer that quickly.

Are you facing difficult circumstances? Do you expect God to deliver you, or are you thinking along the same lines as those who prayed for Peter? God is able to answer your prayer, and He is able to answer quickly—in any situation.

Prayer: Father, I bring my difficult circumstances before
You right now. Thank You that You have promised
to hear and answer our prayers. I trust You and
Your faithfulness for the answer.
In Jesus' name, amen.

Thought: Belief will open doors that hard work cannot unlock.

Reading: **2 Kings 7–9; John 1:1–28**

God's Word Is His Will

*I write these things to you who believe in the name of the Son of God so that you may know that you have eternal life. This is the confidence we have in approaching God: that **if we ask anything according to his will**, he hears us. And if we know that he hears us—whatever we ask—we know that we have what we asked of him.*

(1 John 5:13–15, emphasis added)

First John 5:13–15 pulls together everything we have been discussing about prayer. It begins, *"I write these things to you who believe in the name of the Son of God...."* This verse applies to you if you believe in the name of the Son of God. The passage continues, *"...so that you may know that you have eternal life."* John was saying, "I'm writing these things so that you can know you are connected to God." Then he said, *"This is the confidence we have in approaching God...."* What is that confidence? *"...that if we ask anything according to his will, he hears us."*

Here's that conditional word *"if"* again: *"If we ask anything according to his will...."* God's Word is His will. His Word is His desire, His desire is His intent, and His intent is His purpose. *"If we ask anything according to his will, he hears us."* God always hears your prayers when you pray according to His will. When you pray His Word, He hears Himself. God will hear you when He hears the words He Himself has spoken.

Prayer: Father, I believe that Your Word is Your will.
Through Your Word, show me Your
will for every area of my life.
In Jesus' name, amen.

Thought: God's Word is His desire;
His desire is His intent; His intent is His purpose.

Reading: **2 Kings 10–12; John 1:29–51**

Speak God's Words, Not Yours

God's plan for your life is even bigger than your plan. However, to enter into His plan, you must believe in and affirm it by what you say. Jesus' life was successful because He didn't speak His own words; He spoke God's words.

> For I did not speak of my own accord, but the Father who sent me commanded me what to say and how to say it. I know that his command leads to eternal life. So whatever I say is just what the Father has told me to say. (John 12:49–50)

> The words I say to you are not just my own. Rather, it is the Father, living in me, who is doing his work....He who does not love me will not obey my teaching. These words you hear are not my own; they belong to the Father who sent me. (John 14:10, 24)

This is the secret to living a victorious life of faith. It was a major key to Jesus' power on earth. Jesus Christ didn't invent words to say. He was always praying to God what God had said first. Why? Again, it is because God watches over His Word to fulfill it. Jesus' works were the Father's works because His words were the Father's words. His miracles were the Father's miracles because His words were the Father's words. He knew who He was, what He believed, and what to say, and that combination brought Him victory on earth. The same can be true for us if we follow His example!

Prayer: Father, teach me how to speak and pray
Your Word, so that my words are Your words,
and my works are Your works.
In Jesus' name, amen.

Thought: Speaking the Father's words was the primary
secret of Jesus' power.

Reading: **2 Kings 13–14; John 2**

Faith-Filled Prayers

One reason the Bible builds faith—and therefore gives power—is that it records how God answers the faith-filled prayers of His people. Hebrews 11:1 says that *"the ancients"* were commended for living by what God told them rather than by what they could see. They believed His words and acted upon them, and He responded accordingly.

The men and women of the Bible were not super-saints. They were people, just like us, who received answers to prayer as they put their faith in God, trusting His character and Word. The Bible makes this very clear:

> *Elijah was a man just like us. He prayed earnestly that it would not rain, and it did not rain on the land for three and a half years. Again he prayed, and the heavens gave rain, and the earth produced its crops.* (James 5:17–18)

Acts 10:34 says, *"God does not show favoritism."* He will not treat us any differently from believers in ancient times, except that now we have an additional advantage—the atonement and prayers of Christ on our behalf and the intercession of the Spirit. The powerful examples of believers in the Bible encourage us to have faith that God can and will intervene on our behalf.

We know from reading about the lives of these believers that many of them struggled with doubts, were inclined to mistakes and failures, and had to learn by experience. However, we also see God's faithfulness and love in teaching them His ways, coming to their aid, and strengthening them for the purposes He planned for them.

Prayer: Father, Your Word gives us examples of faith-filled believers. Even though they had weaknesses as I do, they learned to rely on You and Your Word. Teach me to rely on Your faithfulness, as well. In Jesus' name, amen.

Thought: Examples of answered prayer build faith for my own circumstances.

Reading: **2 Kings 15–16; John 3:1–18**

Heroes of Faith

The Bible is filled with examples of faithful men and women of God who believed Him to the end and experienced His power to bless, heal, and save.

A servant (Abraham's chief servant) and a king (Solomon) both asked for wisdom, and God gave it in each case. (See Genesis 24:1–27; 1 Kings 3:4–14.) Hannah asked God for blessing and deliverance from her distress, and God granted her request. (See 1 Samuel 1:1–20.) Moses and Daniel interceded for the nation of Israel, and God heard and answered in mercy. (See Exodus 32:1–14; Daniel 9.)

Nehemiah prayed for the restoration of Jerusalem (see Nehemiah 1:1–11) and was protected as he rebuilt the walls. After lifetimes of devotion to God, Anna and Simeon received signs confirming God's promise of a Redeemer. (See Luke 2:25–38.) Paul and Cornelius received understanding about the way of salvation after they prayed. (See Acts 9:1–20; Acts 10.)

Jesus at His baptism (see Luke 3:21–22) and the disciples at Pentecost (see Acts 1:14; 2:1–4) received the Holy Spirit after prayer. Peter and John received prophetic insight and revelation while they prayed. (See Acts 10:9–15; 11:1–18; Revelation 1:9–10.) Paul and Silas were delivered from prison after praying and singing to God. (See Acts 16:16–34.)

Through these examples, God tells us that He will intervene on our behalf, too. We are His beloved children, redeemed by His Son and undergoing preparation to rule and reign with Him in eternity. *"He who did not spare his own Son, but gave him up for us all—how will he not also, along with him, graciously give us all things?"* (Romans 8:32).

Prayer: Father, thank You for being a God who intervenes on my behalf as I put my faith in Your Word. In Jesus' name, amen.

Thought: The Word says much about how God answers the prayers of believers.

Reading: **2 Kings 17–18; John 3:19–36**

Preparing Us for Prayer

The Word prepares us for prayer and helps us maintain communion with God. The Psalms say that when we embrace the Word, it will keep us aligned with God's will:

> Blessed are they who keep his statutes and seek him with all their heart. They do nothing wrong; they walk in his ways....I have hidden your word in my heart that I might not sin against you.
> (Psalm 119:2–3, 11)

Aaron had to prepare himself to enter God's presence before offering sacrifices on the day of Atonement. We need to offer ourselves daily as living sacrifices to God so we can have continual fellowship with Him. "*Offer your bodies as living sacrifices, holy and pleasing to God—this is your spiritual act of worship*" (Romans 12:1). As our minds are transformed by reading and meditating on the Word, we will know the will of God and will pray confidently and effectively:

> Do not conform any longer to the pattern of this world, but be transformed by the renewing of your mind. **Then you will be able to test and approve what God's will is—his good, pleasing and perfect will.**
> (v. 2, emphasis added)

The Word of God is a tremendous gift that gives us the power to know and do the will of God, the power to pray with certainty and boldness, and the power to know that God hears us when we pray according to His will. "*And if we know that he hears us—whatever we ask—we know that we have what we asked of him*" (1 John 5:15).

Prayer: Father, as I learn Your Word, please help me to hide it in my heart so I won't sin against You. I desire continual communion with You as I dwell in Your Word.
In Jesus' name, amen.

Thought: The Word gives us the power to know and do the will of God.

Reading: **2 Kings 19–21; John 4:1–30**

Putting Prayer into Practice

D o you believe God will keep His Word? Do you think of the Word as alive and active on your behalf? Or is reading the Bible just a religious obligation to you? When you read biblical accounts of God answering the prayers of His people, does your faith grow? Focus this week on abiding in Christ and having His words abide in you (see John 15:7) so the Word will work powerfully in your life. Spend time worshipping and fellowshipping with God, reading and mediating on His Word, praying, and fasting.

Meditate on verses relevant to your needs in order to build your faith in God and His Word: *wisdom*—James 1:5; *salvation*—John 3:16; *healing*—1 Peter 2:24; *finances*—Philippians 4:19; *prosperity*—Isaiah 1:19–20; *provision*—Matthew 7:11.

Choose three people in the Bible who offered effectual prayers to God and discover how they prayed, how they lived, what God promised them, and how He answered their prayers. Record your findings and refer to them when you face similar situations.

Let's pray together:

Prayer: Heavenly Father, Jesus said that those who hear the Word and receive it are like good soil. We ask You to fulfill Your Word in our lives. Let us be fertile soil that produces good fruit. Your Word says You will answer prayer offered in faith and according to Your will. We will expect and prepare for the answer, confident that if You said it, You will do it; if You promised it, it will come to pass.
Thank You for the faith You have given us.
Help us to expect a miracle.
We pray in the name of Jesus, our High Priest,
who sits at Your right hand and intercedes for us. Amen.

Thought: The Word will bring forth good fruit from us.

Reading: **2 Kings 22–23; John 4:31–54**

Principles of the Word in Prayer

Reflect on the power of the Word and its relationship to effective prayer today:

1. Whatever we ask God to do in our lives, in the lives of others, or in the world, must be based on His Word. God's purpose is to be both the motivation and the content of our prayers.
2. Without God's Word as their basis, our prayers have no foundation. They are based merely on our opinions, desires, and feelings. Such prayers are powerless to effect change.
3. Prayer is speaking the Word to God exactly as He gave it to us.
4. There is no difference between what God gave the people in the Bible as the basis for their effective prayers and what He gives us to work with. Both rely on what God has given all mankind—His Word.
5. God wants to use His power in the world; however, for Him to do so, we must know how to appropriate His Word. We must understand it and apply it properly.
6. God Himself is speaking in the Word.
7. God's Word is the foundation of His power. His power is a reflection of His greatness.
8. The Word reveals God's nature to us.
9. A cardinal principle of answered prayer is belief in the trustworthiness of the One to whom you're praying. Belief is trust in action.
10. The Word is alive and active on our behalf.
11. The Word builds faith in us.
12. The Word says much about how God answers the prayers of believers.
13. The Word prepares us for prayer.

Reading: **2 Kings 24–25; John 5:1–24**

The Impact of Sin

Spiritual and emotional hindrances block true fellowship with God and answers to prayer. We must recognize and remove them to live in harmony with Him and to have confidence in prayer.

The first hindrance is the impact of sin, which corrupts our faith, obedience, and prayers. *"Therefore, get rid of all moral filth and the evil that is so prevalent and humbly accept the word planted in you, which can save you. Do not merely listen to the word, and so deceive yourselves. Do what it says"* (James 1:21–22).

When you sin—especially willfully—and disobey the Word, God will not hear you; you will not receive His favor. Isaiah 59:2 tells us, *"Your iniquities have separated you from your God; your sins have hidden his face from you, so that he will not hear,"* and Psalm 66:18 says, *"If I regard iniquity in my heart, the Lord will not hear me"* (KJV). First John 3:22 says, *"And whatever we ask we receive from Him, because we **keep His commandments and do those things that are pleasing in His sight**"* (NKJV, emphasis added).

When we repent, however, 1 John 2:1 assures us, *"If anybody does sin, we have one who speaks to the Father in our defense—Jesus Christ, the Righteous One."* Scripture promises that God will forgive us and hear us again:

> *If my people, who are called by my name, will humble themselves and pray and seek my face and turn from their wicked ways, **then will I hear from heaven** and will forgive their sin and will heal their land.*
>
> (2 Chronicles 7:14, emphasis added)

Prayer: Father, thank You for forgiving my sins.
Please hear my prayers and give me the strength to avoid sin.
In Jesus' name, amen.

Thought: Clearing out hindrances in our lives enables us to live in harmony with God.

Reading: **1 Chronicles 1–3; John 5:25–47**

Fear Is Faith in the Negative

Fear is another hindrance because it keeps us from believing we can approach God in prayer. First John 4:18 says, *"There is no fear in love. But perfect love drives out fear, because fear has to do with punishment* ["*because fear involves torment*" NKJV]. *The one who fears is not made perfect in love."* We're afraid to approach God when we think He will remember our sin or failure and hold it against us. This prevents freedom and confidence in prayer; it blocks faith and renders prayer ineffective.

The Bible says that *"fear involves torment."* Fear immobilizes you. Fear is faith in what could go wrong rather than faith in what could go right. It is believing the devil and other people rather than God.

When you go before God, your sins do not matter if you confess them to Him, appropriating the cleansing blood of Jesus to purify you from all unrighteousness. (See 1 John 1:9.) He will forgive you, and you can approach Him as if you never sinned. No fear should inhibit your prayers.

When we realize that God loved us first and desired a relationship with us even when we didn't know Him and lived in sin, we will understand that we can come to Him and ask for forgiveness. Romans 5:8 echoes this idea: *"But God demonstrates his own love for us in this:* **while we were still sinners**, *Christ died for us"* (emphasis added).

God wants you to be assured of forgiveness and to move forward in His purposes with confidence. *"For God has not given us a spirit of fear, but of power and of love and of a sound mind"* (2 Timothy 1:7 NKJV).

Prayer: Father, thank You for Your love and forgiveness.
Help me never to be afraid to approach You.
In Jesus' name, amen.

Thought: Fear is faith in what could go wrong rather than faith in what could go right.

Reading: **1 Chronicles 4–6; John 6:1–21**

Do You Struggle with Guilt?

S ome people are hindered by a constant sense of guilt, but Romans 8:1-2 tells us, "Therefore, **there is now no condemnation** *for those who are in Christ Jesus, because through Christ Jesus the law of the Spirit of life set me free from the law of sin and* [its consequence] *death"* (emphasis added).

"*There is now no condemnation*" (Romans 8:1). I once spoke at a prayer meeting about Christ freeing us from condemnation. After the meeting, someone told me, "That word was so important for me. I thought that because I'd done some terrible things..., God wouldn't want me to be a part of His work any longer. I asked for forgiveness, but I just needed to hear God say, 'It's okay. You're forgiven.'"

Even after some people have been forgiven, they may go to church, worship, and seem happy, but inside they still feel guilty. Their spiritual growth is stunted because they think God holds their sins against them, and they no longer approach Him in faith and perfect love. God has forgiven and forgotten your sin if you have confessed, repented, and believed in the cleansing blood of Jesus. Hebrews 8:12 says, *"For I will forgive their wickedness and will remember their sins no more."*

Guilt sometimes stems from distrust. If you have asked God to forgive you, He has forgiven you. If you still carry around the sin in your heart and mind, your doubt that God really forgave you brings the guilt back to life. Put away your distrust. You can trust God, who is faithful to forgive your sins and cleanse you from unrighteousness. (See 1 John 1:9.)

Prayer: Father, I can cast off guilt because of Your forgiveness. Help me to trust You always and to realize there is no condemnation because of Jesus Christ. In His precious name, amen.

Thought: Guilt is related to the fear of not being forgiven.

Reading: **1 Chronicles 7–9; John 6:22–44**

The Sea of Forgetfulness

The Bible says, "[God] *will tread our sins underfoot and hurl all our iniquities into the depths of the sea*" (Micah 7:19), and "*I, even I, am he who blots out your transgressions, for my own sake, and remembers your sins no more*" (Isaiah 43:25). God forgets your sins once He forgives them. Since He has chosen to forget them, He doesn't want you to remind Him about them.

One of my college professors used to say, "After we ask for forgiveness, God puts up a little sign that says, 'No fishing.'" He has cast our sins into the sea of forgetfulness, and we aren't to go fishing there. Thank God that everything in the past is forgiven and forgotten. We have been cleansed by the blood of Jesus.

Accept that God has cast your sin into the sea of forgetfulness so you can have power in prayer. Seek reconciliation in your broken relationships and restitution for wrongs you have committed. In the future, if you sin, ask God to forgive you and to continue the process of sanctification in your life. Receive His forgiveness and draw near to Him again in confident faith:

Therefore, brothers, since we have confidence to enter the Most Holy Place by the blood of Jesus, by a new and living way opened for us through the curtain, that is, his body, and since we have a great priest over the house of God, **let us draw near to God** *with a sincere heart in full assurance of faith, having our hearts sprinkled to cleanse us from a guilty conscience and having our bodies washed with pure water.*
(Hebrews 10:19–22, emphasis added)

Prayer: Father, I desire to draw near You with a heart
fully assured by faith. You have cleansed me
from sin, and I praise Your name!
In Jesus' name, amen.

Thought: You can walk into God's presence without feeling
condemned.

Reading: **1 Chronicles 10–12; John 6:45–71**

Do You Feel Unworthy?

F eelings of unworthiness will sabotage your prayer life. You cannot pray effectively if you feel ashamed of yourself and unworthy to receive what you request of God. If you have a low opinion of yourself, you don't know God's true regard for you as revealed in His Word. Here is a marvelous Scripture that describes how God sees us:

> *In love [God] **predestined us to be adopted as his sons** through Jesus Christ, in accordance with his pleasure and will—to the praise of his glorious grace, which he has freely given us in the One he loves. In him we have redemption through his blood, the forgiveness of sins, in accordance with the riches of God's grace that he lavished on us with all wisdom and understanding....In him we were also **chosen**.*
> (Ephesians 1:4–8, 11, emphasis added)

We were chosen in Christ long before the earth was made. God lavishes His love on us. Self-loathing is not from God, but from the enemy. Satan doesn't want you to realize that your value to God is incalculable.

The book of Hebrews says we're so precious to God that He gave Jesus to be the sacrifice, or propitiation, for our sin. (See chapter 10.) Hebrews 4:16 says, *"Let us then approach the throne of grace with confidence* ["come boldly to the throne of grace" NKJV], *so that we may receive mercy and find grace to help us in our time of need."* In light of our value to God, we can respect ourselves and approach Him as chosen children who have received *"the riches of God's grace"* (Ephesians 1:7).

Prayer: Father, thank You for the riches of Your grace.
Please guide me into Your truth so that I will always approach
Your throne with the confidence of being Your child.
In Jesus' name, amen.

Thought: A low opinion of yourself is not from God.

Reading: **1 Chronicles 13–15; John 7:1–27**

Do Your Prayers Deserve Answers?

S elf-image plays a significant role in how we approach God in prayer. When you have a proper estimation of yourself as a redeemed child of God, you don't come to prayer as a beggar. Instead, you present your case confidently. Prayer does not mean appealing to God's sympathy; rather, prayer means coming to Him knowing you deserve what you request *because of the righteousness of Christ* and because the request is *based on His Word.*

You must present the evidence of God's Word as in a court of law. In addition, you must believe that when you walk into the courtroom of Jehovah, Jesus is at your left, the witness side, and the Holy Spirit is at your right, as your counsel. (See Hebrews 7:25; John 14:16–17.) In God's courtroom, with your heavenly Father as Judge, your Elder Brother (Jesus the Son) as witness, and the Holy Spirit as your personal counselor, how can you lose the case?

Jesus goes before the Father and testifies to your faith in Him. When you don't know how to plead, or when you aren't sure how to quote the promises, the Holy Spirit intercedes: *"In the same way, the Spirit helps us in our weakness. We do not know what we ought to pray for, but the Spirit himself intercedes for us with groans that words cannot express"* (Romans 8:26). He speaks to God directly from the heart of a legal counsel. Therefore, when your efforts are inadequate, you have heavenly assistance to help you pray.

Prayer: Father, please help me to remember that my prayers deserve an answer when I come to You in Christ's righteousness and according to what You have promised in Your Word. In Jesus' name, amen.

Thought: You need to present the evidence of God's Word as in a court of law.

Reading: 1 Chronicles 16–18; John 7:28–53

Come Boldly to Pray

S ome people believe they shouldn't come to prayer boldly. They are mild-mannered and fawning, thinking God will see them as humble and grant their requests. Yet true humility is not pretentious or feigned; a humble person knows who he is, and he is honest. However, you can't *be* who you are if you don't *know* who you are. And if you don't know who you are, it's difficult to approach God in prayer. We are God's own children, and we need to approach Him as His children.

How would you feel if your child crawled into the room and timidly asked, "Would you please feed me today?" That would be an affront to your love. Something is wrong if your child is afraid to ask you for food. As a child of God, you can walk boldly into the throne room and say, "Hello, Abba." Your Father will say, "What can I do for you, My child? Remind Me of what I promised you." Then, you can present your case.

A lawyer representing you in a court of law wouldn't merely beg, "Please, judge, I plead with you to let him go." He would bring facts and evidence. Likewise, pleading your case before God doesn't mean saying, "O God, *please* forgive me!" It means telling Him, "According to Your Word, You have said, *'This righteousness from God comes through faith in Jesus Christ to all who believe'* (Romans 3:22), and I'm presenting Your words as evidence. I believe; therefore, I ask You to justify me." You can't pray like that if you feel afraid and inferior. You pray like that when you have assurance of who you are in Christ.

Prayer: Father, You have invited me to come boldly to Your throne through Christ. You have called me Your child. May I never forget that You see me with the eyes of a Father. In Jesus' name, amen.

Thought: You can't *be* who you are if you don't *know* who you are in Christ.

Reading: **1 Chronicles 19–21; John 8:1–27**

You Are My Beloved Child

M ost of us don't understand what prayer signifies about our relationship with God. The parable of the prodigal son illustrates this relationship for us. (See Luke 15:11–24.) God says to each of us, in effect, "You aren't a servant; you are a son." Too often we come to prayer and say, "Lord, I am Your unworthy servant." God responds, "What are you talking about? You are My beloved child!"

When you pray, keep in mind who you are in Christ and what God has promised you. If you do not immediately receive an answer, don't allow feelings of unworthiness to make you think nothing happened. It did. It may take a week. It may take twenty-one days, as in the case of Daniel. It may take longer. However, your prayer has been answered and will be manifested.

Remember—you are not a servant, but a child of God. *"He has made us accepted in the Beloved"* (Ephesians 1:6 NKJV). God loved you before laying the earth's foundation. When you were estranged from Him by sin, He sent His Son to die for you. He has made you worthy in Christ Jesus. He has made you a coheir with His Son. He sends His angels to minister to you. Therefore, live and pray accordingly.

Prayer: Father, You have assured me in Your Word that
I am Your child. Please help me to walk as someone who is
accepted by You, loved by You, and listened to by You.
In Jesus' name, amen.

Thought: When you pray, keep in mind
who you are in Christ.

Reading: 1 Chronicles 22–24; John 8:28–59

What Are Your Motives?

W hat motivates you to pray? Are you asking God for something just to boost your own ego or to achieve other selfish purposes, or are you asking God to fulfill His Word so that His kingdom can come on the earth? If your motives are wrong, your prayers will be hindered, according to James 4:3: *"When you ask, you do not receive, because you ask with wrong motives ["ask amiss" NKJV], that you may spend what you get on your pleasures."*

God knows we have needs, and it's not wrong to ask Him to fulfill them based on His Word. Jesus said, *"Your Father knows what you need before you ask him"* (Matthew 6:8). Yet our main focus should be honoring God and promoting His purposes. When our priorities are right, we can trust Him to meet our daily needs. Jesus promised us,

> *Do not worry, saying, "What shall we eat?" or "What shall we drink?" or "What shall we wear?" For the pagans run after all these things, and your heavenly Father knows that you need them. But seek first his kingdom and his righteousness, and all these things will be given to you as well.* (Matthew 6:31–33)

When you pray, ask God to forgive you for any impure motives and to enable you to develop the right motives through the work of the Holy Spirit. *"For it is God who works in you to will and to act according to his good purpose"* (Philippians 2:13).

Prayer: Father, please check the motives of my heart.
Reveal when I pray with impure motives, so that I might confess
them. I want to make Your purposes my own.
In Jesus' name, amen.

Thought: God is the one who enables us to have the right motives.

Reading: 1 Chronicles 25–27; John 9:1–23

The Danger of Bitterness

Bitterness is dangerous, especially in regard to prayer. Bitterness accumulates when you withhold forgiveness. It often indicates a hidden hatred that hurts you more than it does the other person. When you harbor bitterness, it goes to the very source of your life and dries it up. You will not only suffer spiritually, but you will also wither mentally, socially, and physically. Bitterness is like a cancer.

Psalm 66:18 says, *"If I regard iniquity* [perversity, moral evil] *in my heart, the Lord will not hear me"* (KJV). Iniquity is a secret sin—not because it's something you commit in private, but because it's unseen and intangible, such as having jealousy in your heart. You may smile at someone to conceal that you are envious of him. You may hug somebody you despise and say, "God bless you." This is iniquity. If we willfully hold such things in our hearts, it doesn't matter how long we pray; God won't listen.

Bitterness is an especially hideous, dangerous sin. *"See to it that no one misses the grace of God and that* **no bitter root** *grows up to cause trouble and defile many"* (Hebrews 12:15, emphasis added). To guard against this sin and keep our prayers from being hindered, we must maintain pure, transparent hearts before God and men. *"Let all bitterness, wrath, anger, clamor, and evil speaking be put away from you, with all malice. And be kind to one another, tenderhearted, forgiving one another, just as God in Christ forgave you"* (Ephesians 4:31-32 NKJV).

Prayer: Father, I never want to open my heart to bitterness.
Please convict me of any sins of jealousy and
unforgiveness that I may be hiding.
In Jesus' name, amen.

Thought: Bitterness can grow like a deep root into our hearts.

Reading: **1 Chronicles 28–29; John 9:24–41**

Forgive as You Are Forgiven

And when you stand praying, if you hold anything against anyone,
forgive him, so that your Father in heaven may forgive you your sins.
(Mark 11:25)

An unforgiving spirit can be a destructive presence in our lives, even when we don't realize we're harboring one. Have you forgiven your ex-husband, ex-wife, or whoever makes you angry every time you think about him or her? What about someone on the job who wronged you—someone you're still mad at after three weeks, three months, or three years?

Nurturing an unforgiving spirit can block your prayer life. The Bible says, *"'In your anger do not sin': Do not let the sun go down while you are still angry, and do not give the devil a foothold"* (Ephesians 4:26–27). Withholding forgiveness does not reflect the character of Christ, and it demonstrates ingratitude for the vast forgiveness God has given you.

Jesus made this point in the parable of the unforgiving servant in Matthew 18:23–35. In this story, the king forgives one of his servants and cancels a great debt he owed him. However, this same servant refuses to forgive a fellow servant of a lesser debt. In the end, the king throws the first servant into jail for his lack of mercy. Jesus concludes by warning His disciples, *"This is how my heavenly Father will treat each of you unless you forgive your brother from your heart"* (v. 35). Withholding forgiveness is a serious matter. You need to forgive others if you want God to forgive you and to hear your prayers.

Prayer: Father, I do not want to be captive to an unforgiving spirit. Help me forgive everyone who wrongs me with the same forgiveness that You have offered me in Christ.
In Jesus' name, amen.

Thought: Withholding forgiveness does not reflect the character of Christ.

Reading: **2 Chronicles 1–3; John 10:1–23**

Do Your Relationships Need to Be Repaired?

F irst Peter 3:7 says, *"Husbands, in the same way be considerate as you live with your wives, and treat them with respect as the weaker partner and as heirs with you of the gracious gift of life, so that nothing will hinder your prayers."* Peter was saying, "Husbands, treat your wives with understanding, and don't let there be any animosity between you, or your prayers will be hindered."

Broken relationships hinder prayer. Peter specifically addressed husbands, but the same principle applies to relationships between all family members. As believers, we are to demonstrate the nature of God to one another. Psalm 103:8–10 tells us, *"The Lord is compassionate and gracious, slow to anger, abounding in love. He will not always accuse, nor will he harbor his anger forever; he does not treat us as our sins deserve or repay us according to our iniquities."* If we do not practice the same compassion, grace, mercy, and love to others, we misrepresent God. How can we ask Him to answer our prayers and fulfill His purposes when we violate those very purposes in our treatment of others?

Matthew 5:23–24 says, *"If you are offering your gift at the altar and there remember that your brother has something against you, leave your gift there in front of the altar. First go and be reconciled to your brother; then come and offer your gift."* God is saying to us, "Reconcile your broken relationships at home before you come to church to pray." We are to put our relationships right first, and then go to worship the Lord.

Prayer: Father, my family relationships are so important.
Please help me to forgive others so that I can maintain
communion with my loved ones and with You.
In Jesus' name, amen.

Thought: *"If it is possible, as far as it depends on you,
live at peace with everyone."*

Reading: **2 Chronicles 4–6; John 10:24–42**

Idols of the Heart

Son of man, these men have set up idols in their hearts and put wicked stumbling blocks before their faces. **Should I let them inquire of me at all?** (Ezekiel 14:3, emphasis added)

In this sobering verse, God is saying, "I will not answer your prayers if you are seeking idols." He is referring to idols of the heart. We must be careful not to set up idols in our lives, however subtle they may be.

An idol is anything we give higher priority than God. We live in a culture filled with potential idols—things we make so important that we push God and His purposes for us to the back burner.

For example, we often make idols out of wealth or possessions. This can make us greedy or stingy, and an ungenerous heart hinders prayer. Proverbs 21:13 says, *"If a man shuts his ears to the cry of the poor, he too will cry out and not be answered."* How can we ask God to meet our needs if we're not concerned about the needs of the less fortunate? If we are compassionate and generous, our prayers will be answered. *"A generous man will prosper; he who refreshes others will himself be refreshed"* (Proverbs 11:25).

Idols can displace God from His rightful place in our lives if we don't examine our priorities. God deserves our utmost love, devotion, and respect. *"Love the LORD your God with all your heart and with all your soul and with all your strength"* (Deuteronomy 6:5). Let us determine, through God's grace, to remove all idols from our lives so we can truly love God and others—and have confident and effective prayer.

Prayer: Father, please help me by Your grace to remove idols from my heart. I want to love You and show Your love to others. In Jesus' name, amen.

Thought: Let us throw off everything that hinders us.

Reading: **2 Chronicles 7–9; John 11:1–29**

Putting Prayer into Practice

As you seek to remove hindrances to prayer from your life, ask yourself these questions: Is anything in my life keeping me from a clear conscience and unbroken fellowship with God? Have I accepted God's forgiveness, or am I holding on to past sins and guilt? Have I recognized that I am a child of God? What are my motives for praying? Am I harboring bitterness toward anyone?

Now, take some steps to overcome these hindrances. If you are plagued with feelings of condemnation, consciously replace these feelings with what the Word of God says about God's love and forgiveness toward you. If your relationships need mending, ask God to help you release your bitterness. Take a step toward repairing a broken relationship by forgiving someone or asking for forgiveness. Write down anything you have put before God, such as money, a relationship, or your career. Offer it to God and renew your love and commitment to Him, spending time in worship and acknowledging His Fatherhood and sovereignty.

Let's pray together:

Prayer: Heavenly Father, as Your Word says, we are burdened by things that hinder us spiritually and emotionally, and we too easily become entangled with sin. These encumbrances keep us from having a joyful, unbroken relationship with You and with our families, friends, and coworkers. Enable us to have a true understanding of who we are in Your Son, Jesus Christ. Help us to clear away every hindrance so we can live freely as Your children and pray in harmony with Your will and purposes. We ask this in the name of Jesus, who is our Burden-Bearer— who has carried our sins and sorrows, who has healed us by His wounds, and whose suffering on our behalf brought us peace with You. Amen.

Thought: *"By his wounds we are healed."*

Reading: **2 Chronicles 10–12; John 11:30–57**

Principles for Overcoming Hindrances to Prayer

Today, reflect on these major hindrances to answered prayer and how to overcome them:

1. *Sin:* If we humble ourselves, seek God, and turn from sin, God will forgive us and hear our prayers. (See 2 Chronicles 7:14.)

2. *Fear:* Fear blocks our prayers by undermining our faith. We must accept God's forgiveness and the new spirit He has given us—one of power, love, and a sound mind.

3. *Guilt:* To conquer feelings of condemnation, we must realize that God has forgiven us and has forgotten our sins; therefore, we can pray with assurance.

4. *Feelings of Inferiority:* As God's beloved children, we are not beggars. We can pray confidently based on God's Word, Jesus' testimony, and the Spirit's advocacy.

5. *Wrong Motives:* When we have our priorities right and put God's kingdom first, He will hear our prayers and meet our daily needs.

6. *Bitterness:* God will not hear our prayers if we hold iniquity in our hearts. We need to maintain pure, transparent hearts before God and men.

7. *An Unforgiving Spirit:* Withholding forgiveness blocks our relationship with God and others. Ephesians 4:26–27 says, *"Do not let the sun go down while you are still angry, and do not give the devil a foothold."*

8. *Broken Family Relationships:* God will not answer our prayers if we fail to demonstrate His love and grace to our family members. We must reconcile broken relationships as soon as we can.

9. *Idols:* We must examine our priorities. Anything we value more than God is an idol that will hinder our prayers.

10. *Stinginess:* Proverbs 21:13 says, *"If a man shuts his ears to the cry of the poor, he too will cry out and not be answered."* Our prayers will be answered if we are compassionate and generous rather than greedy and stingy.

Reading: **2 Chronicles 13–14; John 12:1–26**

Do You Understand Fasting?

There is power in prayer and fasting. All the great saints in the Bible fasted—Moses, David, Nehemiah, Jeremiah, Daniel, Anna, Paul, Peter, and even Jesus Himself. A fast is a conscious, intentional decision to abstain for a time from the pleasure of eating in order to *gain vital spiritual benefits.*

Have you ever thought something like the following? *I wish I had the faith of Joshua, who made the sun stand still. I wish I could be like Paul, whose very clothes caused the people who touched them to be healed or delivered. I'd like to be like John, who received the Revelation from God.* We admire these believers, but we don't understand how they manifested such spiritual power. It was because they committed themselves to high standards in the practice of their faith so God could use them to fulfill His purposes; in accordance with this, prayer and fasting were an integral part of their lives.

Fasting is mentioned in Scripture one-third as many times as prayer. It is a pillar of the Christian faith that was once recognized as valuable and significant in the church. For example, early church leaders prayed and fasted in order to receive direction for ministry. (See Acts 13:2–3.) Throughout Scripture, people of God fasted in times of crisis or danger. (See, for example, Esther 4:15–16.) Yet most Christians deemphasize fasting. Many consider the regular practice of fasting to be almost fanatical. So little is taught about fasting that it is not understood by many believers, especially Christians new to the body of Christ, who conclude the practice has only historic significance.

Fasting has become a lost art.

Prayer: Father, I want to follow Jesus' example of fasting.
Open my spiritual eyes to understand the
importance of this practice.
In Jesus' name, amen.

Thought: Fasting is a pillar of the Christian faith.

Reading: **2 Chronicles 15–16; John 12:27–50**

Fasting: A Natural Part of the Christian Life

When I talk to believers about fasting, they ask many questions. "Should every believer fast?" "How does fasting enhance our prayer lives?" "Does fasting simply mean abstaining from food?" "When are we to fast?" "Can a person fast but not pray?" "What is the spiritual significance of fasting?"

Fasting has been part of my walk with the Lord since I was fourteen, and I've developed a tremendous love of this wonderful experience. For the next week or so, we'll explore guidelines to help you understand how and why to fast.

First, *fasting should be a natural part of the Christian life.* In the same way that we develop habits of reading the Bible and praying, we should develop the habit of fasting. Prayer and fasting are partners in a single ministry. In Matthew 6:5-6, Jesus said, "**When** you pray..." (emphasis added), not "If you pray." In the same passage, He said, "**When** you fast..." (vv. 16-17, emphasis added). Just as prayer is not optional for believers, fasting is not optional. God expects His people to fast. At times, the Holy Spirit moves upon a person or group and supernaturally gives them a desire to fast. Most of the time, however, fasting is an act of faith and will. It's a decision we make in obedience to Christ. Even if we want to eat, we temporarily choose not to because of our love for Him.

Prayer: Father, I know that believers in the Bible often prayed and fasted. Lead me by Your Spirit to a time of prayer and fasting with You.
In Jesus' name, amen.

Thought: Fasting is a natural part of the Christian life.

Reading: 2 Chronicles 17–18; John 13:1–20

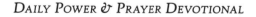

Fasting Puts God First

I n the Old Testament, the Hebrew word for fast is *tsum*. It means "to cover over the mouth." In the New Testament, the Greek word is *nesteuo*, meaning "to abstain from food." Remember, a fast is a conscious, intentional decision to abstain for a time from the pleasure of eating in order to gain vital spiritual benefits.

What does true fasting include? Today, let's look at two aspects of this practice. First, a fast is a time set apart to seek God's face. You abstain from things you enjoy in order to give your whole heart to Him in prayer. Fasting tells God, "My prayers and the answers I'm seeking are more important than my pleasure in eating."

Second, a fast puts God first; it focuses all attention on Him—not on His gifts or blessings, but on God Himself. It shows Him how much you love and appreciate Him. In this way, a fast brings intimacy with God. God reveals Himself only to people who want to know Him. He says, *"You will seek me and find me when you seek me with all your heart"* (Jeremiah 29:13). A fast is a purposeful commitment to God. If you tell Him, "Lord, I want to see Your face," but your mind wanders, He will say, "I cannot show you My face when you're not looking at Me."

Fasting is not a matter of trying to get something *from* God; it's a matter of trying to get *to* God. When you find God Himself, you will discover that everything you need comes with Him.

Prayer: Father, I desire to put You first in my life.
Help me to understand the role of fasting in my pursuit of You.
In Jesus' name, amen.

Thought: Fasting brings intimacy with God.

Reading: **2 Chronicles 19–20; John 13:21–38**

Fasting Creates an Environment for Prayer

Yesterday, we saw that fasting is a time set apart to seek God's face, and that fasting puts God first. A third characteristic of true fasting is that it fosters a sensitive environment for prayer.

In the Old Testament, people fasted in conjunction with wholehearted prayer in times of repentance. Fasting was also used as a point of deliverance from situations. When an enemy threatened God's people, the Israelites often committed themselves to fast. They would say, in effect, "We will fast until the Lord tells us what to do." The Lord would respond with a strategy, and they would win the battle. Fasting, therefore, creates an environment for God to work. We see God's Word and purposes fulfilled for us as individuals and as the collective body of Christ.

Fourth, fasting is an avenue of intercession. The majority of fasts in the Bible were observed on behalf of others' needs, such as national problems or family situations. I believe those who fast reap personal benefit from their obedience. The main purpose for fasting, however, is to benefit others.

Just before beginning His ministry, Jesus fasted forty days and nights to consecrate Himself for the difficult task of redeeming the world to fulfill God's purpose. (See Luke 4:1–2.) Before choosing His twelve disciples, Jesus spent the night in prayer. (See Luke 6:12–16.) Right before His crucifixion, Jesus prayed for His disciples and those who would believe because of their testimony. (See John 17:6–26.) Jesus prayed and fasted for others, and we should do the same.

Prayer: Father, lead me in a time of consecration and fasting so I can put others' needs before my own. Make me more like Jesus. In His precious name, I pray. Amen.

Thought: Fasting fosters a sensitive environment for the working of prayer.

Reading: **2 Chronicles 21–22; John 14**

Fasting Helps Us Hear from God

Fasting—emptying ourselves of food and filling ourselves with God—increases our spiritual capacity. As human beings, we are spirits, but we dwell in bodies that control us most of the time. When you fast, your spirit increases its control over your body. Fasting enables you to discipline your body to be a servant of the Lord rather than the master of your spirit. Your body submits to your spirit rather than pursuing its own impulses. *Fasting does not change God; it changes us and transforms our prayers.*

Much power flows through fasting. Fasting enables us to better discern God's voice to receive guidance, wisdom, instruction, and knowledge. When Moses went up on Mount Sinai, he was seeking God's will for the Israelites. God took him on a forty-day fast and gave him a powerful revelation—the Law, with its Ten Commandments—which many nations have used as the foundation of their societies. Our penal codes are based on the Law that Moses received during his fast. That's how powerful the fast was. When you fast, God will speak to you, giving you a revelation you couldn't otherwise receive.

During a fast, the time you would normally spend on meals should be spent in prayer and Bible study so you can hear what God wants to say. It's amazing how many hours are spent on food each week. Planning meals, shopping, cooking, eating, and cleaning up are time-consuming. When you fast, use that time to seek God. He has always desired a close relationship with you, and fasting allows time for you to develop true intimacy with Him.

Prayer: Father, I desire to receive guidance, wisdom, instruction, and knowledge from You. Increase my spiritual capacity to hear from You through prayer and fasting.
In Jesus' name, amen.

Thought: Fasting increases your spiritual capacity.

Reading: **2 Chronicles 23–24; John 15**

Fasting Brings Power from God

Sometimes prayer alone isn't enough to accomplish God's purposes. The Bible tells of a man who had a demon-possessed son. Jesus' disciples failed to cast out the demon; it laughed at them. Why? They were unprepared. After Jesus cast out the demon, he explained to His disciples, *"This kind does not go out except by prayer and fasting"* (Matthew 17:21 NKJV).

Christ could cast out any demon He encountered because He had spent forty days fasting and praying in preparation for ministry, and because He continued to fast and pray regularly. Spiritual powerlessness can come from feeding your flesh and neglecting your spirit. Even though God created our bodies to require food, He wants them to be controlled by our spirits. I teach the Word of God almost daily, and I eat very little beforehand. If you eat before speaking the Word, your flesh can get in the way of the flow of the anointing.

When Jesus told His disciples that the demon could come out only by prayer and fasting, He was saying, in effect, "Prayer is good, but sometimes you need to add something to your prayers: a spirit of consecration to God and an abstinence from what can interfere with the flow of God's power in your life."

If you have ever thought, "I've been a believer for many years, but God seems so far away. I feel like I'm in the desert. I have no spiritual zeal," fasting with prayer can draw you close to God, revive your spirit, and give you spiritual power.

Prayer: Father, I have walked with You for some time but I have lost my zeal for You. Please draw me to you and fill me with Your power as I fast and pray.
In Jesus' name, amen.

Thought: Fasting with prayer helps to prepare you for a more powerful ministry.

Reading: **2 Chronicles 25–27; John 16**

Christ Is Our Example

W e should model Christ's example when fasting. When He was on earth, He had God's anointing to meet people's needs, but He still needed to fast. The Bible says,

> Jesus, **full of the Holy Spirit**, *returned from the Jordan and was led by the Spirit in the desert, where for forty days he was tempted by the devil. He ate nothing during those days....When the devil had finished all this tempting, he left him until an opportune time. Jesus returned to Galilee* **in the power of the Spirit.**
>
> (Luke 4: 1–2, 13–14, emphasis added)

The Holy Spirit had come upon Jesus when He was baptized. (See Luke 3:21–22.) Yet after fasting, He returned *"in the power of the Spirit."* Jesus didn't *receive* the Holy Spirit after He fasted, but the Spirit within Him was manifested *with new power*. Although you received the Holy Spirit when you were born again, fasting ignites His power within you; you develop a hunger for intimacy with God, and the work of the Holy Spirit is manifested in your life. Witnessing about God's love and grace brings you joy, and you serve God in ways you never expected.

Soon after His forty-day fast, Jesus encountered a demon-possessed man. When you fast, God sends you challenges because you're ready to handle them now through His Spirit. There are people to whom God wants you to minister, but they won't cross your path until you're equipped to help them. Fasting prepares you for ministry.

Prayer: Father, thank You for teaching me about the
power that accompanies fasting. Please equip me for
ministry as I consecrate myself to You.
In Jesus' name, amen.

Thought: A fast ignites the power of the Spirit within you.

Reading: **2 Chronicles 28–29; John 17**

Breakthrough in Difficult Situations

F asting often brings a breakthrough in difficult circumstances or in the lives of those resistant to the gospel. In the book of Joel, we read,

> *The vine is dried up and the fig tree is withered; the pomegranate, the palm and the apple tree—all the trees of the field—are dried up....Come, spend the night in sackcloth, you who minister before my God; for the grain offerings and drink offerings are withheld from the house of your God. **Declare a holy fast**; call a sacred assembly. Summon the elders and all who live in the land to the house of the LORD your God, and cry out to the LORD.* (Joel 1:12–14, emphasis added)

This seems like a depressing passage of Scripture, doesn't it? It lists all the things that are lacking. Everything had gone wrong for the Israelites, but the Lord had the answer. He said, *"Declare a holy fast."* Likewise, when nothing seems to be going right for us, God says, "Stop everything and consecrate yourself. Come to Me."

> *"Even now," declares the LORD, "return to me with all your heart, with fasting and weeping and mourning." Rend your heart and not your garments. Return to the LORD your God, for he is gracious and compassionate, slow to anger and abounding in love, and he relents from sending calamity.* (Joel 2:12–13)

Later, God said, in essence, "After you fast, get ready, because something good is going to happen. Start making some noise, because I'm getting ready to break forth." (See Joel 2:18–32.)

Prayer: Father, You are always there for my deliverance. Please help me turn to You and consecrate my heart through prayer and fasting. In Jesus' name, amen.

Thought: After sincere fasting and prayer, God responds with deliverance and blessing.

Reading: **2 Chronicles 30–31; John 18:1–18**

Only Prayer and Fasting

Have you been praying about something for a long time? You may need to add fasting to your prayers. I used to wonder why my mother would say to my siblings and me, "All of you are going to get saved. I'm fasting for you all." My mother would often fast, especially when one of her sons was getting into trouble. She called it "paying the price for him." Today, every one of her eleven children is born again. She saw us all saved before she went to be with the Lord. Praying isn't enough for some children. They're so tough that you have to go a little deeper and fast for them to be delivered.

James reminds us of the importance of consecration in prayer: *"The prayer of a righteous man is powerful and effective"* (James 5:16). A fervent, heartfelt prayer from a believer in Christ has power and accomplishes much.

Perhaps you have been trusting God to bring certain family members, friends, and acquaintances to Christ. It is possible that evil spirits from the enemy are deceiving them, and that they won't leave unless you add fasting to your prayers. (See Matthew 17:21 NKJV.) Perhaps you have been praying for a breakthrough at your workplace—you can fast for that, too. You can pray, "Father, I'm consecrating myself. I'm setting myself apart for this situation at work." When you "pay the price" by praying and fasting, God will respond.

Prayer: Father, thank You for Your Word, which assures us You will respond to fervent, consecrated prayer. Help me to rely on the Holy Spirit as I fast and pray for my loved ones. In Jesus' name, amen.

Thought: In some circumstances, only prayer and fasting can bring deliverance.

Reading: **2 Chronicles 32–33; John 18:19–40**

The Right Way to Fast

Fasts must be observed in the right spirit. Isaiah 58 tells us right and wrong ways to fast. In verse three, God quoted the Israelites: "'Why have we fasted,' they say, 'and you have not seen it? Why have we humbled ourselves, and you have not noticed?'" His reply was,

> Yet on the day of your fasting, you do as you please and exploit all your workers. Your fasting ends in quarreling and strife, and in striking each other with wicked fists. You cannot fast as you do today and expect your voice to be heard on high. (Isaiah 58:3–4)

The Israelites' fasting was characterized by injustice to others, and it ended in *"quarreling and strife."* It sounds as if the Israelites were competing with one another—even in spiritual matters. That's strife.

When God says, *"Declare a holy fast; call a sacred assembly"* (Joel 1:14), He is saying, "Call people away from their regular duties and have them fast as a holy duty to Me." To get serious with God, we must commit to the things we should be doing—with the right attitude. If we "do as we please" instead of seeking and obeying God when we fast, He will ask us,

> Do you expect Me to answer your prayers while you have this attitude? This is no game. Either you are fasting or you are on a diet. To consecrate yourself before Me, you have to set yourself apart and seek Me rather than your own interests.

Prayer: Father, I desire to have the right spirit before You when I fast. Show me how to fast in a way that pleases You. In Jesus' name, amen.

Thought: When we earnestly seek God's ways, He will pour out His power on us.

Reading: **2 Chronicles 34–36; John 19:1–22**

Fasting Brings Restoration

Is not this the kind of fasting I have chosen: to loose the chains of injustice and untie the cords of the yoke, to set the oppressed free and break every yoke? Is it not to share your food with the hungry and to provide the poor wanderer with shelter—when you see the naked, to clothe him, and not to turn away from your own flesh and blood? Then your light will break forth like the dawn, and your healing will quickly appear; then your righteousness will go before you, and the glory of the LORD will be your rear guard. Then you will call, and the LORD will answer; you will cry for help, and he will say: Here am I. (Isaiah 58:6–9)

I saiah says a fast pleasing to God has the power to break the chains of injustice and destroy the yokes of the oppressed. God's anointing—which comes through fasting consecrated to Him—can deliver people. A true fast causes you to value what's important, such as giving to those in need and having a burden for souls.

Isaiah 58:12 describes the outcome of such a fast: "*Your people will rebuild the ancient ruins and will raise up the age-old foundations; you will be called Repairer of Broken Walls, Restorer of Streets with Dwellings.*" Lives will be restored to God and you will receive God's blessings. Verse eight says, "*Then your light will break forth like the dawn, and your healing will quickly appear.*" Fasting activates faith for healing. Isaiah 58:8 also says, "*Your righteousness will go before you, and the glory of the LORD will be your rear guard.*" Protection and other blessings result from fasts that please God.

Prayer: Father, help me turn to You in a time of fasting
that breaks the yokes of the oppressed and
restores the lives of people around me.
In Jesus' name, amen.

Thought: Fasting restores people's lives and brings God's blessings.

Reading: **Ezra 1–2; John 19:23–42**

Putting Prayer into Practice

W hen you fast, prepare for answers to prayer. God has promised that if you fast in the right way, He will hear and answer. Your spiritual capacity to hear and receive will be increased. Emptied of your own comforts and interests, you will be ready for Him to fill you.

Ask yourself these questions: Do my prayers tend to focus on myself or on others? Is there a situation in my life, or a person for whom I am praying, that is resistant to prayer? Do I hear from God and experience the power of His Spirit to meet the needs of myself and others? Is fasting a regular practice in my life?

Compare Isaiah 58:6-9 with 1 John 3:14-19 and Matthew 25:31-40. How do the New Testament passages reinforce what God said is important to Him during a fast, which He described in the passage from Isaiah? Considering the kind of fast that pleases God, how can you help meet someone's spiritual or physical needs this week? Set aside a time to consecrate yourself in prayer and fasting on behalf of someone who needs a breakthrough.

Let's pray together:

Prayer: Heavenly Father, You have taught us that
when we pray, we are to bring other people's needs before You. We
want to be empowered by Your Spirit through
fasting so we can minister to others and counteract
the work of the enemy. We consecrate ourselves
to You in prayer and fasting, setting ourselves
apart to seek Your will rather than our own interests.
Use us to fulfill Your purposes for Your glory.
We pray this in the name of Jesus, who fasted and prayed
not only for His disciples, but also for us who have
believed in Him through their testimony. Amen.

Thought: *"You will cry for help, and he will say: Here am I."*

Reading: **Ezra 3–5; John 20**

Principles of Fasting

Today, reflect on these principles of fasting:

1. God expects His people to fast; it's not optional. In the same way we practice the habits of reading the Bible and praying, we should also practice the habit of fasting.

2. A fast is a conscious, intentional decision to abstain for a time from the pleasure of eating in order to gain spiritual benefits.

3. The following are characteristics of fasting:
   • Fasting is a time set apart to seek the face of God and to abstain from other things in order to give one's whole heart to God in prayer.
   • Fasting puts God first, focusing one's attention on Him alone.
   • Fasting fosters a sensitive environment for the working of prayer.
   • Fasting is a form of intercession for others.

4. Fasting does not change God; it changes us and our prayers.

5. The results of fasting are:
   • *Hearing from God:* We receive guidance, wisdom, instruction, and knowledge.
   • *Power from God:* We receive the fullness of the Spirit for ministry.
   • *Breakthroughs in Difficult Situations:* Fasting brings breakthroughs in tough circumstances and in the lives of those who are resistant to the gospel.

6. According to Isaiah 58, right and wrong ways to fast are:
   • *Right:* Being consecrated and committed to God, having the right priorities, lifting people's burdens, showing love and generosity to others, and having a burden for souls.
   • *Wrong:* treating others with injustice, quarreling and striving with others, pursuing our own pleasures rather than God's will.

7. The outcomes of a true fast are:
   • People are delivered and restored to God.
   • The one who fasts receives God's blessings.

Reading: **Ezra 6–8; John 21**

Not a Magic Formula

Using the name of Jesus is crucial for effective prayer. In conjunction with praying according to the Word, praying in the name of Jesus gives our prayers tremendous power.

Many believers have unanswered prayers because they misunderstand what it means to pray in the name of Jesus. We tend to think the phrase "In the name of Jesus, amen" makes any prayer effective with God, but it doesn't work that way.

We can't sanctify our prayers simply by tacking on Jesus' name at the end. His name is not a magic formula that guarantees automatic acceptance. When the Bible tells us to pray in the name of Jesus, it doesn't mean the word *J-e-s-u-s* as such—that's just the English word for the name of the Son of God; other languages translate His name using different words. It's not the word, but what the word represents, that makes the difference.

Naming your son Bill Gates won't make him an automatic billionaire. The name doesn't mean anything unless there is substance behind it. Likewise, we do not pray effectively just by using the word *Jesus*, but by understanding the significance of who He is and appropriating His power through faith in His name. As Peter said of the man crippled from birth who was healed at the temple gate, *"It is Jesus' name **and the faith that comes through him** that has given this complete healing to him"* (Acts 3:16, emphasis added).

Prayer: Father, help me see the significance of faith in
the name of Your Son, Jesus, so I can pray prayers
of substance and reality that You can answer.
In Jesus' name, amen.

Thought: Jesus is the name above all names.

Reading: **Ezra 9–10; Acts 1**

The Power of Jesus' Name

*Some Jews who went around driving out evil spirits tried to invoke the name of the Lord Jesus over those who were demon-possessed. They would say, "In the name of Jesus, whom Paul preaches, I command you to come out." Seven sons of Sceva, a Jewish chief priest, were doing this. One day the evil spirit answered them, "Jesus I know, and I know about Paul, **but who are you**?" Then the man who had the evil spirit...gave them such a beating that they ran out of the house naked and bleeding. When this became known to the Jews and Greeks living in Ephesus, they were all seized with fear, and **the name of the Lord Jesus was held in high honor**.*   (Acts 19:13–17, emphasis added)

We can use the name *Jesus* all we want, but we have no authority over the devil unless we are in proper relationship with Christ and understand how to use His name. *We must be able to legally use the authority behind the power of Jesus' name in order to obtain results in prayer.*

If someone uses another name without legal authority, the law calls it fraud. Suppose you attempted to withdraw money from my bank account. The bank teller would ask for proof of identification.

Most of us wouldn't think of committing fraud on a bank, but we do try to commit fraud in prayer. We pray hard, saying, "In the name of Jesus." The Father says, "Show me some ID. Are you in right relationship with My Son? Do you understand who He is, and do you believe in His authority and power?" As the sons of Sceva discovered, praying in Jesus' name without knowing who He is doesn't work.

Prayer: Father, open my heart to the power
and authority of Jesus' name.
In His name I pray, amen.

Thought: Praying in Jesus' name without knowing
who He is doesn't work.

Reading: **Nehemiah 1–3; Acts 2:1–21**

Use Your Covenantal Rights

Anyone who is not in proper relationship with God through Christ cannot legally do business with God. Jesus cancelled our sins with His sacrifice on the cross, providing us with forgiveness and legal access to God through His name. Only the children of God can claim power through Jesus' name. *"But as many as **received him**, to them gave he power to become the sons of God, even to them that believe on his name"* (John 1:12 KJV, emphasis added).

The authority we have in Jesus' name through prayer is based on our covenant relationship with God through Christ. *"But the ministry Jesus has received is as superior to theirs [the priests of Israel] as the covenant of which he is mediator is superior to the old one, and it is founded on better promises"* (Hebrews 8:6). We can pray directly to God in Jesus' name because Jesus has given us authority to do so. In the New Testament, Jesus made seven statements like the following, authorizing us to use His name with God:

> *I tell you the truth, my Father will give you whatever you ask in my name. Until now you have not asked for anything in my name. Ask and you will receive, and your joy will be complete. Though I have been speaking figuratively, a time is coming when I will no longer use this kind of language but will tell you plainly about my Father. In that day you will ask in my name.* (John 16:23–26)

Prayer: Father, thank You for being true to Your Word and allowing me to pray in the power and authority of the name of Jesus. In His precious name I pray, amen.

Thought: The authority we have in Jesus' name is a covenantal authority.

Reading: **Nehemiah 4–6; Acts 2:22–47**

What's in a Name?

"A t the name of Jesus every knee should bow, in heaven and on earth and under the earth" (Philippians 2:10). Since Christ restored our relationship with God, His name is our legal authority to transact all spiritual business.

Today, most people name their children based on how the names sound or look. In Scripture, however, names usually symbolize a person's attributes and characteristics—his nature, power, and glory.

First Corinthians 15:41 says, "There is one glory of the sun, another glory of the moon, and another glory of the stars; for one star differs from another star in glory" (NKJV). The glory of something is its best expression of itself. A flower is in true glory when it's in full bloom. A lion is in true glory when it's at peak strength. The sun is in its true glory at noon. Again, when the Bible refers to a name, it is generally talking about that person's true nature, or glory.

God gave Adam the privilege of naming Eve—of encapsulating her attributes. Adam actually named Eve twice—first to describe her origin, second to describe who she would become to fulfill her purpose. First, he said, "This is now bone of my bones and flesh of my flesh; she shall be called 'woman,' for she was taken out of man" (Genesis 2:23). Later, the Bible says, "Adam named his wife Eve, because she would become the mother of all the living" (Genesis 3:20). The Hebrew word for Eve is chavvah, meaning "life-giver." Her name describes the essence of her nature as the mother of mankind.

Names are important to God, and no name is more important than that of His only-begotten Son.

Prayer: Father, Thank you for my redemption and authority in Jesus, whose name means "salvation." In His precious name, amen.

Thought: We pray in the name of Jesus Christ, who is Lord over the new covenant.

Reading: **Nehemiah 7–9; Acts 3**

Names Signify Purpose

Sometimes God *changed* the names of His people to reflect promises He made and purposes He had for them, which far exceeded their expectations or their parents' expectations.

In Genesis 17:4-5, Abram's name, which meant "exalted father" or "high father," was changed to Abraham, meaning "father of a multitude," reflecting the promise that *"Abraham will surely become a great and powerful nation, and all nations on earth will be blessed through him"* (Genesis 18:18). In Genesis 32:27-28, Jacob's name, which meant "supplanter," was changed to Israel, meaning "he will rule as God" or "a prince of God." This reflected the fact that the nation of Israel—the nation intended as God's earthly representative, *"a kingdom of priests and a holy nation"* (Exodus 19:6)—would come from his line.

In John 1:42, Jesus changed Simon's name, which is derived from a Hebrew word meaning "hearing," to Cephas, meaning "a rock" or "a stone." In English, this name is "Peter." Peter's new name signified his role in establishing and leading the church in its infancy. (See Matthew 16:18.)

God puts emphasis on people's names because He places great significance on His own name, and mankind is made in His image. Using our definition from yesterday, God's name symbolizes the essence of His nature. It represents His collective attributes—His nature, power, and glory. What God says is consistent with what He does; He has complete integrity, or wholeness—the definition of holiness. The main reason we are commanded not to use the name of God in vain (see Exodus 20:7) is that His name does not just *represent* who He is, but it *is* who He is.

Prayer: Father God, I desire to honor Your name in
my every word, action, and prayer.
In Jesus' name, amen.

Thought: God's purposes for us far exceed our own expectations.

Reading: **Nehemiah 10–11; Acts 4:1–22**

    Daily Power & Prayer Devotional

"I Am Who I Am"

Moses said to God, "Suppose I go to the Israelites and say to them, 'The God of your fathers has sent me to you,' and they ask me, 'What is his name?' Then what shall I tell them?" God said to Moses, "I Am Who I Am. This is what you are to say to the Israelites: 'I Am has sent me to you.'" God also said to Moses, "Say to the Israelites, 'The Lord, the God of your fathers—the God of Abraham, the God of Isaac and the God of Jacob—has sent me to you.' This is my name forever, the name by which I am to be remembered from generation to generation." (Exodus 3:13–15)

God was saying, "I *am* My name. Whatever I am, that's what I'm called." Translated into English, this concept basically means, "My name is whatever I am at the time I am it." God is our all-sufficiency, and His name differs according to what we need at a specific time. God says, "If you need bread, then pray, 'Father, You are my Bread.' When you acknowledge that I am your Provider and Sustenance, then I become Bread to you. If you are thirsty, pray, 'Father, You are my Water.' I manifest the qualities of whatever you need."

By calling Himself *"the God of Abraham, the God of Isaac and the God of Jacob"* (Exodus 3:15), God affirms that He is a personal God who meets individual human needs. He desires to be your God and to meet your individual needs. This is why so many names are attributed to God in the Old Testament. Yet I Am encompasses all His nature and attributes.

Prayer: Father, Creator, Sustainer, Healer, Provider,
thank You for being my All in All.
In Jesus' name, amen.

Thought: God says, *"I Am Who I Am."*

Reading: **Nehemiah 12–13; Acts 4:23–37**

Son of God, Son of Man

How does the Bible's emphasis on the meaning of names—especially God's name—apply to praying in the name of Jesus? Since a person's name represents his collective characteristics, the names of the second person of the Trinity convey all that He is, both as the Son of God and as the Son of Man—His nature, power, and glory.

Like God the Father, the Son has a variety of names that describe who He is. In the Old Testament, some of His names are the *"Seed"* (Genesis 3:15 NKJV), *"the Branch"* (Zechariah 6:12), and *"Immanuel* ["God with us"]" (Isaiah 7:14). In the New Testament, the Son has many designations, but the first we read of is the name *Jesus*.

Jesus' earthly parents didn't name Him—His name was given by God, His heavenly Father. (See Luke 1:31; Matthew 1:21.) God named Jesus to affirm Jesus was His Son and to express His identity and role. The name *Jesus* means "Savior"—He came to earth as a human to accomplish the salvation of the world. Therefore, *Jesus* is the name of Christ in His humanity—as the Son of Man. However, *I* AM is the name of Christ in His divinity—as the Son of God. *"'I tell you the truth,' Jesus answered, 'before Abraham was born, I am!'"* (John 8:58). Jesus Christ is the revelation of God in human form. Because He is fully divine as well as fully human, He is ascribed a variety of names, just as God the Father is. Praying in the name of Jesus, therefore, means calling on all His attributes.

Prayer: Father, Jesus' name is above every other name.
May I always bow to His name, remembering that there is
no other name by which I can be saved.
In Jesus' name, amen.

Thought: Jesus Christ is the revelation of God in human form.

Reading: **Esther 1–2; Acts 5:1–21**

Jesus' Name Meets Our Needs

Jesus said, "*I am the bread of life*" (John 6:35). He is also the water of life: "*If anyone is thirsty, let him come to me and drink*" (John 7:37). The attributes Jesus manifests reveal His glory and correspond to His people's needs. He called Himself "*the way and the truth and the life*" (John 14:6) because He gives us spiritual life and access to the Father. He called Himself "*the true vine*" (John 15:1) because in Him we bear spiritual fruit.

To pray "in the name of Jesus," we must pray based on the divine name that meets our particular need. If you know Jesus only as Savior, that's probably all He will be to you. If you know Him only as Healer, that's all He will be to you. Martha's knowledge of Jesus was limited: when Jesus said her brother would rise again, she answered, in effect, "Someday in the *future* when God raises the dead, my brother will rise." (See John 11:23-24.) Jesus replied, "*I am the resurrection and the life. He who believes in me will live, even though he dies; and whoever lives and believes in me will never die. Do you believe this?*" (vv. 25-26, emphasis added). He was prompting Martha to call Him by the necessary name: *Resurrection*. "'Yes, Lord,' she told him, 'I believe that you are the Christ, the Son of God, who was to come into the world'" (v. 27). Her word of faith helped bring Jesus' resurrection power into the family's situation, and Lazarus' life was restored.

Prayer: Father, I long to know You and Your Son, Jesus, in all the ways You are revealed in Your Word. Teach me every name and characteristic that describes who You are to us. In Jesus' name, amen.

Thought: We can pray based on the divine name that meets our need.

Reading: **Esther 3–5; Acts 5:22–42**

Call on His Name

You can depend on Jesus for anything when you're living the way you're supposed to. The Bible says, *"The righteous will live by faith"* (Romans 1:17). Have faith in Jesus and the many attributes His names convey.

If you want a friend or family member to be saved, pray the name *Savior*—"Jesus, Savior, save Judy." Pray for others using the name that designates Jesus as the One who can save them. Acts 2:21 says, *"Everyone who calls on the name of the Lord will be saved."* Call on the name of the Lord on behalf of others.

Living by faith sometimes involves saying things that seem strange. For example, the Bible says, *"Let the weak say, 'I am strong'"* (Joel 3:10 NKJV). We're weak, but God tells us to say the opposite. He says, "Call on My strength. Call Me Jehovah Omnipotent." He doesn't just want us to use His name; He wants us to understand His nature and to appropriate it in faith. If you are weak, call on the Lord your Strength. (See Psalm 18:1.) If you are in poverty, call on Jehovah-Jireh, your Provider. (See Genesis 22:8.) If you are sick, call on Jehovah-Rapha, the God who heals. (See Exodus 15:26.) God tells us to dwell not on the problem, but on His attribute that addresses the problem. Since He is the I AM, His attributes are as numerous as your needs—and beyond!

Prayer: Father, I believe Jesus will meet all my needs.
Even if the words You want me to say seem strange, I want
to speak Your truth. Teach me to pray and believe
according to Your marvelous attributes and power.
In Jesus' name, amen.

Thought: The name of Jesus is given to us to use
in relation to our needs.

Reading: **Esther 6–8; Acts 6**

Jesus Has Power of Attorney

When you give power of attorney to someone, you appoint that person to represent you, granting him legal authority to speak for you and to do business in your name. Praying in the name of Jesus gives Him power of attorney to intercede on your behalf when you make requests of the Father.

Jesus said,

I tell you the truth, my Father will give you whatever you ask in my name. Until now you have not asked for anything in my name. Ask and you will receive, and your joy will be complete. (John 16:23–24)

While Jesus was on earth, the disciples didn't need to pray to the Father. When they needed food, Jesus provided it. When Peter's mother-in-law was sick, Jesus healed her. When they needed to pay taxes, Jesus supplied the money. With Jesus, they had everything they needed; requests were made directly to Him. After His resurrection, Jesus would return to the Father, however, meaning they would no longer be able to ask Him for anything directly. They would need to pray to the Father, and Jesus instructed them to do so in His name, because the Father works through Christ.

Jesus works on our behalf from His position at the right hand of the Father. (See Romans 8:34.) He represents our interests to God: *"Therefore he is able to save completely those who come to God through him, because he always lives to intercede for them"* (Hebrews 7:25). He brings glory to the Father by fulfilling the prayers we pray according to the Word.

Prayer: Father, thank You that Jesus sits at Your right hand
and intercedes for me. He is the only representative
I need to bring my requests before You.
In Jesus' name, amen.

Thought: Jesus actively works on our behalf at the
right hand of the Father.

Reading: **Esther 9–10; Acts 7:1–21**

The Holy Spirit Helps Us to Pray

I tell you the truth, anyone who has faith in me will do what I have been doing. He will do even greater things than these, because I am going to the Father. And I will do whatever you ask in my name, so that the Son may bring glory to the Father. You may ask me for anything in my name, and I will do it. (John 14:12–14)

A fter Jesus told His disciples to pray in His name, He talked about the Holy Spirit, who continues Jesus' ministry on earth. *"If you love me, you will obey what I command. And I will ask the Father, and he will give you another Counselor ["Comforter" KJV] to be with you forever—the Spirit of truth"* (vv. 15–17).

Jesus said, in effect, "The Holy Spirit will be your Counselor. He will assist in exercising power of attorney by helping you bring your case to God. He will sort out your situation so you can present it to the Father in My name."

One of the repeated themes about the Holy Spirit in the New Testament is that He helps us when we do not know how to pray:

We do not know what we ought to pray for, but the Spirit himself intercedes for us with groans that words cannot express. And he who searches our hearts knows the mind of the Spirit, because the Spirit intercedes for the saints in accordance with God's will.

(Romans 8:26–27)

Prayer: Father, thank You for sending the Holy Spirit,
to whom I can turn for help when I do not know how to pray.
Show me the power the Holy Spirit brings to my prayers.
In Jesus' name, amen.

Thought: The Holy Spirit will help you present
your case to the Father.

Reading: **Job 1–2; Acts 7:22–43**

The Key to Heaven

J esus emphasized that *"the Father loves the Son"* (John 3:35; John 5:20). If the Father loves the Son, the Father will do what He asks. With the Son as your Representative, you know your case will be heard.

Don't try to do business with the Father without the name of Jesus, because *His name is the key to heaven.* Jesus didn't say to bring a list of saints to the Father when you pray. Why would we want their help when we have the Son? Martha, Mary, Luke, Bartholomew, John, James, and others were faithful believers. Yet when Peter encountered the man at the gate Beautiful, he healed him in the name of Jesus, not in the name of the believers. He said, in effect, "All I have is a name, *the name,* and I'm about to do business with heaven. The Father is working, and I see you healed already. Therefore, I will bring to earth what I see in heaven, but I must do it through the legal channel." (See Acts 3:1–8.) Jesus is the sole legal channel to the Father.

If we want to do business with the Father, we must come in Jesus' name alone. *"There is no other name under heaven given to men by which we must be saved"* (Acts 4:13). Our laws say that only the person whose name is on the document as power of attorney can legally give representation. According to God's Word, Jesus is the only one who can speak for you: *"For there is one God and one mediator between God and men, the man Christ Jesus"* (1 Timothy 2:5).

Prayer: Father, thank You for the name of Your Son,
the key that opens the gates of heaven to You.
In Jesus' name I pray, amen.

Thought: Jesus is our only legal channel to the Father.

Reading: **Job 3–4; Acts 7:44–60**

Every Knee Will Bow

Therefore God exalted [Jesus] to the highest place and gave him the name that is above every name, that at the name of Jesus every knee should bow, in heaven and on earth and under the earth.
(Philippians 2:9–10)

To make the knee of poverty, sickness, or depression bow, use Jesus' name. Proverbs 18:10 says, *"The name of the LORD is a strong tower; the righteous run to it and are safe."* If you need healing, apply Jesus' name to your situation. Perhaps you need deliverance from bad habits. To break them, you must use the power of His name. Sometimes people give testimonies that they were nearly robbed, but they said, "Jesus!" and the robbers fled because the Savior's power was present.

Jesus' name is power in heaven, and every tongue will eventually confess that Jesus is Lord—Lord of everything. This truth is the basis on which we are to fulfill the Great Commission, telling others about the power of Jesus' name to save and deliver.

Then Jesus came to [His followers] and said, "All authority in heaven and on earth has been given to me. Therefore go and make disciples of all nations, baptizing them in the name of the Father and of the Son and of the Holy Spirit."
(Matthew 28:18–19)

Acting on Christ's authority, the apostle Paul *"preached fearlessly in the name of Jesus"* (Acts 9:27). Our authority in Jesus gives us the courage and boldness we need to make disciples of all nations.

Let's call on the name of the Lord.

Prayer: Father, I call on the name of the Lord to be saved, protected, healed, and set free. I call on that name knowing that You are my everything.
In Jesus' name, amen.

Thought: *"The name of the LORD is a strong tower."*

Reading: **Job 5–7; Acts 8:1–25**

Putting Prayer into Practice

Have you prayed in the name of Jesus without considering what it really means? What specific attributes of Jesus meet your needs today?

Jesus' name is the only name that can activate power in heaven. Since He is the great I AM, His attributes are as numerous as your needs. He is Savior, Healer, Strengthener, Vision-Giver, Sustainer, Rent-Payer, Business-Grower, and so much more. He gives freedom, joy, wisdom, kindness, friendship....

Take time this week to worship the Lord for His marvelous attributes. Ask Him to forgive you for taking His name lightly or misusing it. Determine in your heart to honor His name always.

Whenever you encounter difficult situations, don't be fearful, anxious, or angry; run to the Lord in prayer and call on Him as your Salvation and Righteousness, as your Protector and Defender. (See Proverbs 18:10.)

Prayer: Heavenly Father, how majestic Your name is! Your Word says that at the name of Jesus, every knee will bow and every tongue will confess that He is Lord over everything. Jesus said if we ask for anything in His name, You will do it. We know that we cannot ask in Jesus' name unless we ask according to Your will. However, we also know that when we ask in your Son's name, He will present our requests to You properly. He will pray for us when we don't know how. Lord, we ask that Your will be done. There is no name by which we make our requests but the name of Jesus. We call on the power of His name to meet all our needs. We pray in the name of Jesus, whose name is above all names. Amen!

Thought: Jesus is Lord over everything.

Reading: **Job 8–10; Acts 8:26–40**

Principles of Praying in Jesus' Name

Jesus' name is not a magic formula that guarantees automatic acceptance of our prayers.

- We must be able to legally use the authority behind the power of Jesus' name in order to obtain results in prayer.
- The authority we have in Jesus' name through prayer is based on our covenant relationship with God through Christ.
- In the Scriptures, a person's name symbolized the essence of his nature. It represented his collective attributes and characteristics—his nature, power, and glory.
- God's overarching name, I AM, encompasses His nature and attributes.
- The names of the second person of the Trinity refer to all that He is, both as the Son of God and as the Son of Man—all of His nature, power, and glory.
- *Jesus* is the name of Christ in His humanity—as the Son of Man. *I AM* is the name of Christ in His divinity—as the Son of God.
- If we want God to meet a need when we pray "in the name of Jesus," we must pray based on the divine name that meets our particular need at that time.
- To pray in the name of Jesus is to give Him power of attorney on our behalf when we make requests of the Father.
- The Holy Spirit continues Jesus' ministry on earth. He assists in exercising power of attorney by enabling us to pray when we don't know how.
- Jesus' name is the *only* name that can activate power in heaven.
- The authority of Jesus' name is the basis on which we are to fulfill the Great Commission.

Reading: **Job 11–13; Acts 9:1–21**

Become a Person of Prayer

I n the first half of this devotional book, we have explored many powerful prayer principles. By praying, we invite God to intervene in the affairs of earth, we agree with His sovereign will, and we ask Him to work His ways in this world. Prayer is a vital part of God's purpose in creation; it is something we're called to pursue.

I challenge you to test the principles of this book. Begin praying according to God's Word and in Jesus' name. Review the questions and action steps at the end of each segment and put them into practice. Discover your power, your authority, and your rights as an intercessor for the earth.

Become a person of prayer who—

- knows that prayer is a sacred trust from God.
- understands his or her purpose in life as God's priest, or intercessor, for the world.
- has a relationship of trust with the heavenly Father and desires the world to experience the power of His presence and life.
- knows that the will of God will flow from heaven to earth only through his or her prayers and the prayers of all God's people.

If we know God's plan for prayer but fail to pursue it, we are like the person who sees his reflection in the mirror, but then immediately forgets what he looks like. (See James 1:22–25.) Prayer is mandatory, not optional. If we want to see God's will done on earth, we must do our part—we must *pray*.

Prayer: Father, You have called me to be a person of prayer
and have equipped me with prayer principles from Your Word.
Enable me to be a person of prayer all my life.
In Jesus' name, amen.

Thought: Discover your power, your authority, and your rights
as an intercessor for the earth.

Reading: **Job 14–16; Acts 9:22–43**

God Desires You as His Partner

G od wants you to partner with Him to reclaim and redeem the world. The Bible says, *"If my people, who are called by my name, will humble themselves and pray and seek my face and turn from their wicked ways, then will I hear from heaven and will forgive their sin and will heal their land"* (2 Chronicles 7:14). Once again, God has called His people to be His priests, or intercessors—this refers to the entire body of Christ, not just an elite group of "Intercessory Prayer Warriors" in the church. We all have the power to bring God's will on earth so the world can be healed and transformed by His grace.

God's will can be executed only through mankind's cooperation. Prayer is this medium of cooperation and is therefore the most important activity of humanity. Use the purpose and position God has given you to invite heaven's intervention on earth. Prepare your heart, mind, soul, and strength to agree wholly that God's will be done on earth until *"the kingdom of the world has become the kingdom of our Lord and of his Christ"* (Revelation 11:15).

The earth is depending on you to pray. Your children's children are depending on you to pray. All creation is depending on you to pray. Heaven is depending on you to pray. I challenge you: *Pray!*

Prayer: Father, here I am; send me. Use me in prayer
to touch the people around me; use me in prayer to see
Your will accomplished in my family, my church, my job,
my school, my neighborhood, my state, and my country.
I am Yours, Lord; use me.
In Jesus' name, amen.

Thought: Heaven is depending on you to pray!

Reading: **Job 17–19; Acts 10:1–23**

God's Purpose in Vision

We have seen that God has given us authority over the earth and communion with Him through our prayer lives. Our destiny on this earth is to rule with Christ through prayer.

God has also given each of us specific purposes to fulfill in life. These purposes come to us in the form of a vision or plan for our lives that God places within our hearts. It is His gift to us—to allow us to fulfill our roles in His kingdom on earth. The second half of this devotional book will therefore focus on *discovering your personal vision for life.*

I am excited to share these biblical principles on vision, for they will enable you to realize your destiny! Through these devotionals, you will understand why vision is essential to your success, identify your vision's goals and stay on course, overcome obstacles to your vision, develop a specific plan for achieving your vision, and live for the purpose you were meant to fulfill in God's kingdom.

Why should we focus on vision and destiny? Because God has an exciting plan for your life! You are a joint-heir with Christ (see Romans 8:16-17), and you were created with God-given authority to rule the earth with Him. My desire is that you will be inspired, motivated, and challenged to fulfill your dream. I want you to achieve your greatest in God's purpose for your life.

Prayer: Father, please open my heart to the principles
of vision. My desire is to discover Your purpose
for my life and to walk in it.
In Jesus' name, amen.

Thought: God has given each of us specific purposes
to fulfill in life.

Reading: **Job 20–21; Acts 10:24–48**

Vision as the Source

V ision is a conception that is inspired by God in the heart of a human. The greatest gift God ever gave humanity is not sight, but vision. Vision is the source and hope of life. No invention, development, or great feat was ever accomplished without the inspiring power of this mysterious source called vision. Civilizations were born and developed through the driving power of visionary leaders. Social, economic, architectural, medical, scientific, and political achievement and advancements owe their conception and birth to the power of vision.

It was vision that inspired Abram to leave the land of Ur in search of the "Promised Land." Vision inspired the Greeks to produce philosophy and art that still impact the thinking of our world. Vision motivated the great Roman empire to expand its influence and colonize the known world. Vision inspired the explorers who circumnavigated the globe and ignited the creation and expansion of many of the nations that we know today. Vision transformed the agricultural world into the industrial age. Vision gave birth to the thousands of inventions in the last two centuries that have transformed our lives. For example, it was the vision of flight that inspired the Wright brothers to invent the airplane.

Vision is the energy of progress. Vision is the foundation of courage and the fuel of persistence. Vision is a gift from God.

Prayer: Father, You have given us the gift of vision.
You have placed visions in men's hearts since the
beginning of time. Please enable me to
understand Your gift of vision better.
In Jesus' name, amen.

Thought: Nothing noble or noteworthy on earth was
ever done without vision.

Reading: **Job 22–24; Acts 11**

Our Need for Vision

The wise king of Israel, Solomon, stated in his book of Proverbs, *"Where there is no vision, the people perish"* (Proverbs 29:18 KJV). These words have been quoted and repeated by millions of people over the years because they capture the significant role vision has in our individual, corporate, and national lives. The full essence of his statement implies that where there is no revelation of the future, people throw off self-control, personal discipline, and restraint. Simply put, vision is the source of personal and corporate discipline.

Our world today is in desperate need of vision. Even a casual look at the prevailing conditions in our twenty-first century world is enough to produce fear, hopelessness, and uncertainty.

There are many who have no vision for their lives and wonder how to obtain one. There are others who have a vision but are stuck in the mud of confusion not knowing what to do next. Then there are those who had a vision but abandoned it because of discouragement, disillusionment, some measure of failure, or frustration. If you are in one of these categories, you will soon understand the nature of vision, how to capture or recapture your personal vision, how to simplify your vision, and how to document your vision.

How can I know what my vision is? How can I make my vision a concrete reality? Let's uncover the answers together in the following pages!

Prayer: Father, You have said in Your Word that
without a vision, Your people will perish. I want
to walk in the abundant life that Jesus came to give me.
I ask You to answer my questions concerning
vision today and in the days to come.
In Jesus' name, amen.

Thought: Our world today is in desperate need of vision.

Reading: **Job 25–27; Acts 12**

The Gold inside You

In the mid-twentieth century, in Bangkok, Thailand, the government wanted to build a large highway through a village. In the path of the planned road was a Buddhist monastery with a little chapel, so they had to relocate the monastery—including a heavy, eleven-foot clay statue of Buddha—to another place. When the workers transported the statue of Buddha to the new location and began to lower it into place, unexpectedly, the clay on the statue started to crumble and fall off. The people were afraid because this was a precious religious symbol to them, and they didn't want it to be destroyed. Suddenly, the workers stared in amazement because, as the clay fell away, they saw that the statue was pure gold underneath! Before the statue was moved, people thought it was worth about fifty thousand dollars. Today, that golden Buddha is worth millions and, because of the story behind it, is visited by hundreds of thousands of people every year.

This story illustrates that what we can see is not necessarily what really is. I believe that many of us are living as clay vessels when, in reality, we are pure gold inside. This gold is the dreams we have—or once had—for our lives that are not yet reality, the God-given gifts and talents that we have not yet developed, the purpose for our lives that is not yet fulfilled. How do you remove the clay and uncover the gold within you? Your dreams, talents, and desires can be refined in a process of discovering and fulfilling your life's vision so that the pure gold of your unique and personal gifts to this world can truly shine forth.

Prayer: Father, You have created me with unique and precious gifts, like gold. Help me to discover these gifts and use them to bless the world around me. In Jesus' name, amen.

Thought: Many of us are living as clay vessels when we are pure gold inside.

Reading: **Job 28–29; Acts 13:1–25**

You Have a Unique Vision

G od created each person with a unique vision. No matter who you are or what country you live in, you have a personal purpose, for every human being is born with one. Every person is a leader in his or her own vision, because that person is the only one who can imagine, nurture, and fulfill it. God has tremendous plans for you that no one else can accomplish. The tragic thing is that many people live their whole lives without ever recognizing their visions.

What does it mean to capture the vision for your life? Ted Engstrom, the former president of World Vision, told a story that went something like this: A little girl was on a cruise ship, and she and her father were standing on the deck. It was a beautiful clear day, and the air was crisp and fresh. The little girl, standing on tiptoe, said to her father, "I can't see anything." The father picked her up and put her on his shoulders, so that she was higher than everyone else on the deck and was able to see everything around her. "Daddy!" she exclaimed. "I can see farther than my eyes can look!"

That little girl's statement captures the essence of vision: the ability to see farther than your physical eyes can look—to see not just what is, but also what can be, and to make it a reality.

The ability to see your vision has been given to you by the Father. Begin trusting Him to help you see it.

Prayer: Father, it is my desire to trust You today.
Please allow me "to stand on Your shoulders" to see
my vision. Through faith in You and Your Word,
I want to "see farther than my eyes can look."
In Jesus' name, amen.

Thought: Vision sets you free from the limitations of
what the eye can see.

Reading: **Job 30–31; Acts 13:26–52**

Vision Is Inspired by God

S ight is a function of the *eyes*, but vision is a function of the *heart*. You can have sight but no vision. God gave humanity the gift of vision so we would not have to live only by what we see.

God has given us birth for a purpose. As far as He is concerned, that purpose is already finished because He has placed within us the potential for fulfilling it. We can see that purpose through faith. To paraphrase Hebrews 11:1, faith is the substance of things you hope to accomplish, the evidence of things you can see even when others cannot.

For true visionaries, the imaginary world of their visions is more real to them than the concrete reality around them. There is a story about when Disney World had just opened and had only one ride. Walt Disney was sitting on a bench on the grounds, seeming to just stare into space. One of his workers, who was manicuring the grass, asked him, "Mr. Disney, what are you doing?" "I'm looking at my mountain," he answered. Walt died before Space Mountain was built, so he never saw it constructed. When Space Mountain was dedicated, the governor and the mayor were present, and Walt's widow was also there. One of the men stood up to introduce her and said, "It's a pity Walt Disney is not here today to see this mountain, but we're glad his wife is here." Mrs. Disney walked up to the podium, looked at the crowd, and said, in effect, "I must correct this young man. Walt already saw the mountain. It is you who are just now seeing it."

Prayer: Father, my vision, whether large or small, is the vision You have given me. Let me be a visionary and see with eyes of faith so that my vision will be accomplished. In Jesus' name, amen.

Thought: Sight is a function of the eyes, but vision is a function of the heart.

Reading: **Job 32–33; Acts 14**

The Force of Vision

O ne of the most powerful forces in life is the force of vision. A young man did a college paper in his Yale economics class on his vision for overnight mail. The professor gave him a "C" and wrote, "Do not dream of things that cannot happen." After the young man left school, he started Federal Express. Your vision determines your destiny. At age thirteen, I wrote down my vision for my life. I carried it with me all through junior high and high school. Much of what I'm doing right now was on paper when I was a young teenager. Vision makes you persistent.

I believe with all my heart that when you have no vision, you will simply relive the past with its disappointments and failures. Therefore, vision is the key to your future. In Numbers 13 and 14, Joshua and Caleb and ten other men were sent by Moses into the Promised Land as spies. They all saw a rich land flowing with milk and honey that was being given to the Israelites by God. Ten spies were afraid to enter that land, afraid to pursue the dream. However, Joshua and Caleb believed God and had the vision and faith to go into it and take it. Because of their vision, they did not die in the wilderness with the unbelieving Israelites. They were allowed to move into the Promised Land with the next generation and see God's promises to the people of Israel fulfilled.

Prayer: Father, Joshua and Caleb saw beyond the giants and beyond their fears; they saw the vision of Your Promised Land. Please let me see the vision You have given me. I want to have the faith and courage to see and pursue it. In Jesus' name, amen.

Thought: One of the most powerful forces in life is the force of vision.

Reading: **Job 34–35; Acts 15:1–21**

Your Purpose in Life

Years ago, during the Christmas season, my wife and I took our children to a large toy store. At the time, my son Chairo was about four years old, and his eyes lit up when he spotted a rocking horse. He climbed on, held tightly to the ears of the horse, and began to rock back and forth. After a few minutes, I tried to get him off, but he became angry. When we were about ready to leave, he was still having a wonderful time on that rocking horse, so we let him continue while we walked through the store one last time and told our daughter it was time to go. When we came back, Chairo was rocking even faster. By then, he had been going for about half an hour, and he was soaking wet with sweat. As I watched him, I felt as if God was saying to me, "That's how most people live. They're working hard, sweating hard, but they're making no real progress in life. They're not going anywhere."

What about your own life? What are you using your precious energy on? What are you accomplishing? Remember, God has told us that *"where there is no vision, the people perish"* (Proverbs 29:18 KJV). Now is the time to find the special vision God has for you. I want you to get off the rocking horse and find a living stallion—your life's vision.

Prayer: Father, thank You for giving each of us a vision
for this life. Please open my spiritual eyes so
I can see the plans You have for me.
In Jesus' name, amen.

Thought: God has placed within each person a vision
designed to give purpose and meaning to life.

Reading: **Job 36–37; Acts 15:22–41**

A Sense of Personal Purpose

"I know the plans I have for you," declares the LORD, "plans to prosper you and not to harm you, plans to give you hope and a future." (Jeremiah 29:11)

If you ask people, "Why do you exist?" most cannot tell you. They can't explain their purpose in the world. They have no vision for their lives.

Do you have a sense of personal purpose? Do you know why you were born? Does your purpose give you a passion for living? You may ask me, "Do I really need to have a reason for my existence?" My answer is, "Absolutely!" Life is intended to have meaning; you were not born just for the fun of it. You were meant to be going somewhere, to be headed toward a destination.

I want to help you understand the principles of vision and to provide the practical tools and skills necessary to bring your vision into reality. You were born to achieve something significant, and you were destined to make a difference in your generation. Your life is not a divine experiment, but a project of Providence to fulfill a purpose that your generation needs. This personal purpose is the source of your vision and gives meaning to your life.

I therefore encourage you to believe in your daydreams and to reconnect with your passion; your vision awaits your action. Your future is not ahead of you—it lies within you. See beyond your eyes and live for the unseen. Your vision determines your destiny. God truly has plans for you.

Prayer: Father, thank You for giving me meaning in life. You have created me with a purpose; I desire to understand that purpose and to follow it all the days of my life. In Jesus' name, amen.

Thought: Life is intended to have meaning; you were not just born for the fun of it.

Reading: **Job 38–40; Acts 16:1–21**

A Clear Purpose

P resident Ronald Reagan had a clear sense of his life's purpose: the elimination of Communism. He desired to lift totalitarian oppression from millions of people who were suffering under its ideology and policies. His purpose became his passion, and it influenced his thinking, his pursuits, and his foreign policies as president of the United States. Unlike previous American leaders, he believed that Communism not only could be contained, but that it could also be defeated. Reagan said,

> It is time that we committed ourselves as a nation—in both the public and private sectors—to assisting democratic development....What I am describing now is a plan and a hope for the long term—the march of freedom and democracy which will leave Marxism-Leninism on the ash heap of history as it has left other tyrannies which stifle the freedom and muzzle the self-expression of the people....Let us now begin a major effort to secure the best—a crusade for freedom that will engage the faith and fortitude of the next generation. For the sake of peace and justice, let us move toward a world in which all people are at last free to determine their own destiny.

Like Winston Churchill, Reagan became the leader of his country late in life, but everything he experienced and accomplished up to that point seemed to prepare him for his final and essential role. Reagan believed in his purpose so much that he inspired not only his nation, but also the world, and he lived to see the collapse of Communism.

Prayer: Father, please give me a clear sense of my vision.
Help me to keep that vision as the guiding purpose of my life.
In Jesus' name, amen.

Thought: When your purpose is your passion, it influences
your thinking and your pursuits.

Reading: **Job 41–42; Acts 16:22–40**

What Is Your Dream?

Having a vision is inherent in being human. Maybe you once had ideas of what you wanted to be and do, and you still have those ideas. Do you see yourself becoming a lawyer and starting your own firm? Do you think about owning a day-care center that has a first-class curriculum and services two hundred children? Do you want to write a novel? Do you dream about going back to school and doing something with your education and academic abilities?

I have come to the conclusion that the *poorest* person in the world is the person without a dream. A dream, or vision, provides us with direction. It has been said that if you don't know where you're going, any road will take you there. We don't want to end up on just any road in life.

While the poorest person in the world is the one without a dream, the most *frustrated* person in the world is someone who has a dream but doesn't know how to bring it to pass. Yet if you can have hope for the future, you have true riches, no matter how much money you have in your bank account. It doesn't matter what you currently have or don't have, as along as you can see what you could have. This vision is the key to life because where there's a dream, there's hope, and where there's hope, there's faith—and faith is the substance, or fulfillment, of what you are hoping for. (See Hebrews 11:1.)

Prayer: Father God, I don't want to be directionless in life. Keep me from walking on a road to nowhere. Help me stay focused on You and the purpose You have for me. In Jesus' name, amen.

Thought: Vision generates hope and provides endurance in difficult times.

Reading: **Psalm 1–3; Acts 17:1–15**

Born to Be Distinct

Y ou were designed by God to stand out, not to blend in. Think of the thousands of kinds of flowers in the world. They are all flowers, but each one is unique in its species. Think of a forest. At first glance, the trees all seem to blend together. When you get closer, however, you see that the shape of each tree is unique. Every type of tree has leaves with a distinct design. Why? Uniqueness is part of God's creation.

Individual design is as true of humanity as it is of nature. We read in the Psalms, *"For you created my inmost being; you knit me together in my mother's womb. I praise you because I am fearfully and wonderfully made"* (Psalm 139:13-14). God doesn't want any one person to get lost in the midst of everyone else. There are over six billion people on the planet—and not one of them has your fingerprints. We can become complacent about this astonishing truth, yet it is something we must continually remind ourselves of since it is easy to feel lost in the crowd. You are one of a kind, irreplaceable, original; you are *"fearfully and wonderfully made."*

If you go to a sale at a discount store, you'll notice that many of the dresses, sports coats, or ties on the racks are just alike. They're inexpensive because they were mass produced. If you want an original dress, however, you have to go to a designer. You are not like mass-produced clothing; God has not placed you on a sale rack. You are Designer-made.

Prayer: Father, help me to remember I am uniquely
designed by You. Since I am unique, You have given me
a unique vision. May I discover and walk in it.
In Jesus' name, amen.

Thought: Your uniqueness is part of God's creation.

Reading: **Psalm 4–6; Acts 17:16–34**

What Has God Wired You For?

G od not only created each person on earth with a distinct design, but He also placed in everyone a unique vision. No person can give you this vision. It is only God-given. You can go to as many seminars as possible and receive all kinds of wonderful instruction, but no one except God can give you the idea you were born to fulfill.

The poor man, the rich man, the black man, the white man—every person has a dream in his heart. Your vision may already be clear to you, or it may still be buried somewhere deep in your heart, waiting to be discovered. Fulfilling this dream is what gives purpose and meaning to life. In other words, the very substance of life is for you to find God's purpose and fulfill it. Until you do that, you are not really living. You need to make sure you can say at the end of your life, as Jesus did, *"It is finished"* (John 19:30) and not just, "I am retired," for your dream is much bigger than mere retirement.

Jesus said, *"For this reason I was born, and for this I came into the world, to testify to the truth"* (John 18:37). You must have a clear reason for your life, as Jesus did. I know what mine is. I was born to inspire and draw out the hidden leader in every human being I meet. If you stay around me long enough, you'll start being your true self. Why? I was born for that. I was wired for that. What has God wired you for?

Prayer: Father, what have You wired me for? I am one of
Your children whose vision is still buried in my heart.
Please draw it out so that I may see it and then fulfill it.
In Jesus' name, amen.

Thought: Fulfilling your vision is what gives purpose
and meaning to life.

Reading: **Psalm 7–9; Acts 18**

The World Can't Forget

E very human being was created to accomplish something specific that *no one else can accomplish.* It is crucial for you to understand this truth: You were designed to be known for something special. You are meant to do something that will make you unforgettable. You were born to do something that the world will not be able to ignore. It may be in your church, your community, your state, or beyond.

The Bible is a great book for recording the stories of people who did little things that the world can't forget. One example is Rahab, the prostitute, who risked her life for people she didn't even know. She was born to hide Joshua's spies so that the Israelites could defeat Jericho. (See Joshua 2, 6.) Everyone who reads the Old Testament knows about her act of courage.

In the New Testament, there is the story of the woman who took an alabaster jar of perfume and anointed Jesus' head with it. This woman was taking a chance by violating the accepted social code of the day and interrupting a group of men who had gathered for a meal. She decided to pour out her life in gratitude to Jesus, no matter what the consequences. Some of those present severely criticized her because she had "wasted" costly perfume on Jesus when it could have been sold for charitable purposes. Yet Jesus said to them, *"Leave her alone....I tell you the truth, wherever the gospel is preached throughout the world, what she has done will also be told, in memory of her"* (Mark 14:6, 9). No matter how small the act may be, if you put your whole life into it, it won't be forgotten.

Prayer: Father, I am encouraged that as I serve You,
I will accomplish things that will not be forgotten.
My desire is to put my whole life into service for You.
In Jesus' name, amen.

Thought: You were designed to be known for something special.

Reading: **Psalm 10–12; Acts 19:1–20**

Known for Her Love

A gnes Gonxha Bojaxhiu, whom the world has come to know as Mother Teresa, was born in Skopje, Macedonia. From the time she was a girl, she felt her life's purpose was to serve God full-time. When she was eighteen, she became a nun and went to India with the Sisters of Loreto and taught in a Catholic high school for many years. Her life's purpose and passion crystallized as she felt called by God to help "the poorest of the poor" and devoted herself to bring hope, dignity, healing, and education to the needy in Calcutta—those whom other people dismissed as being either beyond help or not worthy of it.

Mother Teresa started her own order called "The Missionaries of Charity" and became internationally recognized for her selfless humanitarian work. Her passion to help others led her to identify totally with them: she became a citizen of India and always kept her vow of poverty, even when she became famous. Her work expanded beyond India to other nations of the world, influencing hundreds of thousands of people to join in her vision. She believed in the difference that one person could make in the world, saying, "If you can't feed a hundred people, then just feed one." Mother Teresa was awarded the Nobel Peace Prize in 1979 and continued her work until her death in 1997.

Mother Teresa encouraged others not to wait for well-known leaders to do a job but to follow their visions. By acting when there was a real need and doing what she personally could do to help, Mother Teresa became a leader herself. She influenced numerous others to awaken their own visionary gifts and, in so doing, multiplied her effectiveness thousands of times over.

Prayer: Father, You are a God of love. Help me to be remembered for doing acts motivated out of love for You. In Jesus' name, amen.

Thought: Believe in the difference that you can make in the world.

Reading: **Psalm 13–15; Acts 19:21–41**

Known for Your Vision

A re you in your twenties? What have you done so far with your life? Have you spent so much time trying to please your friends that you don't know who you are or what your life is about? If so, you aren't doing yourself any favors. You aren't fulfilling your purpose. You may say you are just reacting to "peer pressure." In reality, you are allowing others to rule your life.

Maybe you are forty years old. What have you done so far that the world can't forget? How long will you drift along without working toward your dream? Be careful—procrastination can become a full-time occupation! Many people spend a lifetime wandering away from who God made them to be because they have never recognized who they are in the first place. For example, perhaps you have been a secretary for twenty years. You are at the same level as when you started, even though you dream of being an administrator. People don't fulfill their visions because they have no sense of destiny.

We need to be like the apostles, who were known for their acts, not their talk. The biblical book about them is called The Acts of the Apostles because they were doers. They were affecting government. They were transforming the world. Nations were afraid of them, and towns became nervous when they showed up because they were said to have *"turned the world upside down"* (Acts 17:6 NKJV). It's exciting to be around people who know that they are doing what they were born to do. You should be known for your God-given vision, too.

Prayer: Father, I want to be known as a doer of Your Word and not a hearer only. I want to understand the vision You have placed in my heart and move toward the fulfillment of that vision. Please help me to do this.
In Jesus' name, amen.

Thought: Be careful—procrastination can become a full-time occupation!

Reading: **Psalm 16–17; Acts 20:1–16**

JULY 17

Your Purpose Is Your Passion

It has been said that there are three kinds of people in the world: First, there are those who never seem to be aware that things are happening around them. Second, there are those who notice but are continually asking, "What just happened?" Third, there are those who *make* things happen. Ronald Reagan and Mother Teresa belonged to the third group.

I have observed firsthand the truth of this statement, paraphrased from John Stuart Mill: One person with vision is greater than the passive force of ninety-nine people who are merely interested in doing or becoming something. Most people have an interest in their destinies, but they have no passion or drive to fulfill them. They don't really believe the dreams God has put in their hearts. If they do believe them, they don't do the things that will take them in the direction of fulfilling them. Yet that is what separates the people who make an impact in the world and those who just exist on the planet.

When you discover your vision, it will give you energy and passion. Ecclesiastes 9:10 says, *"Whatever your hand finds to do, do it with all your might."* I believe this Scripture expresses a truth that most people miss: You accomplish only what you fight for. If you are willing to put all your energy into your vision, then nobody can stop it from succeeding.

Prayer: Father, may the vision that You have placed in my heart give me the energy to live each day for You. I desire to do everything You have laid before me with all my might.
In Jesus' name, amen.

Thought: When you discover your vision, it will give you energy and passion.

Reading: **Psalm 18–19; Acts 20:17–38**

What Is Godly Passion?

Passion is the juice for living. For many people, life is drudgery. They have no motivation in regard to their jobs, spouses, education, or personal development. Someone once said that the most difficult thing about life is that it is so daily. Passion helps us to rise above our daily routines. Godly passion is a deep motivation to serve the Lord. Remember that the apostle Paul said, *"I press on toward the goal to win the prize for which God has called me heavenward in Christ Jesus"* (Philippians 3:14). If you're not motivated, then you will become a weight or burden to others. When you have passion, you don't need the "right" conditions to move forward because passion is internally generated and is not affected by external conditions.

Where does passion come from? First, it comes from a sense of purpose. You are pursuing something that gives your life meaning. If you become distracted or opposition stands in your way, your destiny still pulls you in the direction of your desire because you can't imagine not fulfilling it.

Second, passion comes from having a sense of destiny. Passion comes from something outside this world and is connected to it. If you get your passion from something on earth, then when it stops, you will stop. Yet if you capture a sense of destiny that existed before you and will continue to exist after you, if you feel you're involved in something that is larger than yourself, then you're on your way to leadership and the fulfillment of your vision.

Prayer: Father, I know that my life and purpose are all a part of Your plan for this earth. This gives meaning to my life each day. Please help me to walk in my destiny. In Jesus' name, amen.

Thought: Passion comes from having a sense of purpose and destiny.

Reading: **Psalm 20–22; Acts 21:1–17**

Purpose of a Heroine

C orrie ten Boom was fifty years old when the Nazis invaded her native Holland. Up to that time, she had lived an obscure life with her sister as they helped their father run his watch shop and quietly but devotedly practiced their Christian faith. After Holland fell, she and her family were confronted with the reality of the Nazis' persecution and murder of the Jews. Through this crisis, they discovered their purpose: preserving the lives of Jews and others persecuted by the Nazis by hiding them in a secret room in their home. Their passion was so strong that they risked their own lives for its fulfillment.

Corrie and several of her family members were eventually turned in. Corrie's father died in prison and her sister died in a concentration camp. After suffering in prison, a work camp, and a concentration camp, Corrie was about to be executed when she was released on a clerical error.

After her release, Corrie found a new purpose. Traveling around the world, she told her story and urged people to find healing and freedom through forgiveness. This purpose was severely tested when she encountered one of the former guards who had beaten her beloved sister. He didn't recognize her, but he had heard her message and been moved to change his life through the hope of forgiveness. He came and extended his hand to her. Corrie underwent intense inner struggle, but her passion was even stronger than her pain, and she offered her own hand in forgiveness.

Prayer: Father, thank You for the testimony of women like
Corrie ten Boom who were driven by a passion to serve You.
May I have this type of passion in my own life.
In Jesus' name, amen.

Thought: When your passion for Christlikeness is stronger than
your pain, you can forgive your worst enemy.

Reading: **Psalm 23–25; Acts 21:18–40**

What If They Had Said No?

I f you do not discover your personal vision, you will not be able to fulfill your life's assignment. The result is that you will deprive your generation and succeeding generations of your unique and vital contribution to the world. The great king Solomon wrote that there is *"a time to be born and a time to die"* (Ecclesiastes 3:2). This means that the timing of your birth was essential to some need in the world that you're supposed to meet.

Suppose Moses had refused to go to Egypt and tell Pharaoh to set the Hebrews free. Consider what the world would be like if, during World War II, Winston Churchill had said, "The survival of Great Britain and the rest of the free world is someone else's problem. I'm going to let the Nazis do whatever they want." Suppose Corrie ten Boom had decided that hiding Jews was too risky a proposition. What if Martin Luther King Jr. had not thought civil rights were worth dying for? What would have happened if Mother Teresa had ignored the poor and sick on the streets of Calcutta?

We may never know in our lifetimes the full impact of our influence and actions, great or small. In light of this truth, developing one's vision should not be an option for anyone. As we come to understand the nature and attitudes of true visionaries, we can remove whatever is hindering us from having the same spirit so that we can make a positive and lasting contribution to our generation.

Prayer: Father, I may never know the impact of my influence
and actions during my lifetime. Help me to trust You
that each thing I do in Your name is contributing
to the plan for Your kingdom on this earth.
In Jesus' name, amen.

Thought: We have a responsibility to find, perform, and
complete our purposes.

Reading: **Psalm 26–28; Acts 22**

You Were Born at the Right Time

I n the book of Ecclesiastes, we read about the revelation of God's purposes to the hearts of human beings. The third chapter begins, *"To everything there is a season, a time for every purpose under heaven"* (Ecclesiastes 3:1 NKJV). God has not only given you a purpose, but, according to this Scripture, He has also determined the time for that purpose to be accomplished. There is *"a time for every purpose."* Whatever you were born to do, God has assigned a season in which it is to be done—and that season is the duration of your life. Do you see why it is crucial for you to know the vision that is in your heart? Your purpose can be fulfilled only during the time you are given on earth to accomplish it.

Within this season called life, God has also appointed specific times for portions of your purpose to be accomplished. As you pursue the dream God has given you, He will bring it to fruition during the period of your life when it is meant to be completed. As Ecclesiastes 3:11 says, *"He has made everything beautiful in its time."*

Some people wish they had been born during a different time in history. Yet if you had been born a thousand years ago, or even a hundred years ago, you would have been miserable because you would have been living in the wrong time to complete your purpose and vision. You were born at the right time to accomplish your vision during your generation.

Prayer: Father, how awesome that You have chosen a
particular place and time for me to be born and to live
on this earth. I will confess in faith that I have been
born at the right time to accomplish my vision.
In Jesus' name, amen.

Thought: You were born at the right time
to accomplish your vision.

Reading: **Psalm 29–30; Acts 23:1–15**

His Eternal Purpose in Your Heart

Ecclesiastes 3:10 says, *"I have seen the burden God has laid on men."* The word *"burden"* in the Hebrew could actually be translated as "a heavy responsibility," "occupation," or "task." It could also be described as a "responsible urge." Every human being comes to earth with a purpose that, in a sense, weighs on him. Whether you are twenty, fifty, or eighty years old, there is a burden within you, a "responsible urge" to carry out all that you were designed to do. Do you sense that burden? Almost everybody does, even if they have never expressed it. That feeling, longing, or burden comes from God. He has placed a "responsible urge" on your heart because of His purpose for you.

In Ecclesiastes 3:11, we read, *"He has also set eternity in the hearts of men."* That is a powerful statement. There is something within you that is being called by eternity. The vision God has put in your heart is "a piece of eternity" that He gave you to deliver in time and space—that is, on the earth during your lifetime. What God put into your heart is also what is in His own heart. I think this is what the Bible means when it talks about "deep calling unto deep." (See Psalm 42:7.) Therefore, God has done something awesome. He lives in eternity, yet He has specifically placed you in time so that others on earth will be able to see a piece of His eternity through your life.

Prayer: Father, thank You for placing
eternity in my heart. I hear You call to me
through Your Holy Spirit and in Your Word.
Help me to walk in the vision You have given me.
In Jesus' name, amen.

Thought: God placed His eternal purpose in your heart.

Reading: **Psalm 31–32; Acts 23:16–35**

Your Gift Will Make a Way

How is the fulfillment of vision meant to work in practical terms? Proverbs 18:16 is a powerful statement that reveals the answer: "A man's gift makes room for him" (NKJV). You were designed to be known for your gift. It is in exercising this gift that you will find real fulfillment, purpose, and contentment in your work. Your gift may be in leadership or organization; it may be in educating adults or children; it may be singing or leading worship in church. God has very specifically placed a purpose and gift *in you*.

It is interesting to note that the Bible does not say that a man's *education* makes room for him, but that his gift does. Somehow we have swallowed the idea that education is the key to success. Our families and society have reinforced this idea, but we will have to change our perspective if we are to be truly successful. While education can't *give* you your gift, it can help you *develop it* so that it can be used to the maximum. If education alone were the key to success, then everyone who has a Ph.D. should be financially secure and happy.

If you are intelligent but are not exercising your gift, you're probably going to be poor. If you're educated but have not developed your talent, you're likely to be depressed, frustrated, and tired. Education, in itself, doesn't guarantee anything; it is your God-given gift that is the key to your success.

Prayer: Father, thank You that You are a gift-giving God.
Thank You for giving me gifts with which to serve You.
Using those gifts will bring me fulfillment in life.
Please continue to reveal these gifts to me.
In Jesus' name, amen.

Thought: Your God-given gift is the key to your success.

Reading: **Psalm 33–34; Acts 24**

The World Will Make Room for You

The second part of Proverbs 18:16 says, *"A man's gift...brings him before great men"* (NKJV). You don't realize that the gift you're sitting on is loaded. The world won't move over for you just because you're smart. Whenever you exercise your gift, however, the world will make room for you. Anyone—yourself included—who discovers his or her gift and develops it will become a commodity. If you're a young person in high school or college who is planning your career, don't do what people say will make you wealthy. Do what you were born to do, because that is where you will make your money and find your life's fulfillment. No matter how big the world is, there's a place for you in it when you discover and manifest your gift.

Michelangelo poured his life into his art. That's why we still remember him five hundred years after he lived. Alexander Graham Bell believed that sound could be converted into electrical impulses and transmitted by wire. No one remembers all the people who thought Bell was crazy; we remember only the man who had vision enough to create the telephone. Thomas Edison reportedly would spend eight or nine days straight locked up in a room working on his experiments. He didn't just happen to make a mistake and create a lightbulb—he had a dream. Although it took him a long time, he believed that we could harness energy and that it could produce light. Because he believed it, he stayed with it until he saw the fulfillment of his vision. That's what makes him unforgettable.

Prayer: Father, I don't want to live a mediocre life. You have placed gifts within me to be used for You. Please help me to exercise those gifts with joy, hard work, and persistence.
In Jesus' name, amen.

Thought: There's a place for you when you discover and manifest your gift.

Reading: **Psalm 35–36; Acts 25**

Stirring Up Your Gift

The apostle Paul wrote to Timothy, *"For this reason I remind you to fan into flame the gift of God, which is in you"* (2 Timothy 1:6). In the *New King James Version*, the verse is translated, *"Stir up the gift of God."* The gift is not something we learn. It is something God gave us. It is something we need to discover and then stir up. No one else can activate your gift for you. You have to do it yourself. You stir up your gift by developing, refining, enhancing, and using it.

I once read an article about Louis Armstrong, the jazz artist, who reportedly applied to go to music school when he was a young man. At his audition, he was given scales to sing, but he could sing only the first two notes properly. He was told he didn't have what it takes to be a musician. The story said that he cried at first because he had been rejected from the music program, but that he told his friends afterward, "I know there's music in me, and they can't keep it out." He eventually became one of the most successful and beloved jazz musicians ever. What made the difference? Louis Armstrong put his life into the gift he knew he had, and this gift made room for him. He was an original, and he knew it.

You are an original, too. God said so. Do you believe it?

Prayer: Father, just as Paul told Timothy to stir
up the gift that was in him, I want to stir up my gift.
Guide me as I step out in faith and develop my gift.
Teach me how to use it with more confidence each day.
In Jesus' name, amen.

Thought: You stir up your gift by developing, refining,
enhancing, and using it.

Reading: **Psalm 37–39; Acts 26**

Don't Be an Imitator

Although we are all born as originals, most of us have become imitators. I used to think about becoming like everyone else and joining the rat race. Yet I soon realized that if all the rats are in a race and you win, you simply become the Big Rat. I recommend that you get out of the rat race, stop being in a contest with society, and stop trying to please everybody.

Moreover, you are not to mimic the gifts of others. You are to stir up your own gift. Unfortunately, many people are jealous of other people's gifts. Let me encourage you not to waste your time on jealousy. You should be so busy stirring up your gift that you don't have time to be jealous of anyone else or to feel sorry for yourself.

Perhaps you are fifty-five, sixty-five, or seventy years old. You're looking back over the last thirty or forty years and asking, "What have I done with my life? I've followed the crowd, and I haven't developed my own gift." If you believe you're too old to use your gift, *you're believing a lie*. We read in the Bible that God went to people who were already past retirement age and recharged them. They have become noteworthy in history because they started over when others (even they themselves) thought their lives were almost over. (See the stories of Abraham and Sarah in Genesis 18:11–15; 21:1–8, and Elizabeth and Zechariah in Luke 1.) Your gift will give you your youth back. Your gift will give you energy and strength. You will be healthier. You will stop talking about dying and start talking about living.

Prayer: Father, I believe that You will allow me to use
my gifts throughout my lifetime. Help me to remember
that there is no "retirement" in Christ. We can use
our gifts for You as long as we are alive.
In Jesus' name, amen.

Thought: If you believe you're too old to be using your gift,
you're believing a lie.

Reading: **Psalm 40–42; Acts 27:1–26**

You Can Be an Innovator

Instead of being an imitator of others, the person with vision should be an innovator. Innovation is the ability to be creative and to think outside the box. Our ability to innovate comes from the fact that we are made in the image and likeness of our Creator. Paul said that we are to *"put on the new self, which is being renewed in knowledge in the image of its Creator"* (Colossians 3:10). This means that the more we are transformed into the image of the One who created us, the more innovative we should be.

In light of the mind-set of the innovator, let's look at some definitions of innovation. Innovation is the capacity to create new approaches and concepts to deal with both old and new challenges, the perceptiveness to see possibilities in the combination of old and new concepts, and the capacity to think beyond the known, defy the norm, and believe in one's abilities to solve problems.

Whenever you encounter a project, a challenge, or a problem in fulfilling your vision, practice thinking in new ways and with a different mind-set. Ask the Creator to give you a fresh perspective, and see what happens! As Paul wrote, *"Now to Him who is able to do exceedingly abundantly above all that we ask or think, according to the power that works in us"* (Ephesians 3:20). Visionaries don't follow paths—they create trails. They venture where others don't dare to tread. Venture into the uncomfortable zone—innovate.

Prayer: Father, You are the wondrous Creator who has given me the ability to innovate. Please help me to use my gifts with Your creativity. I want to fulfill my dream in a way that will be successful and creative and bring You honor.
In Jesus' name, Amen.

Thought: Innovation is the ability to be creative and to think outside the box.

Reading: **Psalm 43–45; Acts 27:27–44**

Jesus, the Greatest Innovator

The greatest example of a person with the spirit of innovation is the ultimate man of vision, Jesus Christ. During His time on earth, He demonstrated the same innovative spirit as the heavenly Father. His creativity was manifested in all His work among men. For example, in performing His miracles, He used a variety of approaches to solve problems.

He healed the blind using several different methods. For some, He merely touched their eyes and they were made well. For one, He laid his hands on the person's eyes and put mud on them. For still another, He simply spoke the words, "Go, your faith has healed you." When Jesus wanted to feed thousands of people who had gathered to hear Him speak, He didn't have his disciples buy food at the market; instead, He multiplied five loaves and two fish so that everyone was fed and had leftovers to spare. When Jesus raised the dead, He did so in several ways. One time He touched a young man's coffin and then told him to get up; in another instance, He took a little girl by the hand and told her to get up; and at another time, He called out to Lazarus, who was still in his grave, and Lazarus walked out of the tomb alive. Every instance was unique and most likely tailored to the individual or to God's specific purposes at the time.

Jesus' innovative spirit shows that true vision demands that we always be open to new ways of fulfilling our purposes.

Prayer: Father, Jesus is a perfect example for every part of my life. Please help me to remember that all means of creativity are open to me as I seek to serve You. In Jesus' name, amen.

Thought: Jesus' creativity was manifested in all His work among men.

Reading: **Psalm 46–48; Acts 28**

Vision Always Comes from Purpose

To understand and develop your vision, you must remember that *vision always emanates from purpose.* Why? God is the Author of vision, and it is His nature to be purposeful in everything He does. Every time God appeared on the scene in human history, it was because He wanted something specific accomplished and was actively working it out through people's lives.

God is a God of action based on purpose. Moreover, His purposes are eternal. Psalm 33:11 says, *"The plans of the LORD stand firm forever, the purposes of his heart through all generations,"* and Isaiah 14:24 says, *"The LORD Almighty has sworn, 'Surely, as I have planned, so it will be, and as I have purposed, so it will stand.'"* Nothing can get in the way of God's purposes; they always come to pass.

God created everything to fulfill a purpose in life. You may have been a surprise to your parents, but you were not a surprise to God! He has given you a special vision to fulfill. The Scriptures say, *"For he chose us in him before the creation of the world..."* (Ephesians 1:4). God planned in advance all that you were born to be and accomplish. I am continually positive about life because I know that God created me for a purpose and that He will bring that purpose to pass. Do you believe that about yourself? Do you *know* that your life has a purpose?

Prayer: Father, You chose me for Yourself before
the creation of the world, and You created me
with a purpose. Reveal Your plan to me;
I desire to live a positive and significant life before You.
In Jesus' name, amen.

Thought: Do you *know* that your life has a purpose in God?

Reading: **Psalm 49–50; Romans 1**

Action Steps to Fulfilling Vision

You are the sum total of the choices and decisions you make every day. You can choose to stay where you are right now, or you can choose to move forward in life by pursuing your dream. I want to challenge you to stop making excuses for why you can't accomplish what you were born to do. Take your life out of neutral. God has given you the power and the responsibility to achieve your life's vision.

Ask yourself some serious questions as you ponder your purpose. What is your dream? Have you truly discovered your purpose and vision yet? Do you know what you want to accomplish in this life? Are you doing what you believe you were born to do?

Most people do things because they have to. Wouldn't you like to do things because you have *decided* to, based on your purpose? You must choose to be on the offensive rather than the defensive. I hope you will decide you have had enough of being "normal" and that you will declare your distinction. Remember, you were created to stand out, not to blend in. You were created to accomplish something that no one else can accomplish because God gave the assignment to you.

Now, let's pray together:

Prayer: Heavenly Father, Your Word says that you have a plan
for each of our lives. You have given us a purpose to fulfill
in this world, and You have redeemed us because of Your
love. I ask You to open our spiritual eyes so that we can
clearly see the specific purposes You have for us.
We want to complete those purposes with joy
and with the knowledge that we have
accomplished Your will for our lives.
In Jesus' name, amen.

Thought: You are the sum total of the choices and decisions
you make every day.

Reading: **Psalm 51–53; Romans 2**

Principles of Purpose and Vision

T oday, reflect on the principles we have learned so far about vision:

1. The poorest person in the world is a person without a dream.
2. The most frustrated person in the world is someone who has a dream but doesn't know how to make it come to pass.
3. God created everything and everyone with a purpose.
4. Every person was created by God to be unique and distinct.
5. Vision comes from purpose.
6. God has placed in every human being a unique vision and call that is designed to give purpose and meaning to life.
7. No person can give you your vision. It is God-given.
8. Every human being was created to accomplish something that no one else can accomplish.
9. Every person was created to be known for something special.
10. You were given a burden or "responsible urge" to complete your purpose.
11. You were born at the right time to fulfill your purpose.
12. One person with vision is greater than the passive force of ninety-nine people who are merely interested in doing or becoming something.
13. Your gift will make a way for you in the world and enable you to fulfill your vision.
14. You are responsible for stirring up the gift within you.
15. As long as a person can hold on to his vision, then there is always a chance for him to move out of his present circumstances and toward the fulfillment of his purpose.

Reading: **Psalm 54–56; Romans 3**

What Is the Heart?

Your entire life is controlled and determined by your heart. What is the heart? The Bible provides us with many truths about it. When it uses the word *heart*, it's usually referring to our subconscious minds and their contents. Historically, the heart has been a metaphor for the center of our being.

Our hearts or subconscious minds are what motivate us in our attitudes and actions, even though we may not be aware of what is influencing us. Jesus Christ emphasized the following.

> For out of the overflow of the heart the mouth speaks. The good man brings good things out of the good stored up in him, and the evil man brings evil things out of the evil stored up in him.
> (Matthew 12:34–35)

> But the things that come out of the mouth come from the heart, and these make a man "unclean." For out of the heart come evil thoughts, murder, adultery, sexual immorality, theft, false testimony, slander. These are what make a man "unclean"; but eating with unwashed hands does not make him "unclean." (Matthew 15:18–20)

In these simple statements, the principle of the heart and its power to control all of one's life is evident. Whatever is in your heart dictates your experience in life. According to Jesus, all our actions are motivated by the content of our hearts or what is stored in our subconscious minds.

This leads us to the following truth to ponder: The way you think about your vision and how you act on it come from your heart, as well.

Prayer: Father, my heart is the center of my being and reflects who I actually am. I want my heart and life to reflect You. May my words and actions reveal the good things You have stored up in me. In Jesus' name, amen.

Thought: Whatever is in your heart dictates your experience in life.

Reading: **Psalm 57–59; Romans 4**

AUGUST 2

The Tablet of the Heart

The Bible has much to say about the importance of the heart. Wise King Solomon spoke of the heart's power and function. In the book of Proverbs, we read, *"Let love and faithfulness never leave you; bind them around your neck, write them on the tablet of your heart"* (Proverbs 3:3). What we "write" on our hearts we use as a reference for our attitudes and actions. Again, in Proverbs, we read, *"To man belong the plans of the heart"* (Proverbs 16:1). The heart is where we sift things over and make decisions about what we want to do and be.

Jeremiah the prophet records, *"I the LORD search the heart and examine the mind, to reward a man according to his conduct, according to what his deeds deserve"* (Jeremiah 17:10). Attitude and behavior are tied together because your actions come from what you think. Finally, the book of Hebrews says, *"The word of God is living and active. Sharper than any double-edged sword, it penetrates even to dividing soul and spirit, joints and marrow; it judges the thoughts and attitudes of the heart"* (Hebrews 4:12). We are held accountable not only for our actions, but also for our thoughts and attitudes. In order to walk successfully in the vision God has given you, you must pay attention to your heart, study what's in it, and make certain that the Word of God is your source of truth.

Prayer: Father, Your Word is living and active as it judges
the intentions of my heart. Please help me to make
certain that Your Word is my source of truth.
Fill my mind and heart with Your Word
so that I cannot be led away from
You or from my vision.
In Jesus' name, amen.

Thought: What we "write" on our hearts we use
as a reference for our attitudes and actions.

Reading: **Psalm 60–62; Romans 5**

Completed in Eternity

We can better understand vision when we realize that our purpose has already been completed in eternity. The following passage entirely changed my perspective on the fulfillment of vision:

> I am God, and there is no other; I am God, and there is none like me. **I make known the end from the beginning**, from ancient times, what is still to come. I say: My purpose will stand, and I will do all that I please. (Isaiah 46:9–10, emphasis added)

In this Scripture, God mentions two things that He does. First, He establishes the end before the beginning. This means that He finishes things first in the spiritual realm, and then He goes back and starts them up in the physical realm. Second, He reveals the end result of something when it is just beginning.

I have noticed in the Scriptures the principle that "purpose is established before production." In other words, God first institutes a purpose, and then He creates someone or something to fulfill that purpose. He is the Alpha and the Omega, the beginning and the end. We often don't recognize the fact that when God starts something, He has already completed it in eternity. *"Yet they cannot fathom what God has done from beginning to end"* (Ecclesiastes 3:11). We can see this principle in creation. Everything was already finished in God's mind before He laid the foundation of the world. In a similar way, the vision He has placed within you has already been completed in eternity.

Prayer: Father, You have already completed my purpose
in eternity. Help me to fulfill Your plan on
earth as I follow Your direction.
In Jesus' name, amen.

Thought: When God starts something, He has already
completed it in eternity.

Reading: **Psalm 63–65; Romans 6**

Purpose before Production

There is a street near my house called Shirley Street. At one time, there was a parking lot there. One day when I was driving along that street, I saw a large sign with a beautifully painted picture of a building. There was no building on the site yet, but there was the big sign and the name of the building. It showed the landscape, the color of the building, the windows, everything; it was a very detailed picture of what the completed building would look like. The sign said, "Coming soon." I drove past the lot and sensed God saying to me, "Did you see that?" I said, "See what?" He said, "Did you see the finish?" So I turned my car around and went back to take a closer look at the sign. By showing the completed picture of the building, the construction company was revealing the end of its purpose.

Again, God essentially completed us before He created us. Not only does He establish our ends, but He also gives us glimpses of them through the visions He puts in our hearts. We must pay attention to His work within us so that we will be able to understand more of what He *"has done from beginning to end"* (Ecclesiastes 3:11). God wants you to "see" the completion of your vision by knowing that He already planned and established it before you were born. Therefore, instead of striving to fulfill what God has given you to do, you can rely on Him to finish it as you allow Him to guide you in the specifics of carrying it out.

Prayer: Father, please help me to "see" the completion
of my vision with the eyes of faith.
In Jesus' name, amen.

Thought: God essentially completed us before He created us.

Reading: **Psalm 66–67; Romans 7**

The Project Start-Up

I n the book of Genesis, which means "origin" or "source," we read
about the start-up of God's project called "earth." Those of you
who are involved in project management know that start-up is a significant step in the process of building. When you reach the start-up
phase, it means that you have all the plans drawn, all the physical
resources in place, and all the management resources in order. Before
you start a project, all these things must be in place. Only *then* can
you begin.

When do you start building a house? Is it when you dig the foundation? Essentially, you begin building whenever the idea for the house is
conceived. Digging the foundation is simply the beginning of bringing
your purpose to pass. Therefore, after you dig the foundation, and somebody asks you, "What are you doing?" your answer is very definite. You
point to the architect's rendering of the house and say, "I am building
this."

God wouldn't have allowed you to start your life and your purpose
unless they were already completed in eternity. You must realize, however, that your end doesn't look anything like your beginning—or like any
other point in the process, for that matter. God redeems you because of
the vision you are carrying, and now you must live out that vision. The
Bible says, *"We are God's workmanship, created in Christ Jesus to do good
works, which God **prepared in advance** for us to do"* (Ephesians 2:10, emphasis added).

Prayer: Father, may I be reminded daily that the good
works I walk in were prepared by You since the
beginning of time. May I do those good works
with joy at being a part of Your plan for the earth.
In Jesus' name, amen.

Thought: You were born to manifest something
that is already finished.

Reading: **Psalm 68–69; Romans 8:1–21**

A Glimpse into the Future

A t this point, I want to clarify the difference between purpose and vision. Purpose is the intent for which God created you—the reason why you were born. Purpose is what God has already decided in His own mind that you're supposed to begin to fulfill. Therefore, we can conclude the following:

- Purpose is when you know and understand what you were born to accomplish.
- Vision is when you can see it in your mind by faith and begin to imagine it.

When you are able to see your purpose, your vision comes to life. For example, my purpose is to identify and encourage leadership and visionary qualities in people throughout the world. My vision is to do it through Bahamas Faith Ministries International, which will include a convention center and a hotel in the future.

We have insight into God's purpose for us based on what we know God has already accomplished in eternity. Vision is a glimpse of our future that God has purposed. We don't know all the details of how our purposes will unfold, but we see their "ends" because God reveals them to us in the visions He gives us. This is why we can be confident that they will come to pass. When God created you with a purpose, He also designed you perfectly to be able to fulfill it. God always gives us the ability to do whatever He calls us to do.

Prayer: Father, my life's vision is an exciting look
into the future that You have purposed for me. Thank You
for assuring me that You have already put the plan
in motion so that I might complete it.
In Jesus' name, amen.

Thought: Vision is foresight with insight based on hindsight.

Reading: **Psalm 70–71; Romans 8:22–39**

Vision Is about God

At its essence, vision isn't about us—it's about God. Proverbs 19:21 says, *"Many are the plans in a man's heart, but it is the Lord's purpose that prevails."* True vision is not a human invention. It's about the desires God imparts to us. His purpose was established well before we had any plans for our lives. We were meant to consult God to find out His purposes for us so we can make the right plans. Ecclesiastes 3:14 says, *"I know that everything God does will endure forever; nothing can be added to it and nothing taken from it. God does it so that men will revere him."*

Let's review the following facts: Purpose is the source of your vision. Your purpose existed before you did. What you were born to do was accomplished by God before you even arrived on the scene, and He ordained your birth in order to carry it out.

We must understand the key to recognizing personal vision. After reading my books on purpose, many people write to me and say, "Okay, I read your book. It's wonderful, it changed my life, and I'm ready to go, except that I don't know what my vision is. Tell me how to find it." To find your vision, *you have to look within yourself, where God has placed it.* The key is this: God's will is as close to us as our most persistent thoughts and deepest desires.

Prayer: Father, I realize that vision is about You
and not about me. Vision is about fitting into
Your plan for establishing Your kingdom on this earth.
Lead me into my part of that plan.
In Jesus' name, amen.

Thought: To find your vision, you have to look within
yourself, where God has placed it.

Reading: **Psalm 72–73; Romans 9:1–15**

The Dream That Won't Go Away

Psalm 37:4 says, *"Delight yourself in the LORD and he will give you the desires of your...."* Desires of your what? *"Your heart."* Wait a minute. Doesn't God give us desires from heaven? Yes, He does. Our desires originate there, but remember that God has placed His desires for you within your heart. He put the plans for your life within you when you were born, and they have never left you. The heart, in this case, means your subconscious mind. Sometimes His ideas come in multiples. God may put five or six things in your mind that He wants you to do, each one for a different season of your life.

Whether He gives you one idea or six ideas, the thoughts of God are consistent, and they will be present throughout your life. No matter how old you grow, the same thoughts will keep coming back to you, and the desires will never leave you. This is because the will of God for you never changes. The Bible says, *"God's gifts and his call are irrevocable"* (Romans 11:29). The specifics of your plans may change as your purpose unfolds, but your purpose is permanent.

I have found that people are constantly waiting for God to tell them what to do when it has been given to them already. At times, Christian people look for God's will everywhere except within themselves. It's necessary for them to realize that they don't receive their purposes after they are born again; they were already given their purposes when they were physically born. You're not saved for the sole purpose of going to heaven; you're saved to finish your assignment on earth.

Prayer: Father, thank You for placing Your desires
within my heart. You saved me so that I could complete my
assignment on this earth; please help me to do this.
In Jesus' name, amen.

Thought: Vision is the idea that never leaves you—the dream
that won't go away.

Reading: **Psalm 74–76; Romans 9:16–33**

God Speaks to You

Many people ask me how God speaks to us. They say, "I want to hear from God. Does He speak in an audible voice? Does He come in the night and whisper in my ear? Will He speak through some animal or write on the wall like He did in the Old Testament?" They don't realize that God has been speaking to them since they were born, and He is still speaking to them now. He speaks to them through the thoughts, ideas, and visions they keep having in their minds. If you are unclear about your vision, you can ask God to reveal to you the deepest desires He has placed within you.

Some people call psychic hotlines to get others to tell them their futures. The sad thing is that some Christians do nearly the equivalent of this when they run from meeting to meeting, asking people to prophesy over them concerning their futures, not understanding that God has given them their visions directly. A prophet can *confirm* your vision, but he or she will not *give* you your vision. God gives you that directly, and He reveals it to you as you listen to Him and follow Him. God says, *"I will put my law in their minds and write it on their hearts"* (Jeremiah 31:33).

Again, one way to discern whether something is a vision from God is to determine whether you have *a real desire* to do it or merely *a passing interest* in it.

Prayer: Father, I am so grateful that You are a God who speaks
directly to His people. Thank You for speaking to me through
Your Holy Spirit, through Your Word, and through
the ideas and dreams You have given me.
I want to use them to Your glory.
In Jesus' name, amen.

Thought: A prophet can *confirm* your vision, but he or she will not
give you your vision; God gives you that directly.

Reading: **Psalm 77–78; Romans 10**

August 10

Vision Is Unselfish

True vision is unselfish. Its purpose is to bring God's kingdom on earth and turn people to Him. A vision should always focus on helping humanity or building up others in some way.

First, this means that God will never have you pursue your vision at the expense of your family. A beloved friend of mine went to a conference where a supposed prophet spoke to him about what God wanted for his life. He came to me and asked, "Did you hear what the prophet said? What do you think?" I replied, "Well, let's pray over that prophecy. Let's take our time, get counsel, and find God's will on it." However, the next time I heard from him, he had already set up a plan to fulfill this prophecy. He went to another country, leaving behind a confused and angry family. Was this really God's purpose?

There are instances when family members will agree to be apart for a time to serve a certain purpose. Moreover, your family will not always understand or support your dream. Yet pursuing it shouldn't destroy their lives. Vision should always be accompanied by compassion.

Second, a true vision will not take the form of building a big business just so you can have millions of dollars for expensive homes and cars. These things may be goals, but they are not vision—in fact, they are probably selfish ambition because they build *your* kingdom rather than *God's* kingdom. Your vision might well involve making a large amount of money. The difference, however, is in your motivation and attitude. You need to treat your finances as a resource God has provided to fulfill your vision, not as a tool to fill your life with luxuries.

Prayer: Father, I know that You want me to pursue
my life's dreams with compassion for others.
Please keep me from selfish motives.
In Jesus' name, amen.

Thought: Vision's purpose is to bring about
God's kingdom on earth.

Reading: **Psalm 79–80; Romans 11:1–18**

Vision Brings Fulfillment

Your life's vision is real when it is the only thing that gives you true satisfaction. Ecclesiastes 3:13 says, *"That everyone may eat and drink, and find satisfaction in all his toil–this is the gift of God."* It is God's desire for us to enjoy our work, but this can happen only when we're doing the right work. Merely working at a job is disheartening. Going to work is a dismal experience for many people because, day after day, they are doing something they dislike. That is not what you were created to do. Again, Proverbs 19:21 says, *"Many are the plans in a man's heart, but it is the Lord's purpose that prevails."* True success is not in what you accomplish; it is in doing what God told you to do. That is why people who build big projects or gain great fame can be successful and depressed at the same time.

Going against your purpose may be a personal issue, but it is never a private one. You can mess up others' lives if you aren't supposed to be where you are, or if you are supposed to be somewhere that you refuse to go. Remember the story of Jonah in the Bible? God told him that his purpose was to go to Nineveh to warn the people there to turn to God. Jonah's response was, in effect, "I'm not going!" He got on a ship headed for Tarshish instead. God had purposed that Jonah would go to Nineveh even before the prophet was born. I urge you not to board the wrong ship, but to remain on course in God's purpose.

Prayer: Father, please help me to stay on course with You.
I don't want to drift to the right or to the left,
but to continue to follow Your direction.
In Jesus' name, amen.

Thought: Until you follow God's dream, you will be unfulfilled.

Reading: **Psalm 81–83; Romans 11:19–36**

A Vital Connection with God

Many people don't recognize the vision God has placed within them because they don't have a vital connection with God. God's purpose never changes, and since His purpose is woven into our desires, our own ways are never ultimately satisfying.

God provided salvation through Christ to salvage His will and purpose in your life. He said, in effect, "I'm not going to lose what I gave you birth to do." He restores us to Himself so we can do the works He had in mind for us before the world began. Remember, *"we are God's workmanship, created in Christ Jesus to do good works, which God prepared in advance for us to do"* (Ephesians 2:10). We are not saved *by* doing good works but *for the purpose* of doing good works. We are saved for relationship with God and to fulfill our earthly visions.

Once we are restored to God, we receive His Holy Spirit and can see and understand the vision He has placed in our hearts. The Bible says, *"Casting down imaginations, and every high thing that exalteth itself against the knowledge of God..."* (2 Corinthians 10:5 KJV). This verse is talking about ideas. It continues, *"...and bringing into captivity every thought to the obedience of Christ."* Any idea that is contrary to the Word of God, or to obedience to Christ's wishes for your life, is not a God idea. You must set it aside. The vision God gives you will always line up with His Word.

Prayer: Father, please help me to maintain a vital
connection with You through Your Holy Spirit
and Your Word. I want to be sensitive
to Your voice and to Your purposes.
In Jesus' name, amen.

Thought: Genuine vision is always in alignment with
God's nature and character.

Reading: **Psalm 84–86; Romans 12**

Vision Is Personal and Corporate

We must realize that vision is both personal and corporate; personal vision will always be found within a larger corporate vision. It is not God's method to give a vision to a group. He gives the vision to an individual who shares his vision with the group and transfers it to them. The members of the group then run with the vision because they find in it a place for their own personal visions to be fulfilled.

Moses was constrained by a vision to deliver the people of Israel and lead them to the Promised Land. Joshua was motivated by a vision to possess that land. David was driven by a vision to settle God's people. Nehemiah was possessed by a vision to rebuild the walls of Jerusalem. In every case, the vision was given to an individual who was ultimately responsible for seeing it through, and the individual transferred the vision to a group.

When a person starts to sense his purpose and gift, he often interprets this as a call to autonomy and separation. However, nothing could be further from the truth. In order to accomplish a corporate purpose or make a larger vision come to pass, God brings together many people's personal gifts and unique visions. God wants you to bring your time, energy, resources, and creative power to be part of a larger vision to which your vision is connected.

Prayer: Father, Your Word says that believers are
the body of Christ. We are many members,
each with different purposes and gifts.
Help us to appreciate one another and the
unique visions You have given us,
so that we will function as a whole body.
In Jesus' name, amen.

Thought: In order to accomplish a larger vision, God brings together many people's gifts and unique visions.

Reading: **Psalm 87–88; Romans 13**

We Need Teamwork

Teamwork is defined as the ability to work together toward a common vision. Because it directs individual accomplishment toward corporate objectives, teamwork is the fuel that allows common people to attain uncommon results. Teamwork intrinsically appreciates the diversity of gifts that the team members bring to a partnership or group. Paul wrote,

> Just as each of us has one body with many members, and these members do not all have the same function, so in Christ we who are many form one body, and each member belongs to all the others. We have different gifts, according to the grace given us. (Romans 12:4–6)

We have seen that while God calls individuals to carry out His purposes, He doesn't want them to pursue their callings alone. Even Moses, who was called the friend of God and did extraordinary things, needed leadership help from his brother Aaron and sister Miriam. We also see the idea of teamwork in the first-century church with the traveling teams of Paul and Barnabus, Peter and John, and Priscilla and Aquila. When Paul worked with the churches he founded, he often had many coworkers who assisted him. Jesus Himself emphasized teamwork. He did not carry out His ministry alone, but instead gathered a group of twelve disciples to assist Him and learn from His example. When He sent out His disciples to minister, He told them to go two by two. (See Mark 6:7; Luke 10:1.)

In the same way, whatever your personal vision is, God wants you to be joined with others as a team to fulfill those plans.

Prayer: Father, may we always be thankful for the gift of one another. Please help me to recognize the people You want me to work with in my vision.
In Jesus' name, amen.

Thought: Teamwork is defined as the ability to work together toward a common vision.

Reading: **Psalm 80–90; Romans 14**

Problems in Corporate Vision

When people don't understand teamwork or accept the relationship between personal and corporate vision, there can be problems. If the members of the group think they are inferior to the person with the original vision, or the leader starts to think he is more important than the members, or if one or more of the members wants to supplant the person who has the larger vision, that is when the trouble will begin.

Moses had the latter problem with Miriam and Aaron, his sister and brother. God had appointed them all as leaders. (See Micah 6:4.) Moses, however, was the one who had received the original vision, and he was the one with whom God met directly and through whom God spoke. When Miriam and Aaron became jealous of Moses and wanted to usurp his role, it caused turmoil within that leadership group. God had to remind Miriam and Aaron in a very graphic way that it is His purposes that prevail, not our private ambitions. (See Numbers 12:4–15.)

We must have an attitude of cooperation with those with whom we share corporate vision. If we are going to do something for God so that the world will be better off because we were here, we can't do that with a private, individualistic attitude. Let us be cognizant of God's ways and work with them rather than against them.

Prayer: Father, we know that Your children
do not get along at times. Please help me to cooperate
with the believers with whom You have placed me.
Help me to join with them in fulfilling
the corporate vision that You have given.
In Jesus' name, amen.

Thought: If we are in line with God's nature and character,
we will desire what He desires.

Reading: **Psalm 91–93; Romans 15:1–13**

Drawing Out the Vision

When we understand the relationship between personal and corporate vision, we will recognize a chief way in which God fulfills people's dreams. Proverbs 20:5 says, *"The purposes of a man's heart are [like] deep waters, but a man of understanding draws them out."* In other words, everyone has a vision in his heart, but a person of understanding causes that dream, that purpose, that vision to be brought out so it can become reality. A person of understanding will figuratively lower a bucket into the deep well-waters of your soul and begin to draw out what you are dreaming and thinking.

What is the process by which this occurs? After God conveys a vision to a leader, you will then somehow come into contact with this person, who will present the corporate vision. You will become excited about participating in it because you will see how your private vision finds fulfillment in it. It is essential for you to understand that God brings the corporate vision into your life not to *give* you vision, which He has already given you, but to *stir up* your personal vision. In other words, you don't receive your vision from other people, but you are enabled to fulfill it through others.

It is my desire to stir up your vision. As I wrote earlier, my own vision is to inspire and draw out the hidden leader in every person I meet. You are a leader in the specific purpose God has given you to accomplish through your gift because no one else but you can fulfill it. Are you beginning to believe in the possibilities?

Prayer: Father, thank You for making me a leader in the vision
You have given me for my life. Please enable me to stir up
that vision and see it come to fulfillment in You.
In Jesus' name, amen.

Thought: God brings the corporate vision into your life
to stir up your personal vision.

Reading: **Psalm 94–96; Romans 15:14–33**

I Need Your Vision, You Need Mine

The corporate vision in which your personal vision will ultimately be fulfilled might be that of a company, a church, a nonprofit organization, or even your own family. That is why, when you hear of something that is related to your vision, you should pay attention to it, because it may be that you're supposed to attach yourself to it. You yourself may be given the corporate vision, such as starting a business or organizing a community project. Yet none of us is meant to complete our visions on our own.

The joy of God's plan for personal and corporate vision is that nothing we are born to do is to be done by ourselves or for ourselves. If you and I are part of the same corporate vision, then I need your vision, and you need mine. I'm not involved in the work that I'm doing to build a name for myself. My life's work is to complete the assignment God gave me. Every member of my staff and organization has a part to play in our vision. My part is to stir up their individual dreams, and their part is to stir up mine. When we stir up each other's visions, the divine deposit of destiny starts flowing. Vision generates vision. Dreams always stir up other dreams.

You need people around you who believe in dreams that are even bigger than your own so you can keep stirring up your vision. There are too many other people who will tell you to settle down and do nothing. Yet no matter where you came from, where you're going is better.

Prayer: Father, help me to stir up the dreams and visions
of those around me. I want to be open to their plans and
to receive their encouragement as well.
In Jesus' name, amen.

Thought: None of us is meant to complete
our visions on our own.

Reading: **Psalm 97–99; Romans 16**

Action Steps in Fulfilling Vision

The first step to fulfilling your reason for existence is realizing that you have been given a vision. Yet how exactly do you receive, recognize, and activate your vision? When you understand God is the source of your vision and that He has placed it in your heart, you learn the secrets to its working in your life. This knowledge helps you take your dream from initial idea all the way to fulfillment.

There are simple action steps you can take as you contemplate the vision God has given you. Take half an hour and allow yourself to dream about what you would like to do in life. What ideas and desires do you have? What have you always wanted to do? Think about your primary gifts or talents. How do your dreams and your gifts go together? Write down your ideas, desires, and gifts and read them over every evening for a week. Then ask yourself, "Do these ideas hold true? Are they what I *really* want to do?" If the answer is yes, keep them where you can refer to them as you read this book; watch them form into a specific vision and concrete goals that will move you along toward the completion of your purpose.

Let's pray together:

Prayer: Heavenly Father, You are the Source of our lives. You have decided, in Your divine purpose, to place a vision within each of our hearts. We know that this vision is to be used for Your glory and to accomplish Your purposes on this earth. We are so thankful that we are Your workmanship, that we have been created to walk in the good works—or vision—that You have given us to fulfill. In Your love and wisdom, please guide us to complete all that You have called us to do. In Jesus' precious name we pray, amen.

Thought: God is the source of your vision.

Reading: **Psalm 100–102; 1 Corinthians 1**

Principles of the Nature of Vision

Today, reflect on these principles of the nature of vision:

1. Your purpose is already completed in God.

2. God completed you before He created you.

3. The fact that you were started is proof that you are completed.

4. You were designed to perfectly accomplish your purpose.

5. When you know and understand what you were born to accomplish, that is purpose. When you can see it in your mind by faith, that is vision.

6. Vision is foresight with insight based on hindsight.

7. Vision isn't about us. It's about God and His purposes.

8. You already know your vision. It is as close as your most persistent thoughts and deepest desires.

9. To have vision is to have more than a mere interest in something; it is to have a real desire and passion for it.

10. Vision persists, no matter what the odds.

11. Vision is unselfish.

12. Vision is the only thing that brings true fulfillment.

13. Vision requires a vital connection with God.

14. Personal vision will always be found within a larger corporate vision.

15. Those who are in the same corporate vision must work together harmoniously to achieve it.

16. The leader of corporate vision "draws out" the personal visions of those in the group by helping them to activate their passions, dreams, gifts, and talents.

17. Vision generates vision.

Reading: **Psalm 103–104; 1 Corinthians 2**

Vision Is Specific

A vital aspect about true vision is that it is *specific*. One of the greatest causes of failure among people who are pursuing their visions is that they don't identify their objective of success.

Suppose I came to you and said, "Let's meet." You say, "Okay; where?" I reply, "Oh, anywhere." You ask, "Well, *when* do you want to meet?" and I say, "Anytime." What do you think are the chances that we will actually meet? Practically zero. Vision must be specific rather than general or vague.

I have asked many people, "What are you going to do with your life? What is your vision?" and I usually receive responses such as these: "I'm going to build a big house, own several cars, and have a good family." "I want to get married." "I want to open a restaurant someday." These are not visions, but mere goals. When I ask pastors the same question, they generally give me one of the following answers: "My vision is to win my city to Christ." "My vision is to *'preach the gospel to every creature'* (Mark 16:15 KJV)." "Our vision as a church is to know Him and to make Him known." "Our vision is to equip people for the work of the ministry."

None of the above answers are visions. They are *missions*. Why? They are too general for visions. A mission is a *general statement of purpose* that declares the overall idea of what you want to accomplish. In contrast, a vision is a *very precise statement* that has a specific emphasis and definable boundaries. God has given you a *specific* vision to fulfill.

Prayer: Father, please help me to identify my specific vision, clarifying any general or vague ideas I have be trying to follow, so I can truly fulfill Your plan for me.
In Jesus' name, amen.

Thought: A vital aspect about true vision is that it is *specific*.

Reading: **Psalm 105–106; 1 Corinthians 3**

Vision versus Mission

God is not vague about your life. Therefore, it is essential that you learn the difference between vision and mission. You were designed to be unique and to fulfill a particular purpose. If you are to carry out this specific purpose, your vision has to be specific. Otherwise, you will be just like everyone else around you. Remember, your vision—like your fingerprints—is meant to distinguish you from every other person in the world.

Let me use the Christian church as an example. The assignment that Jesus gave His followers two thousand years ago—"*Go into all the world and preach the good news*" (Mark 16:15)—is called the Great Commission. It is the "co-mission," the joint or corporate mission of the worldwide church. Therefore, if a local church thinks its particular vision is to preach the gospel, then it has a mistaken idea of vision. It knows its *mission*, but it hasn't yet found its true *vision, that one thing that distinguishes it from all other churches.*

One church is not assigned where another church is assigned. That is why an individual church shouldn't compare itself with other churches in its city or nation or use another church as a measure of its own success. Each church is to fulfill its part of the Great Commission through the specific emphasis or approach that God has given it. The same general principle holds true for you and your personal vision. What is the specific emphasis or approach in life that God has given you?

Prayer: Father, my mission as a believer is to see others won
to the Lord Jesus Christ. Please open my heart to see the
specific vision You have given me to fulfill this mission.
In Jesus' name, amen.

Thought: You were designed to be unique and
to fulfill a particular purpose.

Reading: **Psalm 107–109; 1 Corinthians 4**

No Need for Competition

When we truly understand the difference between mission and vision, we are protected from jealousy. One day, while I was talking with a friend who owns the McDonald's franchise in the Bahamas, the owner of the Kentucky Fried Chicken franchise stopped by. I was curious and asked the Kentucky Fried Chicken man what he was doing there. He responded, "We're going to have lunch." I decided to go with them because I wanted to see where they would end up eating. They went to Pizza Hut!

During lunch, I asked, "Excuse me, gentlemen. Aren't you competitors?" They responded, "No." My friend added, "He doesn't sell what I sell. I don't sell what he sells. How can we be in competition?" Then I asked, "Why did you come here?" He replied, "We didn't feel like eating burgers or chicken. We felt like eating pizza!" There is a place for all three establishments in our city because each has its own specific vision.

I travel around the world and speak at large churches alongside well-known pastors. Sometimes I notice certain approaches or methods their churches are using. I'm tempted to imitate them, thinking, "I should try that. Maybe I can get more people to come if I do what they do." Yet the Lord says to me, "Don't you dare." If I try to imitate others, I won't be fulfilling the specific vision He has given me, and I will no longer have His full blessing. Each of us must measure the success of our visions by God's assignments to us. We need to ask ourselves, "Am I doing what God told *me* to do?"

Prayer: Father, love, and not competition, should abound among Your people. As I seek to fulfill my vision, let me work in harmony with others, respecting their unique contributions.
In Jesus' name, amen.

Thought: When you've discovered your own vision,
you do not need to be jealous of anyone.

Reading: **Psalm 110–112; 1 Corinthians 5**

The Trap of Wishful Thinking

One reason people aren't specific about their visions is that they confuse them with mission. Another reason is that they get caught in the trap of wishful thinking. Their dreaming doesn't go beyond vague ideas of what they would like to do "someday." Yet dreaming is only the beginning of vision. Instead of wishing that things would get better, we must make concrete resolutions. We have to say, "Things *must* get better, and here, specifically, is what I'm going to do about it." For example, instead of saying, "I wish I could go to college," sit down today and send for applications to specific colleges. When they arrive, start filling them out. Instead of saying, "I wish I could lose weight," see your doctor and go on a specific weight-loss plan. Make a decision, and then take the first step.

People's success or failure in life is not dependent on the color of their skin. The real problem is the color of some people's *lives*; their lives are "gray." Such people don't have a precise way of living. They're just here. They drift along, allowing life to happen to them. God doesn't want anyone to live in a gray zone. When someone is living in the gray, it means that person isn't saying "yes" or "no," but "maybe." He has no real intention of doing anything with his life. God has invested so much in us. He doesn't want to see us wasting our lives in wishful thinking. He wants us to place our feet on the solid ground of God-given vision.

Prayer: Father, I don't wish to live in a gray zone.
Help me to make concrete decisions that will help me to
fulfill the vision You have placed within me.
In Jesus' name, amen.

Thought: God doesn't want anyone to live in a gray zone.

Reading: **Psalm 113–115; 1 Corinthians 6**

Are You Committed?

I am committed to fulfilling what God gave me birth to do. I resolved years ago that I would look only to God's Word and the vision He put in my heart to know what I could accomplish. In this way, God's purposes and principles have determined what I'm going to be and do rather than my own fears or others' opinions. The Bible says, *"Now it came to pass, when the time had come for* [Jesus] *to be received up, that He steadfastly set His face to go to Jerusalem"* (Luke 9:51 NKJV). Jesus set His face *"steadfastly"* or *"like flint"* (Isaiah 50:7) in His determination to fulfill His purpose. Flint is one of the hardest rocks you can find. This analogy means that after Jesus had set His goal to go to the cross, it was too late to talk Him out of it.

Sometimes we know what we should be doing, but we're hesitant to take that first step. We intend to do it, but we never do. We make excuses, such as "When my life gets less complicated," "When I feel more confident," or "After I pray about it more." There is a story of two fishermen who were lost in a storm on a lake. The storm was blowing so fiercely that they couldn't see a thing. One of the fishermen said to his colleague, "We have two choices. We can pray or row." The other answered, "Let's do both!" That's the way you need to live. Instead of deliberating about what you need to do, just say, "Let's row." Set a destination even while you're praying, and God will guide you where you need to go.

Prayer: Father, I am committed to Your purposes
and Your Word. Please help me keep the vision
You've given me always before me.
In Jesus' name, amen.

Thought: Are you committed to your vision?

Reading: **Psalm 116–118; 1 Corinthians 7:1–19**

Seeking Balance

Some people don't want to focus on a specific goal because they fear their lives might not be well-balanced. They say things such as these: "I don't really want to go after anything in particular because then I will be closing off other options," "I don't want to become too narrow," or "If I become too serious about something, I might miss what I really want to do in life." The problem is that people will say things like these for forty-five years and never end up doing anything! What they call a pursuit of balance is really an excuse for not making a decision. They end up being average, mediocre people.

True balance is the maintenance of equilibrium while moving toward a destination. A good example of this truth is the way a ship functions on the ocean. A ship always needs to maintain its balance. Wouldn't it be a waste of precious time and fuel, however, for a boat to expend all its energy just trying to balance on the water so that it didn't tip over? Some people live for sixty-five years, seventy-five years, or ninety years just balancing. Yet balance is not an end in itself; it is a means to an end. A ship keeps its balance as it makes its way to a specific port. Likewise, we need to have a destination while we're maintaining balance in our lives.

Prayer: Father, please help me to keep my conviction
about my vision strong. I want to be balanced in my life,
but I want to do so *as* I move forward
boldly in Your purpose for me.
In Jesus' name, amen.

Thought: Balance is not an end in itself;
it is a means to an end.

Reading: Psalm 119:1–88; 1 Corinthians 7:20–40

Trying to Do Everything

Is your busyness keeping you from your vision? Some people aren't specific about their visions because they're trying to do too much. Their problem is not that they're hesitant about getting started, but that they're running around attempting too many things. Even though they are constantly constructing something, they're actually building nothing at all because they never complete anything. Why does this happen? Because most people make the mistake of believing that the main goal in life is to stay busy. This way of thinking is a trap. Staying busy does not necessarily mean that you are heading toward a specific destination.

I have learned this very important truth that has set me free from both indecision and ineffective busyness: *I was not born or created to do everything.* This statement might be a good thing to put at the top of your office or household calendar. When we aim at everything, we usually hit nothing. Yet many of us are breaking our necks trying to hit everything in sight. Let me assure you: you were not born to meet all the needs on earth.

All the needs that you see in your nation cannot be met by you. *All* the trouble that you see in your community cannot be solved by you. God created you for a purpose, and that purpose should be your focus. It will keep you centered on what is most important for you to be involved in.

Prayer: Father, it is a relief to know that
I am not required to meet all the needs on earth!
Show me the needs that I can meet—the works
that You have created me to walk in.
In Jesus' name, amen.

Thought: You were not born to meet all the needs on earth.

Reading: **Psalm 119:89–176; 1 Corinthians 8**

A Jack-of-All-Trades

Has God blessed you with many gifts? Some people never pursue their true visions because they have the "problem" of being multi-talented, of being able to do many things. A misunderstanding of their gifts causes many talented and intelligent people to be ineffective and unsuccessful in life. These people say, "I have so many gifts that I don't know which ones I'm supposed to use. I want to develop all of them." As a result, they develop none of them to proficiency. I have many interests myself. I'm a teacher, a preacher, a speaker, and a writer. I can also paint, sculpt, and compose and play music. However, I have had to focus on specific gifts in order to be effective in life.

Let me ask you this: Have you ever seen anyone who became successful in life by doing everything? When a person tries to do everything, he ends up becoming a "jack-of-all-trades and master of none." I'm sure you know some multi-gifted people who seem to have the best chances of success but who aren't doing anything with their lives. You have to guard against the temptation to try to do everything. No matter how many gifts you have, don't let them distract you. You must decide to concentrate on one or two gifts, and then stir them up. Don't worry about losing the other gifts. As you stir one gift up, the other gifts will follow it. God will not waste what He has given you.

Prayer: Father, please help me to keep focused.
There are things that I *can* do, but I want to do them
only if they are part of Your plan for my life right now.
Help me to decide which gift to begin concentrating on today.
In Jesus' name, amen.

Thought: God will not waste what He has given you.

Reading: **Psalm 120–122; 1 Corinthians 9**

 246

The Cost of Vision

You must recognize the cost of fulfilling your vision. I think many people believe that successful people are born successful. In reality, success comes in installments, similar to a payment plan. It's a process. You receive a little bit of success today, a little more tomorrow, and more next week.

One of the costs of vision is *diligence*. All human beings dream, yet only the few who wake up, get out of their beds of comfort, and work hard will experience the fulfillment of their dreams. For example, if you think you have had a string of bad luck in life or that you are an unlucky person, you will probably not make the effort necessary to cause your vision to succeed. You may think, "Why bother?" This type of reasoning can undermine your entire life, destroying your desire to achieve your goals. You must realize that you are not defined by your past or confined by external factors.

Some people believe that others are responsible for causing their visions to fail. Maybe their parents couldn't afford to send them to college, and now they are bitter and resentful because they didn't pursue the careers they wanted to. Life will present us with challenges, but this fact doesn't have to derail our visions. If you want something badly enough, you will be patient in acquiring it, even if the timetable isn't what you would have wanted. You are not a victim. You are a child of the King, and He has given you a vision for your life that you can fulfill through Him.

Prayer: Father God, everything precious in life comes with a cost.
One cost of fulfilling my vision is diligence.
Help me to be strong and diligent in You.
In Jesus' name, amen.

Thought: Life will present us with challenges, but they
don't have to derail our visions.

Reading: **Psalm 123–125; 1 Corinthians 10:1–18**

Your Purpose Is Greater Than Your Past

Some people think their past experiences or failures—educational, social, or spiritual—preclude them from having a vision for their lives. Please realize this: God is not against you. He is for you. Do you believe that in your heart? God still has a definite plan for your life in spite of your background or your mistakes. We often imagine that our pasts loom larger than our futures. Sometimes we think that what we have done is so bad that it is greater than Jesus' sacrifice for us on the cross. Yet nothing is so bad that it can compete with the forgiveness of Jesus. If you have had a baby out of wedlock, if you have been on drugs, if you have been to prison, if you have betrayed someone, God still loves you and wants to redeem you. He wants to give you back your purpose.

The Bible says, *"Every good and perfect gift is from above, coming down from the Father of the heavenly lights, who does not change like shifting shadows"* (James 1:17). This is a very important statement about God. It says that God gives gifts, and that when He gives a gift, He doesn't change His mind regarding it. Don't ever believe that your failures are greater than what God gave you birth to do. God is a restorer, a reclaimer. Let me urge you not to allow circumstances to destroy your passion for living. The winds of adversity can be very strong, but your God-given vision will be your anchor in life.

Prayer: Father, I will not consider the things that are in my past to be obstacles to my future. I know that You still lead me and will enable me to fulfill my vision by the power of Your Holy Spirit. In Jesus' name, amen.

Thought: Whatever God has invested in you, He wants to see you use.

Reading: **Psalm 126–128; 1 Corinthians 10:19–33**

Let Your Life Be Fueled by Vision

Life was designed to be inspired by purpose and fueled by vision. This means that you don't have to live a defensive life that is made up of crisis management. Instead, you can pursue an offensive life that steadily follows its vision and initiates its own goals and actions. My desire is to help you clarify your vision, formulate a plan for accomplishing it, and bring it to a fulfilling and successful completion.

Ask yourself the following questions concerning vision: What do you think is your greatest obstacle to pursuing and completing your vision? What steps can you take to begin overcoming that obstacle? For example, have you distinguished between your life's mission and its vision? Will you trust that your life is under God's purposes and that you are not a victim of "bad luck"? Will you stop blaming others for the way your life has turned out and start thanking God that He will enable you to complete His vision for your life? Take some time to answer these questions in the next few days. Ask the Lord to help you search your heart for the answers.

Let's pray together:

Prayer: Heavenly Father, You can enable us to overcome any obstacles to knowing and fulfilling our visions. Please search our hearts. You have placed a vision within each of us. Help us to see our visions clearly. Give us the strength from Your Word and Your Holy Spirit to pursue those visions and to see them fulfilled. I desire to see Your purposes accomplished. In the precious name of the Lord Jesus Christ, amen.

Thought: You can pursue a life that steadily follows its vision and initiates its own goals and actions.

Reading: **Psalm 129–131; 1 Corinthians 11:1–16**

Principles for Understanding Vision

Today, reflect on these principles for understanding vision:

1. Two major obstacles to fulfilling vision are not understanding the nature of vision and not recognizing the cost of vision.

2. The essential nature of vision is that it is specific.

3. Mission is a general statement of purpose while vision is a very precise statement with a specific emphasis and definable boundaries.

4. The measure of the success of your vision is God's assignment to you, not what others are doing.

5. Dreaming is only the beginning of vision. Instead of wishing things would get better, we must take concrete steps to change our lives.

6. Indecisiveness is a vision-killer and drains the joy out of life.

7. If you set a destination for your life while you continue to pray about your vision, God will guide you where you need to go.

8. You were not born or created to do everything. You were meant to meet certain needs, not every need.

9. When you have several gifts and talents, focus on one or two of them and stir them up. Don't allow multiple gifts to distract you from taking specific steps toward fulfilling your vision.

10. You are not defined by your past or confined by external factors.

11. God has a definite plan and purpose for your life in spite of what your background is or what mistakes you have made.

12. When God gives a gift to someone, He doesn't change His mind about it. Whatever God has invested in you, He wants to see you use.

Reading: **Psalm 132–134; 1 Corinthians 11:17–34**

Follow His Directions

J eremiah 29:11 tells us, "'I know the plans I have for you,' declares the LORD, 'plans to prosper you and not to harm you, plans to give you hope and a future.'" God has plans for us, and He wants those plans to be fulfilled. Yet for this to happen, we must follow His direction.

When Joshua took over leadership of the Israelites, God said to him, in effect, "Though Moses is now dead, you have a big vision; it's your time now to fulfill your purpose." (See Joshua 1:1-6.) The Lord's advice to Joshua was to obey His Word:

> Be careful to obey all the law my servant Moses gave you; do not turn from it to the right or to the left, that you may be successful wherever you go. Do not let this Book of the Law depart from your mouth; meditate on it day and night, so that you may be careful to do everything written in it. Then you will be prosperous and successful ["have good success" NKJV]. (vv. 7-8)

In other words, God was saying, "You will be successful if you learn and follow My precepts and principles." God guaranteed Joshua success if he would obey the commands that Moses himself had had to obey. Note that God didn't tell Joshua to literally imitate Moses' *life*, but to follow Moses' *principles*, the ones Moses had used in his own work. Likewise, you can never—nor should you ever—imitate another person's life. Follow God's principles in His Word and You will be an imitator of Your heavenly Father while carrying out the vision He has given you. (See Ephesians 5:1.)

Prayer: Father, teach me to follow Your precepts and principles. Help me to be attentive to everything You tell me in Your Word. I believe that success will follow me. In Jesus' name, amen.

Thought: God has plans for us, but they can be fulfilled only as we follow His direction.

Reading: **Psalm 135–136; 1 Corinthians 12**

Principles for Fulfilling Personal Vision

God has never created a failure. He designed you, sculpted you, and gave you birth to be a success. If you have failed, it is only because you are a success who went off track. Remember that you don't have to stay on the sidelines. Redemption restores to you the ability to accomplish your vision.

As I have studied God's Word and the nature of vision, I have developed "Twelve Principles for Fulfilling Personal Vision." These principles will help you to find your specific vision and stay on course. The principles aren't hidden or exclusive to only a few. They may be clearly discerned from the Scriptures and the lives of accomplished visionaries, and they are historically proven. Jesus Himself had to use each one of these principles to be successful in His work of redemption.

Few people seem to be following the principles that lead to success. Either they don't know them, or they have never proven them by putting them into practice. A successful person is someone who understands, submits to, and adheres to the principles that will carry him to success. The twelve principles that follow have been used by people of vision and are designed to protect, preserve, and guarantee the fulfillment of your dream. We will explore these important truths for the rest of the year. If you can capture these principles, you will move beyond survival mode; you will be an overcomer and see your vision come to pass.

Prayer: Father, thank You for giving us principles to live by in Your Word. Open my heart to understand these principles for the protection and fulfillment of my dream. In Jesus' name, amen.

Thought: If you put these principles into practice, you can see your vision come to pass.

Reading: **Psalm 137–139; 1 Corinthians 13**

The First Principle:
Have a Clear, Guiding Purpose

The first principle in our Twelve Principles for Fulfilling Personal Vision is that *you must have a clear guiding purpose for your life*. Every effective leader or group of people in history has had one thing in common: They were directed by a clear vision. Remember that Moses, Joshua, David, and Nehemiah each had visions that drove them and motivated their actions.

I cannot stress enough the need for a guiding vision in life because it is perhaps the single most important key to fulfilling your dream. You personally, as an individual, must have your own guiding life vision. This vision must be *absolutely clear* to you because, otherwise, you will have nothing to aim at, and you will achieve nothing.

As I wrote earlier, when you know and understand what you were born to accomplish, that is purpose. When you can see it in your mind by faith and begin to imagine it, that is vision. You cannot contribute to God's greater purpose if you don't know your personal vision. If you have no sense of focus, you will just drift along. I like what Jesus said in Luke 2:49: *"I must be about my Father's business"* (KJV). There were many other businesses Jesus could have been about, but He identified a specific life work that was His own and that motivated everything He did. Having a clear guiding purpose will enable you to stay on track when you are tempted to be distracted by lesser or nonessential things.

Prayer: Father, please help me to define a clear guiding purpose for my life, according to Your will for me. In Jesus' name, amen.

Thought: Without a clear guiding purpose, you will achieve nothing.

Reading: **Psalm 140–142; 1 Corinthians 14:1–20**

The Why of Existence

One of my undergraduate degrees is in education, and I had to take a course in biology for a full year as part of my degree requirements. I really enjoyed that course because it was extremely detailed; we studied the neurological and circulatory systems of the human body. At the end of the class, a question burst into my mind: "Now that you know *what* the human body is, do you know *why* it is?" Education can give us knowledge, but it can't always give us reasons. *It is more important to know why you were born than to know the fact that you were born.* If you don't know your reason for existence, you will begin to experiment with your life, and that is dangerous.

Let me ask you some difficult but necessary questions: Have you changed jobs several times in the last few years? Do you keep changing your major in college? Do you do one thing for a time and then go on to something else because you are bored or dissatisfied? If so, you lack vision. You were not created to be bored and dissatisfied. I want to squeeze everything I can out of each day because I have a vision that keeps me passionate. Proverbs 6:10–11 says, "*A little sleep, a little slumber, a little folding of the hands to rest—and poverty will come on you like a bandit and scarcity like an armed man.*" You must choose where you want to go in life and then be decisive and faithful in carrying it out.

Prayer: Father God, You have created me to love and serve You.
Please direct me in vision so that I will know the reason
for my existence and be faithful in fulfilling it.
In Jesus' name, amen.

Thought: Having purpose and vision enables you to answer
the question, "Why was I born?"

Reading: **Psalm 143–145; 1 Corinthians 14:21–40**

A Job versus a Purpose

There is an excellent illustration in the Bible that shows the difference between simply having a job and having a clear guiding purpose. It is found in the life of Nehemiah. Nehemiah was in a top position in the court of the Persian king Artaxerxes; he was cupbearer, and he was a highly regarded, trusted, and influential advisor to the king. As prestigious as Nehemiah's occupation was, it was simply a job for him because his mind was occupied with something else.

Nehemiah was a descendant of one of the large number of Jews who had been carried into captivity by the Babylonians. At the time of the Babylonian captivity, the city of Jerusalem had undergone terrible destruction. Yet, when the Babylonians were defeated by the Persians seventy years later, fifty thousand Jews had returned to Judea and had rebuilt the temple. Then, an effort to rebuild the walls of Jerusalem was thwarted by opposition from neighboring peoples who had convinced King Artaxerxes to issue a decree to stop the work.

When Nehemiah heard that *"the wall of Jerusalem is broken down, and its gates have been burned with fire"* (Nehemiah 1:3), the news filled him with grief. He *"sat down and wept. For some days [he] mourned and fasted and prayed before the God of heaven"* (Nehemiah 1:4). Nehemiah's job might have been prestigious, but his life was clearly shifting in another direction. Is God shifting your direction to line up with His purposes?

Prayer: Father, thank You for the job that I have right now.
Yet please reveal to me a purpose beyond my job,
a vision that will bring meaning to my life.
In Jesus' name, amen.

Thought: There is a difference between simply having a job
and having a clear guiding purpose.

Reading: **Psalm 146–147; 1 Corinthians 15:1–28**

What You Were Born to Do

I like to think of Nehemiah's cupbearer job as his preliminary occupation, or his "pre-occupation," because he was born to fulfill another, much more important role. Your true work is what you were born to do. Your job is what you do only until you are ready to fulfill your vision. God had placed in Nehemiah's heart a vision of rebuilding the wall: *"I had not [yet] told anyone what my God had put in my heart to do for Jerusalem"* (Nehemiah 2:12).

Nehemiah 2:1 reads, *"In the month of Nisan in the twentieth year of King Artaxerxes, when wine was brought for him, I took the wine and gave it to the king. I had not been sad in his presence before."* It appears that Nehemiah was doing fine on his job until he heard about the wall. Then he had the idea to rebuild it. His desire to accomplish his life's work began to interfere with his job. The king said to him, *"Why does your face look so sad when you are not ill? This can be nothing but sadness of heart"* (v. 2).

When God gives you a vision and confirms it, nothing can stop it. If He tells you to build, start, invest, create, or manufacture something, then it will bother you deep inside; you will be dissatisfied until you do it. Is your true work—your purpose—making it uncomfortable for you to stay in your present job? That was Nehemiah's situation. Nehemiah saw the wall completed in his mind's eye before he started to work on it, and that vision drove his passion.

Prayer: Father, I was born to love and serve You.
Help me to serve You according to my true purpose.
In Jesus' name, amen.

Thought: Your true work is what you were born to do.

Reading: **Psalm 148–150; 1 Corinthians 15:29–58**

What Do You Want?

One of the most significant questions you can ask a person is "What do you want?" When King Artaxerxes saw Nehemiah's sadness, that is exactly what he asked him. (See Nehemiah 2:4.) What is equally significant is that Nehemiah was able to answer the king specifically. He said, "Let [the king] *send me to the city in Judah where my fathers are buried so that I can rebuild it*" (v. 5). Nehemiah knew his clear guiding vision, and his plan was so specific that he was able to give the king a time frame for completing it. (See verse 6.)

You need to seriously ask yourself the same question: What do I want?

Do you know what you really want out of life? Some people want to indulge in self-serving activities. Others think life begins at retirement, and they miss out on practically their entire lives. Some people just want to own a nice house and car. Fine. Then what? There has to be something more to life than the things we accumulate. In Luke 12:15, Jesus said, "*A man's life does not consist in the abundance of his possessions.*"

In order to find your vision, you must be in touch with the values and priorities of the kingdom of God. Your vision should be something that lives on after you're gone, something that has greater lasting power than possessions. People's lives should be changed by your vision. What do you want? The King of Kings is asking you this question today, and you must be able to give Him an answer.

Prayer: My King and Father, Your Word says that
if we call to You, You will hear us. Please help me
to answer the question, "What do I really want?"
Confirm the vision you have placed in
my heart and give me clear direction.
In Jesus' precious name, amen.

Thought: You need to seriously ask yourself, *What do I want?*

Reading: **Proverbs 1–2; 1 Corinthians 16**

Vision Is Future-Focused

Your vision is a clear conception of something that is not yet reality, but which can exist. It is a strong image of a preferable future. This means that the present is not enough; something else is needed. Vision is always pushing the envelope. It demands change by its very nature.

This is a very important point. Many people don't realize that vision is active even when times are good and things are in a positive state. Why will God activate a vision when things are going well? To stir up your life so that you will move forward and progress rather than becoming complacent. A vision will always take you from good to better and from better to best.

Vision is always future-focused. Sometimes people say, "Let's go back to the good old days." Yet if we do that, we will not progress in what God has planned for us. We need to build on the past, but we cannot return to it. I confess that the temptation to focus on the "good old days" has been one of my challenges in life. Vision does not mean regaining what you had; it means moving forward to gain what you have never had. Vision doesn't try to recapture the good old days; rather, it desires to create days that have not yet existed.

Prayer: Father, thank You for the times in my past,
both good and bad. You have used them to mold me
into the person I am today. Yet I don't want to focus on the past.
Move me forward each day in fulfillment
of the exciting plans You have for me.
In Jesus' name, amen.

Thought: A clear vision gives us a passion that keeps us
continually moving forward in life.

Reading: **Proverbs 3–5; 2 Corinthians 1**

Action Steps to Fulfilling Vision

When you are very close to a visionary, or very close to a vision, you're constantly going to be driven to change. To go to a new place, you have to go to a new location. You also have to think in a new way. That sometimes causes discomfort. Vision can constantly keep you unsettled, but it also keeps you fluid and mobile, ready to take the next step toward your vision. This truth is essential to understand because, when you keep company with God, you have to keep moving. When the Israelites were traveling in the desert, they would put down their stakes and set up their tents, but soon the pillar of cloud would move again, and they would need to follow it.

Have you truly answered the King's question, "What do you want in life?" Write down your answer. What things are distracting you from the real "business" of your life? Take some time to really pray about this important question. It will change your life.

Let's pray together:

Prayer: Heavenly Father, thank You for declaring
in Your Word that You have a plan for our lives
that will bring us a good future and an abiding hope.
You have placed within us a purpose that is exciting
and that goes beyond just working at a job.
Through Your love and Your purposeful design,
You give our lives true meaning.
Please help us to walk in Your purposes,
for Your kingdom's sake.
In the name of Jesus, our wonderful Lord and Savior, amen.

Thought: When you keep company with God,
you have to keep moving forward.

Reading: **Proverbs 6–7; 2 Corinthians 2**

Principles of Vision as Guiding Purpose

Today, reflect on these principles of vision as our guiding purpose and catalyst:

1. You must have a clear guiding purpose for your life.
2. The key to life is not only knowing what you are, but also why you are.
3. Your true work is what you were born to do. Your job is what you are doing just until you are ready to fulfill your vision.
4. When God gives you a vision, it will bother you until you do it.
5. One of the most significant questions we must each answer for ourselves is, "What do you want?" (See Nehemiah 2:4.)
6. Your vision should be something that lives on after you're gone.
7. Your vision is a clear conception of something that is not yet reality, but which can exist. It is a strong image of a preferable future.
8. A vision demands change by its very nature.
9. A vision is active even when times are good and things are in a positive state.
10. Vision doesn't try to recapture the good old days; rather, it desires to create days that have not yet existed.
11. When you keep company with God, you have to keep moving.
12. A clear vision gives us a passion that keeps us continually moving forward in life.

Reading: **Proverbs 8–9; 2 Corinthians 3**

The Second Principle: Understand Your Potential

I n our Twelve Principles for Fulfilling Personal Vision, the second principle is that you will never be successful in your vision until you truly understand your potential. Recall that your potential is determined by the assignment God has given you to do. Whatever you were born to do, you are equipped to do. Moreover, resources will become available to you as you need them.

What this means is that God gives ability to fulfill responsibility. God will never call you to an assignment without giving you the provision for accomplishing it. If you understand this principle, no one can stop you from fulfilling your vision.

We must come into an awareness of our potential. In the biblical story of Gideon, we first see him threshing wheat at the bottom of the winepress, hidden from the Midianites, the enemies of Israel. The angel of the Lord comes to him and says, *"The LORD is with you, mighty warrior"* (Judges 6:12). Gideon's answer is, in effect, "How can you say that? The Midianites are destroying Israel, and I am the youngest man in the smallest clan. What can I do?" (See verses 13–15.) Yet the angel of the Lord knows Gideon's potential because of the purpose the Lord has for him. Through Gideon, three hundred men of Israel defeat thousands of their enemies, and God receives the glory.

What hidden seeds of potential has the Lord placed in you, ready to be revealed through your purpose and vision?

Prayer: Father, so often my own abilities come up short.
Help me to look to You and understand that the ability
to fulfill my vision comes from You. I can truly do everything
You set before me through Christ who strengthens me.
In Jesus' name, amen.

Thought: Whatever you were born to do,
you are equipped to do.

Reading: **Proverbs 10–12; 2 Corinthians 4**

The Power at Work within Us

Now to him who is able to do immeasurably ["exceeding abundantly"*
KJV] more than all we ask or imagine, according to his power that is at
work within us.* (Ephesians 3:20)

Many of us have heard this verse so many times that we think we
know it. Yet I don't believe we really understand what it is saying:
"According to his power [or potential] *that is at work"*—where? It doesn't say
His power is at work in heaven. It says it is at work in us! God put His
vision and His Spirit within us, and that is more than enough potential
for our needs.

What are the implications of this truth? It means that what you are
able to accomplish has nothing to do with who your parents were. It has
nothing to do with your past or with physical factors such as your race or
appearance. Instead, it has to do with *"his power"* working within you.

This Scripture changed my life at a point when I wasn't manifesting much of my purpose. I was brought up with the religious idea that
you receive only what you ask for. Consequently, I didn't receive much.
Then I came to understand that God never promised to give me merely
what I asked for. Instead, He said something truly extraordinary: He will
do *"immeasurably"* or *"exceeding abundantly"* beyond all that I can ask for,
think about, or imagine. Once I grasped this truth, it began to transform
my perspective. It enabled me to progress from the knowledge of my
purpose to the faith that accompanies vision.

Prayer: Father, what an amazing promise You have given us!
You will do more than we can ask or imagine
through the power of the Holy Spirit within us.
Thank You, Father, in Jesus' name.

Thought: God's power is actually working within you for the
fulfillment of your dream.

Reading: **Proverbs 13–15; 2 Corinthians 5**

Take a Tour of Your Vision

We can't begin to imagine all the things God wants to do for us. Yet God gave us the gift of imagination to keep us from focusing only on our present conditions. He wants us to take a "tour" of our visions on a regular basis. What do you imagine doing? Visit everything. See all the details. Then pray, "Let's go there, God!"

The Lord told Jeremiah, *"Before I formed you in the womb I knew you, before you were born I set you apart; I appointed you as a prophet to the nations"* (Jeremiah 1:5). Notice that God used the past tense. He had already set apart and appointed Jeremiah as a prophet. Yet at first, Jeremiah responded, *"I do not know how to speak"* (v. 6). God's reaction was, in effect, "Do not say that! If I built you to be a prophet, don't tell Me you can't talk!" (See verses 6–7.) Once God showed Jeremiah why he was born, Jeremiah discovered what he could do. In other words, when Jeremiah understood his vision, he began to realize his ability. At first he didn't think he could speak publicly for God. Whatever God calls for, however, He provides for. Whatever He requires, He enables us to do. In this case, God gave Jeremiah the ability to speak for Him: *"Then the LORD reached out his hand and touched my mouth and said to me, 'Now I have put my words in your mouth'"* (Jeremiah 1:9).

Whatever God is causing you to dream is a revelation of your ability. Responsibility is really "respond-ability," or the ability to respond to the requirements of your vision.

Prayer: Father, thank You for providing me with the ability
each day to accomplish the works You have given me.
I know I can trust You to supply all that I need.
In Jesus' name, amen.

Thought: Whatever God calls for, He provides for.

Reading: **Proverbs 16–18; 2 Corinthians 6**

Perfect for Your Purpose

Everything about you is determined by your purpose. God built you, designed you, and gave you the right makeup for it. Your heritage and ethnic mix, the color of your skin, your language, your height, and all your other physical features are made for the fulfillment of your vision. You were built for what you're supposed to do. You are perfect for your purpose.

Dreams are given to draw out what's already inside us and to activate God's power in enabling us to achieve our visions. This is why God may give us dreams that are bigger than our educations. For instance, I shouldn't be able to do what I am currently doing, based on my background and the expectations of the society I grew up in. Likewise, you may not have the background to do what you are going to do. People may not believe you can do it, yet what does it matter what they think? Just keep doing what God tells you to do.

God never gives us dreams to frustrate us. He gives us dreams to deliver us from mediocrity and to reveal our true selves to the world. The more I study the Word of God, the more I realize that God appoints, anoints, and distinguishes people to fulfill His will. He doesn't like them to get lost in mediocrity. Therefore, He said, in effect, "Abraham, come out. Moses, come out. David, come out. Gideon, come out. Nehemiah, come out. You are lost among the average."

Prayer: Father, my ability isn't limited to the shortcomings I think I have. I will trust that as You appointed me to work toward my vision, You will anoint me for it well.
May my work bring You glory!
In Jesus' name, amen.

Thought: God appoints, anoints, and distinguishes people to fulfill His will.

Reading: **Proverbs 19–21; 2 Corinthians 7**

Say Yes to Your Dream

The ability to accomplish your vision is manifested when you say yes to your dream and obey God. Nehemiah's job of cupbearer, in itself, did not give him the ability to rebuild the wall of Jerusalem. If he had looked only at the resources he had at that time, he never would have fulfilled his vision. Yet God had placed him in his position for a reason, and Nehemiah trusted God to provide what was needed. You don't know how your present job may contain hidden potential for your true life's work. Nehemiah had favor as a trusted servant of the monarch, and God gave him even more favor with the king so that he could fulfill his vision. God reveals our potential as we act on our dreams.

Note that after Nehemiah had stepped out in faith and articulated his vision in answer to the king's question, *"What is it you want?"* (Nehemiah 2:4), his ability and resources came into place. The king gave Nehemiah letters granting him safe passage to Jerusalem and giving him access to timber from the king's forest for the rebuilding of the wall. The king basically paid for the project. Moreover, the king appointed Nehemiah as governor in the land of Judah so that he had the authority to carry out the reconstruction of the wall. (See Nehemiah 2:7–10; 5:14.)

Have you said yes to your dream? Have you begun to act on it? When you do, the ability and resources to accomplish your vision will begin to be manifested.

Prayer: Father, help me to overcome any negative feelings I may have about my abilities and to rely on You to provide all I need as I step out in faith and obedience.
In Jesus' name, amen.

Thought: The ability to accomplish your vision is manifested when you say yes to your dream and obey God.

Reading: **Proverbs 22–24; 2 Corinthians 8**

Action Steps to Fulfilling Vision

Let's review the second principle for fulfilling personal vision: understanding our potential. Potential is hidden capacity, untapped power, unreleased energy. It is all you could be but haven't yet become. Potential is who you really are, in accordance with your vision, even if you don't yet know your true self. God has created you to do something wonderful, and He has given you the ability and resources you need to do it.

Our lives are like seeds. We were born with the potential for the fulfillment of our destinies that have already been established within us. When God gives a vision to someone, He's simply calling forth what He put into that person. This is why you can always determine what you can do by the dream that is within you. Plant the seed of your vision by beginning to act on it and then nurture it by faith. Your vision will develop until it is fully grown and bears much fruit in the world.

How can you begin to plant the seed of your vision today?

Let's pray together:

Prayer: Heavenly Father, You have placed potential in our lives, just as You did in the great men and women of the Bible. When You called Abraham, Moses, Gideon, Esther, Paul, and Peter to serve You, You always gave them the strength, the power, and the abilities to complete their visions. You acted exceedingly beyond their imaginations. Please enable us to walk in God-given power each day of our lives. Help us to take our ideas from dream to full-fledged reality. In Jesus' name we pray, amen.

Reading: **Proverbs 25–26; 2 Corinthians 9**

Principles of Vision as Potential and Ability

Today, reflect on these principles of vision as the measure of your potential and ability:

1. You will never be successful in your vision until you truly understand your potential.

2. Your potential is determined by the assignment God gave you to do. Whatever you were born to do, you are equipped to do.

3. God gives ability to fulfill responsibility. When you discover your dream, you will also discover your ability.

4. Power or potential is at work in us. God put His vision and His Spirit within us, and that is more than enough potential for our needs.

5. God will do "immeasurably" or "exceeding abundantly" beyond all that we can ask for, think about, or imagine. (See Ephesians 3:20 NIV, KJV.)

6. God gave us the gift of imagination to keep us from focusing only on our present conditions.

7. Whatever God calls for, He provides for. Whatever He requires, He enables us to do.

8. Your ability isn't dependent on what you perceive as your limitations. You are perfect for your purpose.

9. Dreams are given to us to draw out what's already inside us and to activate God's power in enabling us to achieve our visions.

10. God appoints, anoints, and distinguishes people to fulfill His will. God gives us dreams to deliver us from mediocrity and to reveal our true selves to the world.

11. The ability to accomplish your vision is manifested when you say yes to your dream and obey God.

Reading: **Proverbs 27–29; 2 Corinthians 10**

The Third Principle:
Develop a Clear Plan

The third principle in our Twelve Principles of Vision is that you must have a clear plan. There is no future without planning. I've known people who tried to be successful over and over again without a plan. It never works.

When I was a teenager and had been a Christian for only about two years, I kept wondering why God didn't seem to be guiding me in my life. Perhaps you are wondering the same thing about your own life. I used to want God to show me His will, so I would stay up all night with one eye open, just waiting. I used to pray, "Oh, Lord, let the angels show up." Then I would look and there would be nothing but mosquitoes. Whenever they sang a certain song in church, I used to sing it the loudest: "Lead me, guide me, along the way!" One day, as I was singing this song, I felt as if the Lord was saying to me, "Lead you along what way?" I realized then that if you don't have a plan, God doesn't have anything specific to direct you in.

Proverbs 16:1 says, *"To man belong the plans of the heart, but from the LORD comes the reply of the tongue."* That's a very powerful statement. God is saying, in effect, "I gave you the vision. Now you put the plan on paper, and I will work out the details." Proverbs 16:9 says, *"In his heart a man plans his course, but the LORD determines his steps."* If you don't have a plan, how can He direct you?

Prayer: Father, You have given me a clear purpose;
now, please help me to write a clear plan.
Direct me as I articulate the details of my vision.
In Jesus' name, amen.

Thought: For your vision to be successful,
you must have a clear plan.

Reading: **Proverbs 30–31; 2 Corinthians 11:1–15**

Ideas Are Seeds of Destiny

Ideas are seeds of destiny planted by God in the minds of humankind. When ideas are cultivated, they become imagination. Imagination, if it is watered and developed, becomes a plan. Finally, if a plan is followed, it becomes a reality. However, when a person receives an idea from God, it must be cultivated soon or the idea often goes away. If that person doesn't ever work on the idea, God will give it to someone else. Inevitably, if the second person takes the idea, makes a plan, and starts to work on it, the first person will become jealous because he had the idea first! Yet it's not just having ideas that is important. Ideas need plans if they are going to become reality.

Young people often think their dreams will just happen. Yet none of us can move toward our dreams without a plan. Jesus said that a wise person doesn't start to build something unless he first works out the details:

Suppose one of you wants to build a tower. Will he not first sit down and estimate the cost to see if he has enough money to complete it? For if he lays the foundation and is not able to finish it, everyone who sees it will ridicule him, saying, "This fellow began to build and was not able to finish." (Luke 14:28–30)

God Himself had a plan when He created humanity. Ephesians 1:11 says, *"In him we were also chosen, having been predestined according to the plan of him who works out everything in conformity with the purpose of his will."*

Do you have a plan for your vision?

Prayer: Father, You had a plan when You created me.
Thank You for choosing me in You.
Please guide me as I develop a plan for my vision.
In Jesus' name, amen.

Thought: Ideas are seeds of destiny planted by God
in the minds of humankind.

Reading: **Ecclesiastes 1–3; 2 Corinthians 11:16–33**

Don't Float through Life

S omeone once said to me, "You always seem to be going somewhere. Why don't you just relax?" I told him, "I've discovered something about life. Where I live in the Bahamas, when you just sit on a boat in the ocean and relax, the current takes you wherever it's going, even if you don't want to go there. Life is the same way." Too many people float through their lives and still expect to make it to their goals.

A ship has a compass so that the navigator can know what direction he is going in, and it has a rudder so that the pilot can steer it. However, a ship is given a specific course—a plan—by the captain, so that it can arrive at its destination. All three are necessary—the compass, the rudder, and the plan. Just because a ship has a rudder doesn't necessarily mean it is going anywhere specific. It needs to be steered according to the coordinates of the plan.

Are you developing a plan for your vision? Suppose you wish you could start a business, but you've never thought about how you'd go about it. What if someone came to you and said, "I want to invest some money, and I like you. Why don't you develop something with it?" You would probably answer something like, "I'd like to, but right now I'm just a clerk...." However, if you had developed a specific plan, if you were reading the appropriate books and preparing yourself, if you had everything down on paper, you'd be prepared for this opportunity. You could say, "You have the money? Here's the plan. I'm ready to go!"

Prayer: Father, please direct me in developing a plan for my vision so I can sail on a specific course to a clear destination. In Jesus' name, amen.

Thought: Too many people float through their lives and still expect to make it to their goals.

Reading: **Ecclesiastes 4–6; 2 Corinthians 12**

A Blueprint of Your Vision

When a contractor is building a structure, he uses a blueprint. That is his plan for his vision, which is the finished building. The contractor always keeps a copy of his blueprint on site with him. Why? He needs to keep checking it to see if the building is being constructed correctly. If you don't have a plan for your life, you have nothing to refer to when you want to make sure you are on track. How do you begin developing a blueprint of your vision?

Again, you must first secure for yourself the answer to the question "Who am I?" Until you do, it will be difficult to write a plan for your life because such a plan is directly tied to knowing who you are. You will never become really successful in your life if you don't have a clear idea of your own identity in God. Many of us have become what other people want us to be. We have not yet discovered our unique, irreplaceable identity. Yet it is knowing your true identity that gives you the courage to write your life plan.

Next, you must answer the question "Where am I going?" Once you learn God's purpose, you can start planning effectively because you will be able to plan with focus.

Prayer: Father, please continue to reveal to me
my unique, irreplaceable identity so I have
a clear idea of who You have made me and can
write my life plan with courage and confidence.
Thank you, Lord, in Jesus' name, amen.

Thought: You will never become really
successful in your life if you don't have
a clear idea of your own identity in God.

Reading: **Ecclesiastes 7–9; 2 Corinthians 13**

The Importance of Planning

The importance of planning for your vision is evident in Scripture. Note the way Nehemiah planned for his vision of rebuilding the wall of Jerusalem:

> I went to Jerusalem, and after staying there three days I set out during the night with a few men. I had not told anyone what my God had put in my heart to do for Jerusalem. There were no mounts with me except the one I was riding on. By night I went out through the Valley Gate toward the Jackal Well and the Dung Gate, examining the walls of Jerusalem, which had been broken down, and its gates, which had been destroyed by fire....I went up the valley by night, examining the wall. Finally, I turned back and reentered through the Valley Gate. The officials did not know where I had gone or what I was doing, because as yet I had said nothing to the Jews or the priests or nobles or officials or any others who would be doing the work.
>
> (Nehemiah 2:11–13, 15–16)

Nehemiah did not tell everyone about the vision right away because not everyone could have handled it at that point. Sometimes you have to keep your plan secret for a time. Some people will try to talk you out of it, saying, "You can't do that!" If you listen to them, in no time you will throw your plan away and end up an average person. Not everybody will understand what you're dreaming, but put your dream on paper anyway. Why? Your dream is worth writing down. If God gave it to you, it deserves to be done.

Prayer: Father, Nehemiah was wise and did not take action until he first prayed and then developed a plan. Remind me of the need to seek You and to plan before I take action.
In Jesus' name I pray, amen.

Thought: Your dream is worth writing down.

Reading: **Ecclesiastes 10–12; Galatians 1**

 272   DAILY POWER & PRAYER DEVOTIONAL

Acknowledge God's Work

Remember the principle of potential? It's not what you need that is important. Starting with what you have makes your vision successful because God will take care of the rest. I know you have some great ideas. Start right where you are and go where you need to go by making a plan and beginning to implement it.

After Nehemiah had fully made his plan, he was ready to talk to others about it. He talked to those who would be directly involved in carrying it out. *"Then I said to [the Jews, priests, nobles, officials, and others], 'You see the trouble we are in: Jerusalem lies in ruins, and its gates have been burned with fire. Come, let us rebuild the wall of Jerusalem, and we will no longer be in disgrace'"* (Nehemiah 2:17). Nehemiah expressed to them his clear vision. Here was one man, with just a few people, who was planning to do a project that would take thousands of people to accomplish. He was starting out with a seeming impossibility, but he said, "Let's start."

Next, we read, *"I also told them about the gracious hand of my God upon me and what the king had said to me"* (v. 18). Nehemiah gave credit to God for the vision, and in the process built up the faith of those who would work on the project. The statement also shows that Nehemiah was so sure that his vision was from God and that the Lord was with him that he was able to say, in effect, "God told me to do this." I hope you feel the same way about your dream.

Prayer: Father, I give You the credit for
the vision and the plans You have given me.
Help me to always acknowledge You as my source.
In Jesus' name, amen.

Thought: Starting with what you have makes your vision
successful because God will take care of the rest.

Reading: **Song of Songs 1–3; Galatians 2**

Fulfilling Your Destiny

A vision becomes a plan when it is captured, fleshed out, and written down. Anyone who works with me will tell you that I'm a stickler for planning. I have plans for what I'm going to do next week, next month, next year, and five years from now. In fact, the vision for Bahamas Faith Ministries is on paper for the next sixty or seventy years!

When you put your plan on paper, you will find that you have plenty of material for your prayers. If your prayer time is short, maybe it's because you have nothing specific to pray about. If you develop a plan, however, you will never have enough time for prayer.

Your plan will also enable you to fulfill your destiny. In Deuteronomy 30:19, God told the people, *"I have set before you life and death, blessings and curses. Now choose life."* In other words, He was saying, "Stop procrastinating and hoping you will eventually get somewhere in life. Decide whether you're going to get a curse or a blessing." Jesus said in Revelation 3:15–16, *"I know your deeds, that you are neither cold nor hot. I wish you were either one or the other! So, because you are lukewarm—neither hot nor cold—I am about to spit you out of my mouth."*

Are you going to make a plan, or are you going to procrastinate on your dream and drift along, ending up wherever the lukewarm tide takes you? You were not designed to drift. You were designed for destiny. Make a plan and fulfill it!

Prayer: Father, as I place my plan on paper,
confirm Your will in it.
I want to know with certainty that my
plans and desires come from You.
In Jesus' name, amen.

Thought: You were not designed to drift.
You were designed for destiny.

Reading: **Song of Songs 4–5; Galatians 3**

Who Runs Your Life?

If you don't have any goals, other people will run your life. The wise king of Israel, Solomon, declared, *"Whoever has no rule over his own spirit is like a city broken down, without walls"* (Proverbs 25:28 NKJV). If nothing controls and orders your life, then you are fair game for other people to control you, and you won't accomplish your purpose. Remember that the more successful you become, the more people will compete for your time, so you have to guard your plans and goals even more carefully.

Let's define what a goal is. A goal is an established point for achievement that leads to a greater accomplishment. A goal is a point of measure for progress toward an ultimate purpose.

Goals give us a structure for accomplishing our plans one step at a time. They give us a starting place and an ending place, and they help us to focus. There are very clear benefits to having goals: Goals separate achievers from dreamers. Goal setting is the art of discipline. Goals give specifics to the plan. Goals create targets for our energy. Goals protect us from procrastination. If you want to fulfill your vision, make goals for your life. One of the secrets to success in vision is living a very focused life in line with your purpose.

Prayer: Father, I realize that goals are important steps to reaching my vision. Please help me to be more disciplined in setting up a personal plan for my life. In Jesus' name, amen.

Thought: If you don't have any goals, other people will run your life.

Reading: **Song of Songs 6–8; Galatians 4**

Setting the Right Goals

I f you are pursuing a vision, then you are a leader. All true leaders possess a goal-driven attitude. Leaders distinguish themselves from followers by their passion for preestablished goals. They regulate their activities and measure their progress against prescribed objectives and milestones.

Everyone in the world is a goal setter, in one way or another. Even the man who is failing at life is setting goals that cause him to fail. In fact, many of us plan not to do things that would make us successful. Many times, we don't realize that we are setting goals. Whenever we make plans to go to the grocery store, go to school, do the laundry, or meet friends for a meal, we are in reality setting goals. When we don't achieve what we want to achieve or accomplish what we desire to accomplish, the problem is not goal setting, in itself. Instead, it's that we don't set goals for the things we truly care about, or we set the wrong kind of goals.

A leader needs to understand how to set the right goals. This is a vital attitude to cultivate because your future and your life depend on the goals you set—either consciously or subconsciously. Where you end up in life is a result of the goals that you set or did not set for your life.

Success comes from the discipline of goal setting according to one's purpose. This is why it is vital, as we set goals, to remain in communion with the One who gave us our visions.

Prayer: Father, as I work to fulfill my vision, help me to be a true leader—a goal setter who will not roam aimlessly through life but will set specific objectives according to the purpose You have given me. In Jesus' name, amen.

Thought: Where you end up in life is a result of the goals that you set or did not set for your life.

Reading: **Isaiah 1–2; Galatians 5**

Action Steps to Fulfilling Vision

Do you have a plan for your life? Do you know what you want to do next week, next month, next year, and five years from now? Do you have a plan for the next twenty years of your life? God has given you the ability to do that. He has given you a mind, the gift of imagination, the anointing of the Holy Spirit, and the vision of faith. He has also given you the ability to write so that you can put down what you see in your heart. What are you waiting for? God says He will explain how your vision will be accomplished, yet He can't discuss it with you until you have something concrete to talk about.

Have you truly answered the questions "Who am I?" and "Where am I going"? Start the process of developing a blueprint for your vision by writing down answers to these questions. Think seriously about where you want to be one, five, ten, twenty, thirty years from now. Jot down your ideas and continue to think and pray about them. The Lord will be faithful to hear and answer your prayers. He wants to see His purpose fulfilled in your life.

Let's pray together:

Prayer: Heavenly Father, we have much to consider
as we think about our lives and answer these questions.
Prompt us to search our hearts for the thoughts and dreams
You have placed there. Enable us to write down plans
with specific goals for accomplishing our visions.
We will always submit our plans to You, knowing that
You will make any necessary adjustments along the way.
Help us to take concrete action to carry out our plans.
We trust You to give us the abilities we need
to see our visions become reality.
Thank You, Father, for Your guiding hand.
In Jesus' loving name, amen.

Reading: **Isaiah 3–4; Galatians 6**

Principles of Vision Planning

Today, review the following principles for developing a plan for your vision:

1. To be successful, you must have a clear plan.

2. If you don't have a plan, God doesn't have anything specific to direct you in.

3. *"To man belong the plans of the heart, but from the LORD comes the reply of the tongue"* (Proverbs 16:1). God leaves the planning up to the heart of the person, but He will provide the explanation as to how the vision will be accomplished.

4. When a person receives an idea from God, it must be cultivated soon or the idea often goes away.

5. We need to have a plan in place to be ready when opportunities come.

6. If you don't have a plan for your life, you have nothing to refer to when you want to make sure you are on track.

7. You must secure for yourself the answer to the question "Who am I?" You will never become really successful in your life if you don't have a clear idea of your own identity in God.

8. You must answer the question, "Where am I going?" Once you learn God's purpose, you can start planning effectively because you will be able to plan with focus.

9. A vision becomes a plan when it is captured, fleshed out, and written down.

10. You can't tell your plan to everyone because some people won't be able to handle it right away.

11. Your dream is worth writing down. If God gave it to you, it deserves to be done.

12. Your plan is material for your prayers.

13. Your plan will enable you to fulfill your destiny.

14. If you don't have any goals, other people will run your life.

15. Goal setting must be done in accordance with your purpose.

Reading: **Isaiah 5–6; Ephesians 1**

The Fourth Principle:
Possess the Passion of Vision

The fourth principle in the Twelve Principles of Vision is that you'll never be successful without passion. Passionate people are those who have discovered something more important than life itself. Jesus told His disciples, in essence, "If you are not willing to take up death and follow Me, then you can't be My disciples; you can't go on with Me." (See Luke 14:27.) Giving up false visions and ambition for your genuine vision is the path to true life.

Are you hungry for your vision? How badly do you want what God has placed in your heart? Passion is stamina that says, "I'm going to go after this, no matter what happens. If I have to wait ten years, I'm going to get it." Again, let me say especially to young people that if you want to go all the way to your dream, you can't sit back and expect everything to be easy. You must have the attitude of those who worked on the wall with Nehemiah: "*So we rebuilt the wall till all of it reached half its height, for the people **worked with all their heart**"* (Nehemiah 4:6, emphasis added).

Remember that after Nehemiah first saw in his heart a vision of the rebuilt wall, he returned to his job, but he was no longer satisfied with it. He was depressed until he was working on the vision. The depression came from his passion for change. People who are satisfied with less than God's vision for their lives will never go where they need to be.

Will you be a person who works with all your heart on God's vision?

Prayer: Father, I desire to work on my vision with all
my heart, as working for You, Lord, not for men.
In Jesus' name, amen.

Thought: Passionate people are those who have discovered
something more important than life itself.

Reading: **Isaiah 7–8; Ephesians 2**

Enabled by Passion

One reason I stress the need for a clear guiding purpose is that vision is the prerequisite for passion. The majority of people on earth really have no passion for life because there is no vision in their hearts. In 2 Corinthians, we find a unique passage that shows the passion Paul had for his vision. Some false prophets had challenged Paul's right to be an apostle and had drawn people away from the truth. Paul responded by addressing the Corinthian believers:

> I have worked much harder, been in prison more frequently, been flogged more severely, and been exposed to death again and again. Five times I received from the Jews the forty lashes minus one. Three times I was beaten with rods, once I was stoned, three times I was shipwrecked, I spent a night and a day in the open sea, I have been constantly on the move. I have been in danger from rivers, in danger from bandits, in danger from my own countrymen, in danger from Gentiles; in danger in the city, in danger in the country, in danger at sea; and in danger from false brothers. I have labored and toiled and have often gone without sleep; I have known hunger and thirst and have often gone without food; I have been cold and naked. Besides everything else, I face daily the pressure of my concern for all the churches.
> (2 Corinthians 11:23–28)

Paul was saying, "If the vision I received wasn't real, do you think I'd go through all those hardships?" Paul paid a price for his vision, but his passion enabled him to do it.

Prayer: Father, I want to serve You
with passion—to be so focused on Your vision
for my life that I am willing to pay the price for it.
In Jesus' name, amen.

Thought: You know your vision is from God when
you are still at it once the storm clears.

Reading: **Isaiah 9–10; Ephesians 3**

Faithful to the Vision

I t's easy to get excited about a vision, but it's harder to be faithful to it. Faithfulness to vision is one of the marks of its legitimacy.

The apostle Paul was clearly faithful to his mission. In his early life, he was envied by the best. This gifted young man had great power in the religious community and could have been a prominent Pharisee. He also could have had an easy life. His father was a merchant and a Roman citizen, and Paul was born with that citizenship. Paul had his training under Gamaliel, a leading teacher of the Hebrew people. Paul was a *"Hebrew of Hebrews"* (Philippians 3:5). He was so set up to be successful that he could have made it in any category or profession. He really could have been a first-class success story. However, he said,

> *But whatever was to my profit I now consider loss for the sake of Christ. What is more, I consider everything a loss compared to the surpassing greatness of knowing Christ Jesus my Lord, for whose sake I have lost all things. I consider them rubbish, that I may gain Christ.*
> (Philippians 3:7–8)

In essence, Paul said, "I'm going to jail, I'm going to be whipped, I'm going to go through a myriad of problems because the vision God showed me is more important than anything else in my life."

If someone who had the respect of everyone in the community and could have had any job he wanted was willing to go through all that, he had to have vision.

How faithful are you to your vision?

Prayer: Father, I ask You for clarity and direction in my vision, and also that I might be faithful to it throughout my life. In Jesus' name, amen.

Thought: Faithfulness to vision is one of the marks of its legitimacy.

Reading: **Isaiah 11–13; Ephesians 4**

Vision Is the Source of Passion

L ater in his ministry, Paul was on trial before King Agrippa. As he told the king about the purpose that Jesus Christ had given him on the road to Damascus, he made a statement that is very important concerning people with vision:

> Then I asked, "Who are you, Lord?" "I am Jesus, whom you are persecuting," the Lord replied. "Now get up and stand on your feet. I have appeared to you to appoint you as a servant and as a witness of what you have seen of me and what I will show you. I will rescue you from your own people and from the Gentiles. **I am sending you to them** to open their eyes and turn them from darkness to light, and from the power of Satan to God, so that they may receive forgiveness of sins and a place among those who are sanctified by faith in me."
> (Acts 26:15–18, emphasis added)

Paul summed up his account by saying, "So then, King Agrippa, I was not disobedient to the vision from heaven" (v. 19). He said that God had given him a clear guiding vision, which was to preach the gospel to the Gentiles, and that he was not disobedient to it. He reiterated this vision to Timothy: "For this purpose I was appointed a herald and an apostle...and a teacher of the true faith to the Gentiles" (1 Timothy 2:7).

Paul knew what his purpose in life was, and that is what kept him going through all his struggles. When your vision is from God, nothing can stop you. Vision is the source of passion.

Prayer: Father, please help me to have the conviction of purpose that Paul had, so I can say, "For this purpose I was appointed...."
Let my vision from You be the source of my passion.
In Jesus' name, amen.

Thought: When your vision is from God,
nothing can stop you.

Reading: Isaiah 14–16; Ephesians 5

Resistance to the Vision

A passionate person gets up in the morning and says, "Good morning, Lord! Here I am! Thank you for another day that will take me one step closer to where I want to go." Passion means that no matter how tough things are, what I believe is bigger than what I see. It is an urge that is deeper than any resistance it might encounter. People stop too soon. They don't win because they give up when they fall down the first time. In Romans 1:14, Paul said, "'*I am obligated*' to do the work God told me to do." He just had to do it. It was God's will for his life, and he was *"eager to preach the gospel"* (v. 15). He couldn't wait to do it. A person of passion is always eager to fulfill his vision.

Passion meets every problem. It says things such as these:

- "You may say 'no,' but I know it really means 'wait'."
- "Even though you haven't come around to my idea now, you will later."
- "Even though you stop me now, I'm eventually going to jump this wall."

If you're going to be what you see in your mind, if you're going to pursue what's in your heart, believe me, there will be resistance. You overcome that resistance by having passion for your vision. When you are truly passionate about your dream, you can stand strong when trouble comes. Persistence will keep you moving forward, yet you need passion to feed your persistence.

Prayer: Father, I do not want to stop at the first sign
of resistance in my life. Your Word reminds me
that I am more than a conqueror. May my passion
for Christ and for the vision You have given me
help me to overcome all resistance to my purpose.
In Jesus' name, amen.

Thought: The only way to overcome resistance is
to have passion for your vision.

Reading: Isaiah 17–19; Ephesians 6:1–9

Paying the Price

S ometimes people will join your vision for a while and then say, "This vision isn't real" because they don't know what the vision is costing you.

John Mark was a very excited and zealous young man. He worked with Paul and Barnabas on a missionary journey until a certain point when he decided to leave them and return to Jerusalem. Later, when John Mark wanted to accompany them on another journey, Paul said no because he felt John Mark had deserted them and the work. (See Acts 12:25–13:13; 15:36–40.)

Barnabas ended up going with John Mark on a separate journey, and Paul asked Silas to join him. In Philippi, Paul and Silas were beaten and imprisoned when some men incited a mob against them. Silas was committed to the vision. If Paul went to jail, he would go to jail, too. I want you to know that the prison they were thrown into wasn't an ordinary lockup. This "inner cell" has been described as a deep, dark dungeon. Yet this was the place where Paul and Silas sang hymns! (See Acts 16:16–25.) Passion is willing to pay the price.

Passion also helps you to stay focused on your vision. You can see this principle at work in churches. Wherever there is no vision, there is often fighting, gossiping, murmuring, and backbiting. Vision preoccupies people to the point that they have no time to gossip or get angry at the pastor or complain about his preaching. We must rediscover the passion of working together for a common purpose and vision.

Prayer: Father, in my local church, help each believer to rediscover the passion of working together in commitment for a common vision. Remind us to put off anger, bitterness, and slander, and to put on kindness, compassion, and forgiveness.
In Jesus' name, amen.

Thought: We must rediscover the passion of working together for a common purpose and vision.

Reading: **Isaiah 20–22; Ephesians 6:10–24**

Action Steps to Fulfilling Vision

If you become passionate about your vision, you can defy the odds and persevere to the fulfillment of your goals. Whenever you are tempted to quit too soon or to stay down when life knocks you over, remember the examples of Nehemiah and Paul. Capture your vision and stay with it, and you will be rewarded with seeing that vision become a reality, no matter what might try to come against it.

What evidence of a passion for vision do you see in your life? Do you generally give up the first time you fall down? Ask yourself these questions:

- How hungry am I for my vision?
- How badly do I want what I'm going after?
- In what ways might I have become complacent about my vision?
- What will I do to regain my passion for my dreams?

Let's pray together:

Prayer: Heavenly Father, You are a God who is passionate about Your people. You loved us so much that You gave Your only begotten Son for us. Jesus was so passionate about us that He laid down His life for us. We desire to show that passion in our own lives—to have a fervent desire to see the vision You have given us fulfilled. Please help us daily to stir up passion for our visions. In Jesus' name we pray, amen.

Thought: What evidence of a passion for vision do you see in your life?

Reading: **Isaiah 23–25; Philippians 1**

Principles for a Passion for Vision

Today, reflect on these principles for developing a passion for your vision:

1. You cannot be successful without passion.
2. Passionate people have discovered something more important than life itself.
3. Vision is the prerequisite for passion.
4. Vision will be tested by tribulation.
5. Faithfulness to vision is one of the marks of its legitimacy.
6. Passion means that no matter how tough things are, what you believe is bigger than what you see.
7. A person of passion is always eager to fulfill his vision.
8. Passion keeps you focused on your vision.

Reading: Isaiah 26–27; Philippians 2

The Fifth Principle:
Develop the Faith of Vision

The fifth principle in our Twelve Principles of Vision is that you must develop the faith of vision. Remember, sight is a function of the eyes, while vision is a function of the heart. The greatest gift that God gave humanity is not the gift of sight, but the gift of vision.

You have probably heard of the great author and wonderful entrepreneur Helen Keller, who became blind, deaf, and mute as a result of an illness when she was only eighteen months old. She was a powerful, remarkable woman who impacted her whole generation, and she still influences us today. In her old age, she was interviewed by a news anchor about her life. Communicating his questions to her through Braille, he asked, "Miss Keller, is there anything worse than being blind?" She paused for a moment and, in her unique way of talking, said, "What's worse than being blind is having sight without vision."

What a perceptive woman! This woman, who could not see physically, had more vision and accomplishments than the majority of those in her generation who had sight. The Bible says, "As [a person] *thinks in his heart, so is he*" (Proverbs 23:7 NKJV). We must never let what our eyes see determine what our hearts believe. *"For we walk* ["live" NIV] *by faith, not by sight"* (2 Corinthians 5:7 NKJV). In other words, we are to walk according to what is in our hearts. We are to let what is in our hearts dictate how we see life.

Prayer: Father, thank You for reminding me that I am
to walk by faith and not by sight in every part of my life.
Help me never to forget that when it comes to my vision.
In Jesus' name, amen.

Thought: You must develop the faith of vision.

Reading: Isaiah 28–29; Philippians 3

Vision in the Heart

I am convinced that most people have sight but no vision. Physical sight is the ability to see things as they are. Vision is the capacity to see things as they could be, and that takes faith.

God told Abraham something that could be seen, believed, and achieved only through the eyes of vision: He told him that inside him was a nation. He and Sarah were already elderly, and Sarah had been barren throughout their marriage. However, God said, in effect, "I see a nation in you. Everyone else is looking at your barrenness, but I see a nation of descendants as numerous as the stars in the sky and the sand on the shore." (See Genesis 11:29–30; 12:1–3; 17:1–19.)

When we have vision, we are governed by the faith God has put in our hearts. Hebrews 11:1 says that *"faith is the substance of things hoped for, the evidence of things not seen* [that you cannot see]" (NKJV). Therefore, I would define faith as vision in the heart. Faith is seeing the future in the present. When you have faith, you can see things you hope to have and achieve.

If you are operating by sight, you see the problems and challenges all around you. You see how many bills you have to pay; you see that your company is downsizing; you see things that threaten your security. Sight without vision is dangerous because it has no hope. We must live by vision and see with the eyes of faith.

Prayer: Father, as I face the many challenges of life, may
I learn to live by vision and to see with the eyes of faith.
In Jesus' name, amen.

Thought: Vision is the capacity to see things as they could
be, and that takes faith.

Reading: **Isaiah 30–31; Philippians 4**

Things As They Should Be

R emember that sight is the ability to see things as they are, and vision is the ability to see things as they could be. I like to go a step further and define vision this way: Vision is the ability to see things as they should be. The vision in your heart is greater than your environment.

Our spirits were designed to operate as God operates. In Genesis 1:26, God said, *"Let us make man in our image, in our likeness."* The word *"image"* refers to moral and spiritual character, while the phrase *"in our likeness"* means "to function like." In other words, we were created to live according to the nature of God and to function as He functions in the world. The Bible is very clear that *"without faith it is impossible to please God"* (Hebrews 11:6). If you try to function in any other way than faith, you will malfunction. Fear, for instance, will make your vision short-circuit.

Jesus was filled with faith, and He was the calmest person on earth. He slept soundly in the middle of a storm. When His frightened disciples woke Him up, He asked them, *"Do you still have no faith?"* (Mark 4:40). He was telling them, "If you have faith, you'll be able to sleep during a storm as well." I have been living this way—by faith instead of fear—for over twenty years, and it's been so much fun. I don't worry for very long about anything because I believe that, ultimately, everything is on my side. All things work for my good because I am called according to God's purpose. (See Romans 8:28.)

Prayer: Father, I know that faith comes from hearing
the Word of God. As I study and grow through
Your Word, I can count on my faith increasing.
Please help me to continually walk in faith.
In Jesus' name, amen.

Thought: The vision in your heart is greater than
your environment.

Reading: **Isaiah 32–33; Colossians 1**

Creative Thoughts and Words

How does faith for your vision work? Let's look more closely at how God functions. In Jeremiah 1:12, God declared, *"I am watching to see that my word is fulfilled."* The *New American Standard Bible* says it this way: *"I am watching over My word to perform it."* As this verse—along with many others throughout the Bible—demonstrates, God always brings His words into being.

We talked about this truth earlier. What did God use to create the universe? He used words. All through the account of creation, we read, *"God said"* (Genesis 1:3, 6, 9, 11, 14, 20, 24, 26). God had an idea for the universe, and then He saw or visualized it. Finally, He spoke His idea into existence. The result was that everything God saw in His mind's eye for the earth and the rest of the universe became visible reality in the physical world.

Nothing on earth is more important than a thought. Thoughts are even more important than words because words are produced from thoughts. Yet while thoughts are the most important things on earth, words are the most powerful. This point is crucial to understand because, while thoughts design a future, words create that future. You can think about something for twenty years, but that will not bring it to pass. Creative power is in the words (and actions) that come from thoughts. Whether those words are spoken or written, they are full of creative power.

Prayer: Father, the Bible tells us that You will perform
Your word. I trust You to perform Your Word in my life as
I read and apply it. Your promise in Jeremiah 29:11
is true for me: You indeed have a plan for me
that will give me a future and a hope.
Thank You for making my vision a reality.
In Jesus' name, amen.

Thought: While thoughts *design* a future, words *create* that future.

Reading: **Isaiah 34–36; Colossians 2**

The Negative Power of Words

Words have power. Unfortunately, there is a negative aspect to this truth as well as a positive one. You can undermine your vision by what you continually say about yourself, such as "I'm fat," "I'm slow," "I'm not intelligent," "I'm a timid person," "I don't like people," "I'm a failure," or "I'll always have a mortgage." I am. I am. I am. You will become everything you constantly declare about yourself. That is the power of words.

Satan knows that the key to creating anything is having a clear vision of it and speaking it into existence. He wants you to speak negative rather than positive things so that your effectiveness for God's kingdom will be negated. Remember that Satan's desire for your life is exactly the opposite of God's. In John 10:10, Jesus said, *"The thief [Satan] comes only to steal and kill and destroy; I have come that they may have life, and have it to the full ["abundantly" NASB]."*

We can help protect our visions, therefore, by guarding what we say. Instead of saying, "I'll always have a mortgage," say, "I'm going to be debt free." You may have been imagining that you don't owe any bills, but you have to start saying it as well. Say, *"My God will meet all [my] needs according to his glorious riches in Christ Jesus"* (Philippians 4:19), then pray, "Lord, please perform Your Word."

A vision doesn't have any power until you talk about it. As you talk about it, you can develop a plan for achieving it. The Lord will meet you in your words and actions that are spoken and performed according to His Word.

Prayer: Father, thank You for the power of words.
Please help me to speak faith-filled words
over my vision and my life.
In Jesus' name, amen.

Thought: We can help protect our visions by guarding what we say.

Reading: **Isaiah 37–38; Colossians 3**

Life the Way You See It

L ife is the way you see it. When you begin to see with the eyes of faith, you will understand how to make your vision a reality. There is a story of a man and his friend who visited India years ago. They were walking down the streets of Bombay and saw the thousands of poor people on the streets. The man said to his friend, "Look at these people. Isn't it a sad sight? They're without shoes. Isn't it a shame that we have so much at home in our country while these people are poor and without shoes. I'll never forget this sight." By this time, his friend had already taken out a piece of paper and was writing down some notes. He had started working out a plan of how to ship shoes over to India and how to manufacture shoes in India. Instead of saying, "Look at the bare feet," he was saying, "Look at the feet that need shoes!" Today his enterprise is one of the largest shoe companies in America. One man saw bare feet. Another man saw an opportunity for a much-needed business. It's all in how you see.

You can see every problem as an opportunity for ministry, service, or business. That is really how Bahamas Faith Ministries International got started. The number one problem of people in developing nations is ignorance. God raised up BFMI to be one of the solutions to that problem: to bring knowledge, training, and information to the Third World.

Prayer: Father God, if I would see life through Your eyes,
I would see all things as possible, I would have faith
without doubt, and I would not experience fear.
Please help me to see life as You do!
In Jesus' name, amen.

Thought: Life is the way you see it.

Reading: Isaiah 39–40; Colossians 4

OCTOBER 13

Your Vision Should Outlive You

S uccessful men and women who have impressed and impacted their generations weren't "lucky." They didn't just stumble on greatness. They thought great things and expected great things, and greatness found them. Big thinking precedes great achievement. You don't need to be big to think great thoughts. You need to think great thoughts to become big. That is the faith of vision.

You must realize that ideas control the world. Ideas are so powerful that many nations are ruled by the thoughts of men who have long since died. When I went to college, most of the books I read were by people who are no longer living. A vision is an idea that is so powerful it can live beyond the grave. Your own vision should outlive you. In order for that to happen, however, you can't keep your ideas to yourself. You must clearly conceive and express them.

I'll never forget the time I was grappling with the possibility of writing books. I told God that I didn't want to write because so many others were writing, and I didn't want to do it just because everybody else was doing it. I wanted my teaching to be real and genuine. However, when I was preparing my notes one night for a teaching, I felt as if the Lord was saying to me, "If you do not write, what you know will die with you. If you write down the ideas that I have given you, however, your words will live on after you are gone."

Prayer: Father, thank You for the ideas You have placed within me. Please guide me as I write down my vision and fulfill it, so that future generations may benefit from it, for Your glory.
In Jesus' name, amen.

Thought: A vision is an idea that is so powerful it can live beyond the grave.

Reading: **Isaiah 41–42; 1 Thessalonians 1**

Action Steps to Fulfilling Vision

Your success or failure is determined by how you see. Jesus continually dealt with the sight of the disciples because their sight got them into trouble so often. He wanted them to move from sight to vision, and that is why He taught them about faith through life illustrations such as the fig tree, the feeding of the five thousand, and the raising of Lazarus. (See, for example, Matthew 21:19-22; Mark 6:34-44; John 11:1-44.)

The faith of vision is crucial because the way you see things determines how you think and act and, therefore, whether or not your vision will become reality. Remember that Proverbs 23:7 says, "As [a person] *thinks in his heart, so is he*" (NKJV). Do you have sight or vision?

What is your answer to the above question? Are you thinking and speaking in positive or negative terms in relation to your vision? This week, choose one aspect of your vision and practice speaking words of faith regarding it.

Let's pray together:

Prayer: Heavenly Father, we join with the psalmist David
in prayer that the words of our mouths and the meditation
of our hearts would be pleasing in Your sight, Lord.
We know that only words of faith are pleasing to You.
If we are tempted to speak negative words
concerning our lives or visions, please convict us.
Remind us that words of faith reveal that we are
in agreement with You. We know that words of faith
are vital to the fulfillment of our visions.
Help us to function as You do, Lord,
speaking creative words and then
watching them come to pass.
In Jesus' name, amen.

Thought: The way you see things determines
how you think and act.

Reading: **Isaiah 43–44; 1 Thessalonians 2**

Principles of the Faith of Vision

Today, reflect on the following principles regarding the faith of vision:

1. Sight is a function of the eyes, while vision is a function of the heart.
2. Sight is the ability to see things as they are, while vision is the ability to see things as they could (or should) be.
3. We must never let what our eyes see determine what our hearts believe.
4. Faith is vision in the heart.
5. Sight without vision is dangerous because it has no hope.
6. The vision in your heart is greater than your environment.
7. God gave us vision so we would not have to live by what we see.
8. We were created to live according to the way God functions. God functions through faith and His Word.
9. While thoughts are the most important things on earth, words are the most powerful. Thoughts design a future, but words create that future.
10. Whether words are spoken or written, they are full of creative power.
11. Faith sees problems as opportunities.
12. Great thinking precedes great achievement.
13. You don't need to be big to think great thoughts. You need to think great thoughts to become big. That is the faith of vision.
14. A vision is an idea that is so powerful it can live beyond the grave.
15. In order for your vision to outlive you, you can't keep your ideas to yourself. You must clearly conceive and express them.
16. The faith of vision is crucial because the way you see things determines how you think and act and, therefore, whether or not your vision will become reality.

Reading: **Isaiah 45–46; 1 Thessalonians 3**

The Sixth Principle:
Understand the Process of Vision

T he sixth principle in our Twelve Principles of Vision is that we must understand the process of vision. God has a plan for each of our lives, yet He brings those plans to pass in a gradual way. I'm learning that God tells us where we are going with our visions, but He rarely tells us exactly how He will take us there. He gives us purpose but doesn't explain the full process.

Proverbs 16:9 says, *"In his heart a man plans his course, but the LORD determines his steps."* Notice the word "steps." God didn't say He would direct our leaps, but rather our steps. There is no hurried way to get to God's vision. He leads us step-by-step, day-by-day, through trials and character-building opportunities as He moves us toward our dreams. Why does God lead us in this way? Because He doesn't want us only to win; He wants us to win with style. God's desire is to fashion people with character and battle scars who can say, "God didn't just hand me this vision. I have qualified for it."

At the time when we receive our visions, we are not yet ready for them. We don't have the experience or the character for them. God could accomplish quickly what He desires to do through us, yet He wants to prepare us to receive and work in our visions. This is the way in which the Lord worked in the lives of the great Bible leaders, and it is the way He still works today.

Prayer: Father, I have seen in my life that there is
no hurried way to get to Your vision.
You have a step-by-step plan to lead me where I need to be.
Help me to have the patience and faith
to trust You each step of the way.
In Jesus' name, amen.

Thought: We must understand that vision is a process.

Reading: **Isaiah 47–49; 1 Thessalonians 4**

God Chooses the Route

We must learn to train for what God has already told us is coming. We ask God, "Why do I need to go this way? I don't like this route." He answers that the route is going to do two things for us: (1) develop our character, and (2) produce responsibility in us. We weren't born with those things; we have to learn them. Moreover, if God were to show us the full route to where we are going, we might say, "I'll stay right where I am."

Let's look at the life of Joseph as an example. When he was seventeen years old, he had a dream from God in which his father, mother, and brothers were kneeling down before him. (See Genesis 37:9–10.) Joseph thought to himself, "Yes! I like this dream." God had given him a vision, yet He didn't tell him how he was going to get there. Suppose God had said, "Joseph, you're going to become a great ruler, and here is what I have planned to get you there: your brothers are going to tear your favorite clothes right off your back, throw you into a pit, and sell you as a slave. Then your master's wife is going to lie about you, accusing you of rape, and your master is going to have you put in jail, where you will be forgotten for a long time. But eventually you will get there." If God had said that, Joseph probably would have replied, "I'll just stay a shepherd. I'm very happy where I am right now."

God protects us and our visions by leading us according to His route and His timing.

Prayer: Father, You are committed to me
and to completing the work You have begun in me.
Thank You for developing character and responsibility in my life.
In Jesus' name, amen.

Thought: You must learn to train for what God has
already told you is coming.

Reading: **Isaiah 50–52; 1 Thessalonians 5**

OCTOBER 18

In the Midst of the Process

Are you in the midst of the vision process? Are you wondering, "Where is the vision God promised me?" Perhaps you are beginning to wonder if there is a God in heaven.

Joseph likely felt the same way during his ordeals. He found himself sitting in a pit when, just a few days earlier, he had seen himself on a throne. He was probably thinking, "Where is the God who showed me that dream?" If so, I believe God's reply to Joseph was something like this: "I'm with you in the pit, and I'm working on your character because you can't rule well without it."

Suppose Joseph hadn't learned self-control through all his hardships? When Potiphar's wife tried to seduce him, he might have given in to the temptation. Instead, because he had learned discipline and reliance on God, he could be trusted in such a situation.

What if God had told Moses, while he was still one of the most powerful men in Egypt, that in order to fulfill God's vision to free the Israelites, he would lose his position, go through numerous hardships, and eventually not even enter the Promised Land himself? I think Moses would have said, "Lord, You can keep both the people and Pharaoh. I'll pass on this vision." Yet, through a long process, Moses deepened his relationship with God, developed character, and fulfilled his purpose.

Do you really believe that God sees and knows everything? If you do, then you have to trust that your hardships are part of His perfect plan for you.

Prayer: Father, I believe that You see and know everything about me and about the plan You have for my life. Please help me trust You and to face trials joyfully and confidently, knowing that You are perfecting me. In Jesus' name, amen.

Thought: You have to trust that your hardships are part of God's perfect plan for you.

Reading: **Isaiah 53–55; 2 Thessalonians 1**

Preparing for the Purpose

J ust because we're going through difficult times doesn't mean God has stopped working to fulfill our purposes. God is working on us, preparing us for our purposes through the process. However, we often sit back and say, "Why is it taking so long? Why do I have to go through all this?" That attitude of complaint and lack of faith is exactly what God is trying to work out of you. He doesn't want you to go into your promised land dragging bad attitudes behind you. He is working for your good.

Let's talk about the life of Paul again. God told him, essentially, "You will be an apostle to the Gentiles for Me. You will preach to kings." (See Acts 9:15.) Paul might have thought, "That sounds pretty good." However, if God had told him about the fastings, the whippings, the stonings, the hunger, and the prisons, Paul might have said, "I think I'll stay in Jerusalem rather than going on that road to Damascus." As it was, after his conversion, God did warn Paul through Ananias, "*I will show him how much he must suffer for my name*" (v. 16).

God's plan to get you where you are meant to be is unpredictable. He doesn't tell you about it because you might be tempted to quit. You might say, for example, "Isn't there another way to start a business?" God will answer, "No. This is the way I am taking you. You want to have a store? Good. I want you to start by working in one. This is your route. I'm working on your character and your training."

No one can have the vision without being qualified for it.

Prayer: Father, as You conduct my training and
prepare me for my vision, I pray that I may live
and work in a way that honors You.
In Jesus' name, amen.

Thought: God is working on us, preparing us for our
purposes through the process.

Reading: **Isaiah 56–58; 2 Thessalonians 2**

Your Vision Awaits an Appointed Time

T he prophet Habakkuk asked God, *"How long, O LORD, must I call for help, but you do not listen?"* (Habakkuk 1:2). He was referring to all the problems and difficulties that were taking place in his nation. There was disorder, corruption, and murder. The Lord's answer to him was this:

> Write down the revelation and make it plain on tablets so that a herald may run with it. For the revelation awaits an appointed time; it speaks of the end and will not prove false. Though it linger, wait for it; it will certainly come and will not delay....But the righteous will live by his faith.　　　　　　　　　　(Habakkuk 2:2–4)

The vision that you have received awaits an appointed time. This is where walking by faith and not by sight comes in. You must believe in what God has told you because it won't happen overnight. Again, it will occur through a process of character development, which will come as you live by faith and inner vision—not by what you see.

You may not face a life-or-death situation, as some of God's people have, but you will have challenges and difficulties in one degree or another as you move toward the fulfillment of your vision. That is why I want you to be aware of the process of vision and be prepared for it. I don't want you to give up on your vision prematurely. God will continually fulfill a little more of your dream until it comes to pass. It will culminate in His timing. Lamentations 3:26 says, *"It is good to wait quietly for the salvation of the LORD."*

Prayer: Father, it is sometimes so hard to wait,
especially in these days when the world seems to move so fast
around me. May Your Word continue to encourage me
to wait on You with faith and joyful expectation.
In Jesus' name, amen.

Thought: Don't give up on your dream prematurely.

Reading: **Isaiah 59–61; 2 Thessalonians 3**

 　　　　　　　　　　DAILY POWER & PRAYER DEVOTIONAL

Action Steps to Fulfilling Vision

While you are waiting for the fulfillment of your vision, you must realize that regardless of what job you are in right now, purpose gives your job meaning. Being in a pit and in prison didn't stop Joseph because he saw himself as a ruler, and he knew that one day his vision would be fulfilled. God's purpose in your heart is what enables you to keep moving forward.

God places us in jobs that will prepare us for our life's work. Remember that a job is a pre-occupation on the way to true occupation. I'm very glad for each of the jobs I have had, because they all prepared me for what I'm doing right now. What I am doing now is so fulfilling that I could do it for the rest of my life. So get all the knowledge you can from your job, because you're going to move on in a little while.

In the meantime, ask yourself these questions:

- How has God used experiences in my life to build character in me?
- What character qualities has God shown me I need to work on?
- In what specific ways is my job preparing me for my life's work, such as skills, knowledge, and experience?

Let's pray together:

Prayer: Heavenly Father, we are so encouraged by
Your care for us. You have promised in Your Word
to complete the work You have begun in us and to bring us
to maturity. We know that we can trust You in the process
of preparing us for the visions You have given us.
We have seen how You prepared Abraham, Jacob, Joseph,
Moses, Paul, and so many others for their roles
in Your plan for the world.
Prepare us, Lord, so that we will be equipped to do
all that You desire us to do for Your glory.
In Jesus' name we pray, amen.

Thought: Purpose gives your present job meaning.

Reading: **Isaiah 62–64; 1 Timothy 1**

Principles of the Process of Vision

Today, reflect on these principles concerning the process of vision:

1. God has a plan for each of our lives, yet He brings those plans to pass in a gradual way.
2. God will tell you where you are going with your vision, but He will rarely tell you exactly how He will take you there.
3. There is no hurried way to get to God's vision.
4. At the time that we receive our visions, we are not yet ready for them.
5. The process of vision develops our character and produces responsibility in us.
6. God places us in jobs that will prepare us for our life's work.
7. The vision God has given you will come to pass. Until then, you are to live by faith.

Reading: **Isaiah 65–66; 1 Timothy 2**

The Seventh Principle: Set the Priorities of Vision

Principle number seven in our Twelve Principles of Vision is that you must set priorities for yourself in relation to your vision. Understanding priority will help you accomplish your dream because priority is the key to effective decision-making. Both successful and unsuccessful people make decisions every day that influence their chances of achieving their visions. Whether they realize it or not, it is the nature and quality of the choices they make that determine their success or failure.

Life is filled with alternatives; we are constantly bombarded with choices, and our preferences reveal who we are and what we value in life. Remember, your life is the sum total of the decisions you make every day. You have become what you have decided for the last fifteen, twenty, or thirty years of your life. Even more significantly, you can tell the kind of life you're going to have in the future by the decisions you are making today. In this sense, the future really is now. Sometimes we believe that we can make bad choices today and make up for them later on. That thinking is in error. Whatever we are doing now is our tomorrow.

This is why yes and no are the most powerful words you will ever say. God wants you to be able to say them with precision because they will determine your destiny. You will be blessed by saying yes to what is in accordance with your vision and no to anything else.

Prayer: Father, I make many decisions each day.
Please enable me to make decisions that
will benefit the vision You have given me.
My desire is to make godly, good decisions today.
In Jesus' name, amen.

Thought: Priority is the key to effective decision-making.

Reading: **Jeremiah 1–2; 1 Timothy 3**

Not Everything Is Beneficial

If you want to fulfill your dream, you must fix your eyes on it and not get caught up in anything that won't take you there. Please understand that prioritizing creates useful limits on your choices.

In the first part of 1 Corinthians 6:12, Paul wrote, *"Everything is permissible for me'—but not everything is beneficial."* Even though we have permission to do everything we want to, *"not everything is beneficial"* for us. You have to determine what is beneficial based on the needs of your vision. The second part of that verse is a very powerful statement: *"'Every-thing is permissible for me'—but I will **not be mastered** by anything"* (emphasis added). Even though you can do anything in life, the only things that should master you are the things that will take you to your goal. Of course, that goal should be what pleases and glorifies God.

Remember, even if something is good, that does not necessarily mean it is beneficial to fulfilling your God-given vision. For example, when you are traveling along a highway, there are dozens of exits you might take. Is there such a thing as a "bad" exit? No, they're all good, legitimate routes. Many of them lead to helpful services, such as hotels, restaurants, or gas stations. Therefore, is there anything that makes an exit "bad" for you? Yes—if it doesn't lead to your desired destination. Ask yourself, "Which activities are aligned with God's purposes for me? What will move me toward my goal?"

Prayer: Father, please lead me by Your Holy Spirit. Give me the wisdom to choose the things that are truly beneficial to me and not to become involved in things that will pull me away from my goal. In Jesus' precious name, amen.

Thought: *"Everything is permissible for me, but not everything is beneficial."*

Reading: **Jeremiah 3–5; 1 Timothy 4**

The Beneficial Things

W hat is beneficial for you? Obviously, the first thing that you should consider as beneficial is your relationship with God through Jesus Christ. If you want to know where you're supposed to go in life, you have to establish a connection with the Person who gave you the assignment, the Person who created you. It's no wonder the Bible says the greatest commandment is to love God first with all your heart, mind, soul (will), and strength. (See Mark 12:30.) When you do that, He reveals to you the assignment that you were born to fulfill. Once you are certain of where you are meant to go in life and have truly committed to it, then a lot of the extraneous things will fall away on their own.

After you capture your vision, you need to prioritize your life in keeping with that vision. You have to decide how many of the things that you are currently involved in are beneficial to your dream. Again, there might not necessarily be anything wrong with them. They just may not be right for you to be involved in based on what you need to accomplish.

The key is that the vision itself decides what is good for you. You don't just do good things. You do things that are good for your vision. Most of us know the difference between right and wrong. Therefore, your greatest challenge is not in choosing between good and bad but between good and best. A vision protects you from being misguided by good alternatives. It allows you to say no to lesser opportunities, even if there are certain benefits to them.

Prayer: Father, help me to choose between
good and best. Sometimes they are so similar;
please give me discernment by Your Holy Spirit
to know the difference.
In Jesus' name, amen.

Thought: *The vision itself* decides what is best and most
beneficial for your vision.

Reading: **Jeremiah 6–8; 1 Timothy 5**

Good versus Best

W e can see a clear illustration of the principle of priorities in Jesus' reaction to the choices of Martha and Mary of Bethany.

As Jesus and his disciples were on their way, he came to a village where a woman named Martha opened her home to him. She had a sister called Mary, who sat at the Lord's feet listening to what He said. But Martha was distracted by all the preparations that had to be made. She came to him and asked, "Lord, don't you care that my sister has left me to do the work by myself? Tell her to help me!"

(Luke 10:38–40)

Martha had made a very honorable request: "What I'm doing is important; I need help." Yet note the Lord's answer: *"Martha, Martha,... you are worried and upset about many things"* (v. 41). Jesus didn't say "bad" things, just *"many things."* He continued, *"But only one thing is needed. Mary has chosen what is better, and it will not be taken away from her"* (v. 42).

Jesus was saying, in effect, "You're doing what is good, Martha, but Mary has shifted into an area of life that I wish everyone would go to. Don't just do good things. Concentrate on what is best." In the story of Martha and Mary, nowhere does it say that Jesus was hungry. God doesn't want us to start anything, including doing good works for Him, until we consult Him. This is because He doesn't want us to work *for* Him, but *with* Him in partnership. We are *"God's fellow workers"* (2 Corinthians 6:1).

Prayer: Father, I want to focus on what is best.
As I meet with You each day in prayer, reveal to me
the good things I can do that day to serve You.
In Jesus' name, amen.

Thought: Concentrate on what is *best*.

Reading: **Jeremiah 9–11; 1 Timothy 6**

Keep Your Eyes on the Mark

When I was in Israel, I visited a farm that used modern tractors and combines. Nearby, I saw a little field in a valley where a man was tilling the ground using just an ox hooked up to a plow. I was intrigued by the sight, and I said to one of the men from the farm, "He's using an animal and an old, outdated plow, but his field is just as perfect as yours, and you use modern machinery!" The man told me, "That guy's system is better than mine! He keeps his furrows completely straight. At the end of the field, he sets up little sticks and ties red or white flags on them. He sets his eyes on the little piece of cloth at the far end of the field as he controls the movements of the ox. If he didn't use the sticks, his furrows would be crooked."

Then he said something that put the whole thing into perspective for me: "That little stick is called 'the mark.'" That term took me back two thousand years to that same area of Palestine where Jesus had lived. I understood what Jesus meant in Luke 9:62: *"No one who puts his hand to the plow and looks back is fit for service in the kingdom of God."* When you set your hand to the plow, you must put your eyes on the mark and not look to the left, right, or behind you. Then you will hit God's mark for your life.

Prayer: Father, I want to hit the mark for my life!
Please help me to keep my eyes and my heart
focused on the vision You have given me,
without being tempted by what lies to the right,
to the left, or behind. Thank You, Lord.
In Jesus' name, amen.

Thought: When you put your hand to the plow,
you must put your eyes on the mark.

Reading: **Jeremiah 12–14; 2 Timothy 1**

My Yoke Is Easy

When someone sets his eyes on a goal and never takes them off it, he will reach that goal. The apostle Paul talked about focusing on his goal:

> Brothers, I do not consider myself yet to have taken hold of it. But one thing I do: forgetting what is behind and straining toward what is ahead, I press on toward the goal to win the prize for which God has called me heavenward in Christ Jesus. (Philippians 3:13–14)

Do you remember when you were learning to ride a bicycle? You were told to look straight ahead because wherever you looked, that's where you were going. If you looked down, you would fall down. Many of us have set markers in our lives—our visions—claiming we are headed in that direction, but then we keep looking everywhere except at our visions. It doesn't take too long before we're off course.

In Matthew 11:30, Jesus said, "*My yoke is easy and my burden is light.*" A yoke is a single piece of wood that joins two oxen together. It keeps them at the same pace and in the same position. Jesus also said, "*Come to me, all you who are weary and burdened, and I will give you rest. Take my yoke upon you and learn from me*" (vv. 28–29). We are to join with God's plan for our lives and let His yoke guide us. This means that if He turns, we turn; if He stops, we stop. This is the way we hit the mark.

Prayer: Father, I desire to take Christ's yoke upon myself
so that I may learn from Him and rest in Him.
I willingly join with Your plan for my life.
Thank You for guiding me.
In Jesus' name, amen.

Thought: We are to join with God's plan for our lives
and let His yoke guide us.

Reading: **Jeremiah 15–17; 2 Timothy 2**

Vision Protects You

V ision protects us from trying to do everything. The apostle Paul had a deep love and concern for the Jews. They were his people; he was born from among them, and he was one of them. Yet his purpose was to preach to the Gentiles: *"For this purpose I was appointed a herald and an apostle—I am telling the truth, I am not lying—and a teacher of the true faith to the Gentiles"* (1 Timothy 2:7). He knew what he was appointed for, and he stayed in his vision. Paul's vision was his motivating force: *"I am so eager to preach the gospel also to you who are at Rome"* (Romans 1:15).

Perhaps we become involved in too many things because we're trying to impress God and other people by showing them how much we are capable of doing. Yet we must remember that our gifts are the key to fulfilling our personal visions. If we spend time on things that we're not as gifted in, we will wear ourselves down to the point that when we come back to our gifts, we are too tired to use them effectively.

Jesus Himself was born to do one main thing. At one point, one of Jesus' closest friends tried to talk Him out of His vision. Peter said, in essence, "Master, You're talking about how You're going to die. *'This shall never happen to you!'"* (Matthew 16:22). What Peter said wasn't bad, but it wasn't right based on Jesus' vision. We must keep our eyes on God's true purpose for our lives.

Prayer: Father, I have been guilty of being involved
in too many things. Please help me to say yes only
to the things that You have given me to do
based on Your true purpose for my life.
In Jesus' name, amen.

Thought: Vision protects us from trying to do everything.

Reading: **Jeremiah 18–19; 2 Timothy 3**

Vision Disciplines Your Choices

Vision is the key to an effective life because when you see your destination, it helps you to discipline your life in ways that train and prepare you, providing for your vision.

Proverbs 29:18 is often quoted but not fully understood: *"Where there is no vision, the people perish"* (KJV). The word in the Hebrew for *"perish"* means "to throw off constraints." If you don't have vision, there are no real restraints in your life. Yet, when you have vision, you are able to say no with dignity. The *New International Version* reads, *"Where there is no revelation, the people cast off restraint."* The use of the words "revelation" and "restraint" is very significant because the verse may be interpreted as meaning, "Where there is no vision, the people throw off self-control." You will never be disciplined in your life until you have real vision.

Discipline may be defined as self-imposed standards and restrictions motivated by a desire or vision that is greater than any alternatives. According to *Merriam-Webster's 11th Collegiate Dictionary*, the words *discipline* and *disciple* come from the same root word that means "pupil." A disciple is a student who is dedicated to learning to think like his or her teacher. The followers of Jesus, the ultimate Teacher, were called His disciples because they were committed to changing their thinking so that they thought like He did. As You follow the Lord in Your vision, you will become more and more disciplined in the choices you make in life.

Prayer: Father, many choices are available to me.
The most important one is to choose to love and serve You.
Please teach me to be more disciplined so that I might make choices
for the rest of my life that truly honor You.
In Jesus' name, amen.

Thought: Seeing your destination helps you to discipline your life
in ways that train and prepare you, providing for your vision.

Reading: **Jeremiah 20–21; 2 Timothy 4**

Discipline Is a Teacher

How disciplined is your life in relation to your dream? Ask yourself questions such as these: What am I using my energies on? What am I putting my heart and soul into? Is it worth it, based on my purpose? Where am I investing my money? Your vision dictates where you put your resources. Are you buying things that you don't need? Are you so much in debt that you can't channel your money toward fulfilling the vision in your heart?

What movies and television programs am I watching? Are they helping or hindering me? What books am I reading? If you're only reading romance novels, you are living in a fantasy world and not living out your true dream. What am I taking into my body? There are talented, gifted people who are dying prematurely because they consistently eat food that isn't good for them. If you're going to make it to the end of your vision, you must take care of your health.

What is my attitude toward life? If you know where you're going, you can keep your attitude positive. When things go wrong, you can say, "That's okay. This is only temporary. I know where my true destination is." Paul said we should discipline our thoughts to think about what will build us up: *"Whatever is true, whatever is noble, whatever is right, whatever is pure, whatever is lovely, whatever is admirable—if anything is excellent or praiseworthy—think about such things"* (Philippians 4:8).

Choose to live well! Associate with people and be involved in things that are conducive to your dream.

Prayer: Father, all that I have and all that I do
should be dedicated to You and should lead me to my dream.
I submit my energy, my money, my entertainment, my
books, my body, and my heart attitude to You.
In Jesus' name, amen.

Thought: Associate with people and be involved in things
that are conducive to your dream.

Reading: **Jeremiah 22–23; Titus 1**

NOVEMBER 1

Make Your Life Count

Nehemiah made a statement that I believe everyone with vision should learn to make. It's one of the greatest statements of priority that I have ever read anywhere.

Nehemiah was at a place where he had started to rebuild the wall of Jerusalem. He had motivated the people by giving them a renewed purpose, he was able to communicate to them the necessity of doing this great project, and they were working hard at it. Yet, in Nehemiah 6:1, he was confronted by three men who wanted to prevent his vision from being fulfilled. Sanballat, Tobiah, and Geshem were professional distracters. In Nehemiah 6:2, Nehemiah said, *"Sanballat and Geshem sent me this message: 'Come, let us meet together in one of the villages on the plain of Ono.' But they were scheming to harm me."* In verse three, Nehemiah said, *"So I sent messengers to them with this reply: 'I am carrying on a great project and cannot go down. Why should the work stop while I leave it and go down to you?'"* He refused to come down from the wall, and his enemies were thwarted. That's what I call a man who had his priorities set.

Your destination is so perfect for you that God doesn't want you to end up anywhere else. He wants you to find your vision and stay focused on it. If you have gotten off track in life, it doesn't matter how young or old you are: refocus on your vision and make decisions that will lead you there.

Prayer: Father, I know I haven't always made the best use of my time, gifts, and resources in the past, but with Your help I'm going to make the rest of my life count by staying focused on my vision.
In Jesus' name, amen.

Thought: Your destination is so perfect for you that God doesn't want you to end up anywhere else.

Reading: **Jeremiah 24–26; Titus 2**

DAILY POWER & PRAYER DEVOTIONAL

Action Steps to Fulfilling Vision

If you are afraid to take decisive action to move toward your vision, consider this: It is better to make a decision that will prove to be wrong, but which you can learn from, than not to make any decision at all and never learn anything. Someone has said, "I'd rather try and fail than never try and never know I could succeed." People succeed because they try. People who don't try have no chance of success.

As you pursue your vision, review some of the questions from the last few days. Write out your answers to the discipline questions. Then, set priorities in each area of your life in relation to your vision and write them down. What things do you need to eliminate from your life in order to focus on your dream? Bring all these areas before the Lord in prayer and listen closely as He speaks to your heart.

Let's pray together:

Prayer: Heavenly Father, as disciples of Your Son Jesus,
we are learning to walk as mature believers in this world.
You placed a vision in each of our hearts so that Your purposes
on earth would be achieved and so that we would have
an important part in fulfilling those purposes.
You know the importance of discipline in reaching our goals.
Thank you for encouraging us to be self-controlled
and for showing us how to discipline our choices so that
our lives will count for now and for eternity.
In Jesus' name, amen.

Thought: People succeed because they try.
People who don't try have no chance of success.

Reading: **Jeremiah 27–29; Titus 3**

Principles of the Priority of Vision

Today, reflect on these principles of the priority of vision:

1. If you want to be successful, you must set priorities for yourself in relation to your vision.
2. Understanding priority will help you accomplish your dream because priority is the key to effective decision-making.
3. You can tell the kind of life you're going to have in the future by the decisions you make today.
4. *Yes* and *no* are the most powerful words you will ever say. God wants you to be able to say them with conviction because they will determine your destiny.
5. When people don't succeed in their visions, it is often because they don't understand that prioritizing creates useful limits on their choices.
6. You have to determine what is beneficial, defining what is beneficial based on the needs of your vision.
7. The only things that should master you are the things that will take you to your goal.
8. Once you are certain of where you are meant to go in life and have truly committed to it, then many extraneous things in your life will fall away on their own.
9. The vision itself decides what is good for you. You don't just do good things. You do things that are good for your vision.
10. Your greatest challenge is not in choosing between good or bad but between *good* and *best*.
11. To end up where you want to be, keep your eyes on the mark.
12. Vision protects you from trying to do everything.
13. When you see your destination, it helps you to discipline your life in ways that train and prepare you, providing for your vision.
14. You will never be disciplined in your life until you have real vision.

Reading: **Jeremiah 30–31; Philemon**

The Eighth Principle: Recognize the Influence of Others

Principle number eight in our Twelve Principles of Vision is that *we must recognize the influence of others on our visions.* We need other people if we are going to be successful in life because, as I emphasized earlier, we were not created to fulfill our visions alone. As a matter of fact, God specifically said about His first human creation, *"It is not good for the man to be alone"* (Genesis 2:18). We need people to make it in life. For any vision that you have, God has people prepared to work with you, and they will be a blessing to you.

There will always be a need for positive people in your life. When I went to college, I had a dream to get my degree, and there were people who already had been set apart to help me graduate. Some of them helped me academically, others financially, and others with encouragement in my spiritual walk. When you have a dream, that's the way it works. People will always be there, waiting to help you. Therefore, if you have no dream, or if you do not begin to act on it, the people who are supposed to help you won't know where to find you.

The principle of influence has a twofold application, however, because people can have a negative effect on us as well as a positive one. When you begin to act on your vision, it will stir up both those who want to help you and those who want to hinder you. This is why you must learn to recognize the influence of those around you.

Prayer: Father, thank You for bringing people across
my path to be a positive influence on my life and vision.
Help me to recognize them so I may benefit from their help.
In Jesus' name, amen.

Thought: There will always be a need for positive
people in our lives.

Reading: **Jeremiah 32–33; Hebrews 1**

Choosing Your Friends

How do you choose your friends? You should generally choose friends who are going in the same direction you are and who want to obtain the same things you do. In the book of Proverbs, Solomon said, *"He who walks with the wise grows wise, but a companion of fools suffers harm"* (Proverbs 13:20). The *New King James Version* reads, *"The companion of fools will be destroyed."* My version of this maxim is, "If you want to be a success, don't keep company with those who aren't going anywhere in life."

In light of these truths, I want you to ask yourself three questions. First, "With whom am I spending time?" Who are your closest friends; who are the people you are confiding in?

Second, "What are these people doing to me?" In other words, what do they have you listening to, reading, thinking, and doing? Where do they have you going? What do they have you saying? How do they have you feeling? What do they have you settling for? That last one is an important one, because your friends can make you comfortable in your misery. Most important, what is being around these people causing you to become?

Third, ask yourself, "Is what other people are doing to me a good thing in relation to my vision?" When you start telling people where you're going to go and what you're going to do, they may (even unconsciously) begin to say things to try to hinder your dream. Therefore, you need to ask and answer these three questions about your friendships truthfully—and regularly—as you progress toward your vision.

Prayer: Father, thank You for the godly friends that
You have brought into my life. It is good when we can walk
in the same direction, following Your Word and our visions.
Please help me to continue to build godly relationships.
In Jesus' name, amen.

Thought: *"He who walks with the wise grows wise."*

Reading: **Jeremiah 34–36; Hebrews 2**

NOVEMBER 6

The Law of Association

The law of association states that you become like those with whom you spend time. This law corresponds to Solomon's words, *"He who walks with the wise grows wise, but a companion of fools suffers harm"* (Proverbs 13:20).

We often underestimate others' influence in our lives. The two words that most accurately describe influence are *powerful* and *subtle*. The influence of others can be powerful because we all desire to have people like us; therefore, we may start acting more like others to gain their approval. Their influence is also subtle because we may think it has no effect on us. Often, we don't know we're being influenced until it is too late. Whether we realize it or not, however, the influence of those with whom we spend time has a powerful effect on how we will end up in life, on whether we will succeed or fail.

What we call peer pressure is simply this: people with whom we associate exercising their influence on us, trying to direct our lives in the way they want them to go. Adults, as well as young people, experience peer pressure. They find it hard to disregard other people's opinions. There are people who are forty, sixty, and eighty years old who give in to peer pressure. Almost everyone is affected by it.

People have the potential to create your environment. Your environment then determines your mind-set, your mind-set determines your vision, and your vision determines your future. You must choose your friends wisely, selecting those who are truly with you and not against you. Show me your friends, and I'll show you your future.

Prayer: Father, make me sensitive to the influences of those around me. I do not want peer pressure to control my life. I want my influence to come from You, Your Word, and my vision.
In Jesus' name, amen.

Thought: There are two words that most accurately describe influence: *powerful* and *subtle*.

Reading: **Jeremiah 37–39; Hebrews 3**

Vision Wakes Up the Opposition

Nehemiah 4:1 says, *"When Sanballat heard that we were rebuilding the wall, he became angry and was greatly incensed."* People of vision have found that the minute they decide to fulfill their dreams, all their enemies seem to wake up. Again, as long as you're not doing anything about your vision, no one will bother you. If you start to move toward your vision, however, opposition arises.

Suppose you have been a secretary for twenty years, and everybody thinks you're content in your job. One day you decide, "I'm going back to school." When your friends ask you why, you say, "I'm going to get a master's degree in computer science because I want to head a computer company someday." Suddenly, your friends seem to become your enemies. They ask, "Do you know how old you are?" or "Who do you think will become your clients?" By the time they finish, you feel like staying a secretary.

Sad to say, sometimes those who are the most detrimental to the fulfillment of our visions are members of our own families. Some family members may be extremely supportive, but others may not be. The potential for negative influences from family members in regard to vision is probably the reason why the Lord told Abraham, *"Leave your country, your people and your father's household and go to the land I will show you"* (Genesis 12:1).

Your passion for your vision must be more powerful than the opposition of those around you. You must be clear about what you're going to do and persevere in doing it.

Prayer: Father, please help me to persevere in my vision,
even if I encounter opposition from family members
and friends. Help me to continue to show
Your love to them as I pursue my purpose.
In Jesus' name, amen.

Thought: As long as you're not doing anything about your
vision, no one will bother you.

Reading: **Jeremiah 40–42; Hebrews 4**

The Tobiah Syndrome

People who change the world have declared independence from other people's expectations. That's what makes them successful. Even if people tell liesor start rumors about you, keep your eyes on the mark, continue working, and keep on building.

Nehemiah faced this very situation. In Nehemiah 4:2, we read,

And in the presence of his associates and the army of Samaria, [Sanballat] said, "What are those feeble Jews doing? Will they restore their wall? Will they offer sacrifices? Will they finish in a day? Can they bring the stones back to life from those heaps of rubble?"

When people are angry, they ask questions to discourage you. Look at the questions Sanballat was asking the Jews. Consider the words he used. He jeered at their abilities and scoffed at their timetable. In essence, he declared their vision a dead project.

Nehemiah 4:3 says, *"Tobiah the Ammonite, who was at his side, said, 'What they are building—if even a fox climbed up on it, he would break down their wall of stones!'"* In other words, "Don't worry about them. This isn't going to work. It will soon come to nothing." Have you ever heard that before? "Oh, don't worry about that new business. It will last only a couple of months before it folds." That attitude is what I call the "Tobiah Syndrome." When someone says something like that to you, encourage yourself in the Lord and receive strength from His Word. Find brothers and sisters in Christ who will support you. Keep moving forward with your vision!

Prayer: Father, by Your Holy Spirit,
I will move forward in my vision every day.
In Jesus' name, amen.

Thought: People who change the world have declared independence from other people's expectations.

Reading: **Jeremiah 43–45; Hebrews 5**

The Protection of Disassociation

Pursuing your vision means that you will have to disassociate yourself from certain people and places if you're going to make it to your dream. Some people say it doesn't really matter with whom they associate; they wouldn't want to hurt anybody by disassociating from them. Yet Jesus said, *"If the blind leads the blind, both will fall into a ditch"* (Matthew 15:14 NKJV). He was telling us not to be foolish by following those who are spiritually blind. You have to disassociate yourself from people who aren't going anywhere and don't want to go anywhere in life. The sad thing is that some people literally sacrifice their dreams and their lives because they are afraid of having conflict and disagreement with others.

If you need to remove yourself from some people and activities that have been hindering you, stand firm when you tell your former companions, in love, "I don't do that any longer. I can't go out with you tonight. We aren't going in the same direction anymore." Choose friends who have a heart for God and His purposes. Associate with people who want you to move toward your vision. Let them be your encouragement. Disassociation does not need to be confrontational. Sometimes you can ease out of people's lives very quietly and very subtly, just as you eased into them.

If you listen to the critics, you won't do what you were born to do. Remember what Nehemiah said when his critics tried to distract him from his vision: *"I am carrying on a great project and cannot go down. Why should the work stop while I leave it and go down to you?"* (Nehemiah 6:3).

Prayer: Father, help me to stop associating with those who
are a hindrance to my faith or Your purpose for my life.
Help me to speak the truth in love to them.
In Jesus' name, amen.

Thought: If you listen to the critics, you won't do
what you were born to do.

Reading: **Jeremiah 46–47; Hebrews 6**

The Protection of Limited Association

I n considering how people influence my life, I have also learned to protect my vision by limited association. You may not want to completely disassociate yourself from some of the people in your life. It is important, however, that you thoughtfully and prayerfully determine how much time you will spend with them.

For those of you who are dating, please take this to heart: When you have a goal for your life, make sure that the person you are interested in is also interested in your goals. Many people get married and then tell their spouses their goals. Often their spouses say, "I really don't want that." The Bible asks us, "*Can two walk together, unless they are agreed?*" (Amos 3:3 NKJV). Jesus reinforced this theme when He said, "*A house divided against itself will fall*" (Luke 11:17). You don't want to be in a house that is divided. You want to be in a house with one vision.

It's all right to have casual friends as long as you give them casual time. You don't want to spend quality time with casual friends. It's all right to spend two hours with some people, but not two days. It's all right to spend two minutes with some people, but not two hours. It depends on the person and his or her influence on you.

You must protect your mental environment. Here's how to do so: Spend major time with positive influences and minor time with negative influences. Stay away from bad situations. Paul stated the adage, "*Bad company corrupts good character*" (1 Corinthians 15:33). He was telling us, "Choose your company well."

Prayer: Father, you have given me the ability to choose my company well. Help me to continue to choose close friends who love You and are seeking You with all their hearts.
In Jesus' name, amen.

Thought: Spend major time with positive influences and minor time with negative influences.

Reading: **Jeremiah 48–49; Hebrews 7**

Expand Your Association

T he third step in choosing who will influence your life is the most positive of the three: expand your association. If you're going to be successful, you have to spend more time with the right people—people who have the same philosophy and discipline that you do, people who exhibit the kind of character that you want to have. Those are the people with whom you want to expand your relationships.

Spend time with people of vision. When the angel Gabriel announced to Mary that she would become pregnant with Jesus, Mary asked, "How can I have a baby?" God's answer through Gabriel was that this would occur through the power of the Holy Spirit. Yet notice what else the angel said. He mentioned that Elizabeth was pregnant with John the Baptist after she had been both barren and past the age of childbearing. It was as if God was saying, "Mary, to help you stay strong during this time, you need the faith-inspiring testimony of Elizabeth. She has her own miracle baby, and she's six months ahead of you." The Bible says that Mary went straight to Elizabeth's house and stayed with her for three months. (See Luke 1:26–56.)

God doesn't want you to spend time listening to critics because they will talk you out of your "baby." He wants you to be encouraged by someone who has already been through the morning sickness, so to speak, because there will be times when you'll feel like giving up. During those hard times, that person can tell you, "You're going to get through it. Don't give up on your dream."

Prayer: Father, please enable me to surround myself with encouragers, believers who have faith for the vision.
In Jesus' name, amen.

Thought: Spend time with people of vision.

Reading: **Jeremiah 50; Hebrews 8**

Action Steps to Fulfilling Vision

We all need other people to guide, help, and encourage us along the path to fulfilling our visions. Because we need the influence of others, however, we are also in danger of the negative effects they may have on us if we—or they—are not careful. Therefore, it is crucial for us to guard our hearts, thoughts, attitudes, and ideas from being sabotaged by those around us. We must increase the positive influences in our lives and decrease the negative ones as we pursue our individual goals in tandem with others.

To help you progress in your vision, answer the three questions posed in the last few days: With whom am I spending time? Who are my closest friends; who are the people I am confiding in? What are these people doing to me? What do they have me listening to, reading, thinking, doing? Where do they have me going? What do they have me saying? How do they have me feeling? What do they have me settling for? Is what these people are doing to me a good thing in light of my vision? Then, ask yourself: Who can help me toward my goal? What person can I get close to and learn from?

Let's pray together:

Prayer: Heavenly Father, it is crucial for us to guard our hearts. Your Word says that the heart is the wellspring of life. We need the positive influence of others to carry out Your purposes for us. Lord, You created human beings to work together and to live together in harmony. Please help us to discern the positive influences from the negative ones. We want to share Your good news of salvation with those who are negative, but we don't want to absorb their negative influence into our lives. Enable us to honestly answer the questions concerning people's influence on our lives and to make any changes we need to in obedience to You. In Jesus' mighty name, amen.

Thought: Guard your heart, thoughts, attitudes, and ideas from being sabotaged by others.

Reading: **Jeremiah 51–52; Hebrews 9**

Principles of
Influence on Vision

Today, reflect on these principles of influence on vision:

1. When you begin to act on your vision, it will stir up both those who want to help you and those who want to hinder you.
2. The law of association states that you become like those with whom you spend time.
3. There are two words that most accurately describe influence: powerful and subtle.
4. People have the potential to create your environment. Your environment then determines your mind-set, and your mind-set determines your vision and your future.
5. People of vision have found that the minute they decide to fulfill their dreams, all their enemies seem to wake up.
6. Sometimes the people who are the most detrimental to the fulfillment of your vision are members of your own family.
7. People who change the world have declared independence from other people's expectations.
8. Three things that will protect your vision are disassociation, limited association, and expanded association.
9. We must increase the positive influences in our lives and decrease the negative ones as we pursue our individual goals in tandem with others.

Reading: **Lamentations 1–2; Hebrews 10:1–18**

The Ninth Principle:
Employ the Provision of Vision

Principle number nine in our Twelve Principles of Vision is that we must understand the power of provision. People often stop dreaming about what they really want to do in life because of their limited resources. They believe they have to pay for their visions with their present incomes when they can barely make ends meet. Similarly, when young people tell their parents what they dream of becoming, the parents often become nervous because they feel their children's dreams are too expensive for them to finance.

If we believe that we have to use our own resources to accomplish God-given visions, then we are small dreamers. I want to encourage you that the Bible is clear concerning the dreams in our hearts and how they will be provided for. Proverbs 16:1 says, *"To man belong the plans of the heart, but from the LORD comes the reply of the tongue."* This statement has to do with provision. When a person receives a dream from God, it usually seems impossible. Yet God knows that our provisions are never equal to our visions at the moment we receive them. He realizes that we cannot explain to others—or even to ourselves—how we are going to accomplish our visions without the necessary money, people, facilities, or equipment. He knows that often our dreams are big and our bank accounts are small. What is His solution for us? He says that He will give the answer or *"reply of the tongue."*

Therefore, if people ask you how you are going to accomplish your dream, you don't have to try to give them a full answer. Tell them you are trusting God for provision each step of the way.

Prayer: Father, You have placed Your vision within me.
Thank You for promising the provision to match the vision.
In Jesus' name, amen.

Thought: Our provisions are never equal to our visions at the
moment we receive them.

Reading: **Lamentations 3–5; Hebrews 10:19–39**

Everything You Need

Perhaps your dreams are so big they almost frighten you. You don't see how they could ever come to pass. Let me assure you that your initial apprehension is normal. God often gives us dreams that confound us at first. He wants to make sure we don't attempt to fulfill them apart from Him. If we try to do so, we won't succeed, because the resources won't be available.

Rest assured that God will never give you a vision without provision. The ability and resources are available for whatever you were born to do. Your provision, however, is usually hidden until you act on your vision. Whatever you were born to do attracts what you need to do it. Therefore, you first have to establish what you want to do and begin to do it before the need can be met. Most of us work in reverse. We like to see the provisions before we start, but faith doesn't work that way. When we take action, then God manifests the provision.

God has prepared everything you need to complete your purpose because He chose you for your vision. God tells us we don't have to worry about our provision because He has already blessed us with every spiritual blessing in the heavenly places. (See Ephesians 1:3.) Worry is the greatest sign of doubt in God. If He can put Pharaoh's money into the pockets of the Israelites and take His people into the wilderness loaded down with the gold of the enemy, don't you think He can provide for your needs?

Prayer: Father, I trust You to provide everything I need.
You have promised over and over in Your Word
that You will meet the needs of Your children.
Thank You for already blessing me in the heavenly places.
In Jesus' name, amen.

Thought: Rest assured that God will never give you
a vision without provision.

Reading: **Ezekiel 1–2; Hebrews 11:1–19**

Does Prosperity Mean Excess?

Many people, Christians included, have misconceptions about money. We think prosperity means excess, and that is why we worry when we don't have enough money in the bank to fund our visions. Further, our concept of prosperity is more like hoarding. In the Bible, hoarding is referred to as gluttony. A person can be gluttonous even when he has no money or food. Gluttony is a state of mind in which a person never feels he has enough to satisfy him.

Whatever we hoard will begin to destroy us. When we eat more than we need, it creates a problem of excess weight. That weight causes pressure on the heart. Our arteries begin to clog up, putting us in danger of a heart attack or stroke, all because we loaded up on excess food.

The Bible says that people who have excess money have many burdens, worries, and headaches trying to figure out what to do with their riches and how to protect them. (See, for example, Luke 12:16–21; James 5:1–5.) Too much wealth can cause oppression and even depression. Some people own so many gems and other material goods that they put bars on their windows to protect themselves against theft. They worry that someone might break in and take their twenty-thousand-dollar watch, which they rarely wear anyway. To me, this approach to wealth is foolishness because the riches are a burden rather than a blessing.

It is not money itself, but the love of money (its excess) that is the root of all evil. (See 1 Timothy 6:10 KJV.) We should cultivate a love for God rather than for money. We can trust Him to provide whatever we need for our lives and our visions.

Prayer: Father, help me to trust Your provision and not worry about having an excess of money. In Jesus' name, amen.

Thought: Gluttony is a state of mind in which a person never feels he has enough to satisfy him.

Reading: **Ezekiel 3–4; Hebrews 11:20–40**

Does Prosperity Mean Future Needs Are Met Today?

S ome people have the idea that prosperity means all our needs should be provided for well ahead of time. Jesus addressed this misconception when He told His disciples,

> Therefore I tell you, do not worry about your life, what you will eat or drink; or about your body, what you will wear. Is not life more important than food, and the body more important than clothes?...So do not worry, saying, "What shall we eat?" or "What shall we drink?" or "What shall we wear?" For the pagans run after all these things, and your heavenly Father knows that you need them. But seek first his kingdom and his righteousness, and all these things will be given to you as well. (Matthew 6:25, 31–33)

Do people worry about something they already have? No. Worry isn't related to our present supply. It is related to a perceived or potential lack in the future.

Jesus concluded His statements on provision by saying, "*Tomorrow will worry about itself. Each day has enough trouble of its own*" (v. 34). Prosperity doesn't mean that tomorrow's need is met today; it means that today's need is met today. We find the same concept in the Lord's Prayer: "*Give us today our daily bread*" (Matthew 6:11). Jesus tells us not to worry about tomorrow because it has its own supply (see verse 34), and tomorrow we may need even more than we do today. When we get to tomorrow, the supply will be there. We must understand what prosperity really is in order to grasp the foundational principle of how God provides for our visions.

Prayer: Father, Jesus' words from the Sermon on the Mount bring me such freedom from worry. As I seek Your kingdom and Your vision for my life, may I trust You more each day for provision in every way. In Jesus' name, amen.

Thought: Prosperity means that today's need is met today.

Reading: **Ezekiel 5–7; Hebrews 12**

The Nature of Real Prosperity

For the last two days we've been discussing misconceptions about prosperity. What, then, is the nature of real prosperity? One of the Hebrew words that is translated *"prosperity"* in the Bible is *shalev* (see, for example, Psalm 30:6; Psalm 73:3), which means "tranquil," "being at ease," "peaceable," and "quietness." Another Hebrew word for prosperity is *shalom* (see Psalm 35:27; Jeremiah 33:9), which means "peace," "safe," "well," "happy," and "health." The Bible is saying that prosperity is peace. Prosperity is also harmony. When things are in balance, we say they are peaceful. True prosperity frees us from worry and fear; it reflects a state of contentedness that everything necessary is being taken care of.

Jesus used an analogy from nature to help explain prosperity:

Look at the birds of the air; they do not sow or reap or store away in barns, and yet your heavenly Father feeds them. Are you not much more valuable than they? Who of you by worrying can add a single hour to his life? (Matthew 6:26–27)

How does God feed the birds? He provides for them, but He doesn't personally hand-deliver food to their nests! The birds don't just sit around waiting for God to stop by with their meals. When Jesus said His heavenly Father feeds the birds, He meant that everything they need has been made available for them, but they have to go and get it. The bird has to keep working until it finishes building its nest. It has to keep working until it gets the worm. God's prosperity for us is similar: it is peaceful provision as we keep working toward His purposes.

Prayer: Father, the prosperous soul is free from
worry and strife, and that is how I want to be.
Help me to continuously rest in You
as I trust in Your provision.
In Jesus' name, amen.

Thought: True prosperity frees us from worry and fear.

Reading: **Ezekiel 8–10; Hebrews 13**

Prosperity for the Purpose

A fundamental aspect of provision is that God has designed every purpose with its own prosperity. Your purpose has built-in provision for it. God never requires from you what He does not already have in reserve for you.

Here is the key: Your prosperity is directly related to your purpose in life. The nature and degree of your prosperity is determined by what your assignment is. You were not born to have too much or too little. You were born to fulfill God's purpose. When you capture your vision—the part you're supposed to contribute to your generation and succeeding generations, the role you're supposed to play in history—when you capture that and are doing it, you will see that all your provisions are automatically built into it.

In this way, you don't ultimately work for money or food, because you're too busy living. You were not created by God just to pay a mortgage. In your heart, you know that's true. If this is what you're doing, you are probably frustrated with your situation. By the time you turn sixty, you will look back at your life and say, "Did I enjoy any of this?"

Sometimes God doesn't give us all the resources we need to fulfill our visions because He has called other people to provide them for us. God may have provisions all over the world waiting for you. He may move you a thousand miles to get you where you were meant to be, to do things you were born to do, to fulfill the purpose in your own heart while, at the same time, fulfilling the purpose in His heart.

Prayer: Father, You have helped me to realize that You have a
purpose and a plan for everything. I will trust You
to bring all of Your plans to completion.
In Jesus' name, amen.

Thought: God has designed every purpose
with its own prosperity.

Reading: **Ezekiel 11–13; James 1**

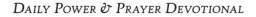

Provision Is Right for the Vision

God is a God of provision. He is Jehovah-Jireh, "The Lord Will Provide." He provides everything, but only after you begin the work of the vision. This means that obedience to vision is not a private issue. It affects everyone who is supposed to work with you and be impacted by your life.

Prosperity means having everything that is needed. It doesn't necessarily mean having a large bank account, several cars, and a large house, although you might need those things to fulfill your vision. For example, because of our purpose, my wife and I need a long dining room table that can seat a large number of people, as we often have guests of the ministry to dinner. That's part of our assignment. It might also be yours, depending on what you are called to do. However, perhaps you need a four-chair table rather than a twelve-chair table because you usually just have your family at dinner. Instead of using the money on a large table, you use it for other things related to your personal or church vision. Similarly, I may not need something that you must have to fulfill your purpose. If I had it, it would be excess.

God provides for all the needs of our visions, no matter what they are, large or small. We are as rich as our purposes, and our visions aren't yet completed. We still have provision coming to us that no one can hold back.

Prayer: Father, may I always remember that my obedience
to my vision is not a private issue; it affects everyone who
is supposed to work with me and be impacted by my life.
Help me to walk in obedience.
In Jesus' name, amen.

Thought: God provides for all the needs of
our visions, large or small.

Reading: **Ezekiel 14–15; James 2**

"Spare Parts" for Your Vision

In 1998, while visiting a friend in Detroit, I toured the Ford Motor Company. We went through what looked like one massive building, but there were smaller storehouses within it. Every section had a different name, and there were millions of parts stored in each section. I pointed to one section and asked the guide, "What is this?" and he said, "These are the cars we're preparing for 2005." I said, "Wait a minute; it's only 1998." He said, "Yeah, but we are at least five years ahead. This one is for 2002, this is for 2003, this is for 2004, and this one is for 2005." When I asked if I could see the cars, he said, "No, the cars themselves are not yet made. We make the parts first. However, these are not the parts we will use on the new cars. These are the replacement parts in case any repairs would be needed." The company makes the spare parts before they build the new cars. That's why, when anything needs to be replaced on your car, the part is already available.

As I listened to our guide explain this, I felt as if the Holy Spirit was speaking to me right in that warehouse. He said, "That's exactly the meaning of Ephesians 1:3: *'Praise be to the God and Father of our Lord Jesus Christ, who has blessed us in the heavenly realms with every spiritual blessing in Christ.'* Everything you're going to need for your vision is already provided for. I have it all reserved in big storehouses in heaven. Even before you came on the scene, I had it all prepared."

Prayer: Father, thank You for preparing all the "parts" that I will need before I need them. Nothing ever happens without Your knowledge or Your purpose.
In Jesus' name, amen.

Thought: God says, "Even before you came on the scene, I had it all prepared."

Reading: **Ezekiel 16–17; James 3**

Warehouses in Heaven

My good friend Jesse Duplantis once told me about a spiritual vision he had in which Jesus took him on a tour of heaven. At one point, Jesus led him to a large area of heaven where there were massive warehouses. There were names on the warehouses, and he saw one with his name on it. Inside, piled up to the ceiling, was what looked like billions of dollars' worth of things. In the corner was a small, empty space. He asked, "Lord, the whole place is filled with all these magnificent things, but what's that empty spot right there by the door?" Jesus said, "That's all you've asked for so far."

After he told me that story, I said to myself, "I'm going to clean out my warehouse before I leave planet earth." When we go to heaven, most of us are going to be shocked at what was ours for use on earth that we never asked for. Daily, we should ask God, "Deliver to me what I need today." Everything you need is waiting for you, available when you ask for it with confidence. God is not short of anything you need.

I'm concerned that you may be asking for some things that aren't yours. Let me explain. If you pursue the wrong assignment, you're going to need things you can't get, because the provision isn't there unless the vision is yours. It's someone else's assignment, and he has his own warehouse. Again, knowing God's will for your life is the key to your prosperity.

Prayer: Father, help me to go beyond my limited understanding so I can pray for the things that are available to me and that I need to fulfill my vision. I want my heavenly warehouse to be empty because I have used it to build Your kingdom.
In Jesus' name, amen.

Thought: God is not short of anything you need.

Reading: **Ezekiel 18–19; James 4**

The Inherent Wealth of Land

I believe there are five specific ways that the Scriptures teach us God provides the resources—financial and otherwise—that we need to fulfill the visions He gives us. We will look at these five ways over the next few days.

The first way God provides for our visions is through our ability to obtain and use land and the resources inherent in it. Land is God's concept of wealth. Note that the first thing God placed man in was the garden of Eden, or real estate. Genesis 2:8-12 says,

> Now the LORD God had planted a garden in the east, in Eden; and there he put the man he had formed. And the LORD God made all kinds of trees grow out of the ground—trees that were pleasing to the eye and good for food....A river watering the garden flowed from Eden; from there it was separated into four headwaters. The name of the first is the Pishon; it winds through the entire land of Havilah, where there is gold. (The gold of that land is good; aromatic resin and onyx are also there.)

This passage describes the wealth of the land surrounding Eden. There was gold, resin, and onyx. Resin is a fragrant gum, similar to myrrh. Onyx is a type of gem. God was saying, "Adam, there's richness in the land." Not only do we as human beings have use of what is on the surface of the earth, but we also have use of what is under the ground. There is special prosperity in owning land and using the rich resources of the earth.

Prayer: Father, please show me how land and its
inherent wealth may be involved in the fulfillment
of the vision You have given me.
In Jesus' name, amen.

Thought: Land is God's concept of wealth.

Reading: **Ezekiel 20–21; James 5**

God's Promise of Land

L et's look at another example from Genesis that shows us wealth is inherent in land. What was God's first promise to Abraham?

"Go to the land I will show you."...Abram traveled through the land as far as the site of the great tree of Moreh at Shechem. At that time the Canaanites were in the land. The LORD appeared to Abram and said, "To your offspring I will give this land." (Genesis 12:1, 6-7)

God made the same promise of inheritance of land to Abraham's son Isaac (see Genesis 26:2-4) and grandson Jacob (see Genesis 28:10-15). He also reaffirmed this promise of land to the Israelites through Moses. (See Exodus 3:7-10, 15-17.) In Genesis 13:15, God said the land would forever belong to Abraham's descendants. Even today, in the state of Israel, land is leased, rather than sold, to the citizens. A person can build and own a house, but he doesn't own the property upon which it stands. The government owns the land. It is considered God's property and therefore is secured for Him.

According to the biblical record, land seems to be God's first order of prosperity. I think it is desirable for most people to own land. Young people, if your parents left you land, don't exchange your perpetual inheritance for a "pot of soup." (See Genesis 25:29-34.) Live very simply, if you have to, but keep the land because there's wealth in it. Christians tend to think in terms of heaven because that is where their focus is. Yet God didn't create humanity for heaven alone—He created us to fulfill His purposes on earth.

Prayer: Father, You have given us this beautiful earth to be nurtured and cultivated. Help us to see how special it is and to treat it accordingly as we fulfill our visions.
In Jesus' name, amen.

Thought: Land seems to be God's first order of prosperity.

Reading: **Ezekiel 22–23; 1 Peter 1**

The Ability to Work

The second way God provides for our visions is through our ability to work. When you decide to move forward with your dream, it will often take a great amount of work. I define work as the passion that is generated by a purpose.

Many people misunderstand the nature of work. They don't realize that work was given to mankind before the fall: *"The LORD God took the man and put him in the Garden of Eden to work it and take care of it ["cultivate it"* NASB]*"* (Genesis 2:15). Cultivation involves both creativity and effort. Work is not a curse, but a great blessing. Genesis 1:28 says that God blessed the male and female and gave them dominion over the earth. He blessed them in all their dominion assignments—including work.

God Himself worked when He created the world, and He still works to carry out His purposes. Because you are made in God's image and likeness, you are designed to work. Remember that work is meant to include creativity and cultivation, not drudgery.

Moreover, work needs to be kept in its proper place. The Bible says that God worked hard and completed His work, but that He also stopped His work and rested. (See Genesis 2:2–3.) He didn't work seven days a week just for the sake of working. He stopped when it was appropriate, and He has instructed us to do the same. (See Exodus 20:9–10.)

Prayer: Father, Your Word gives us such a balanced
picture of work. You worked, so we should work.
You were creative, so we can be creative.
You rested, so we should rest as well.
May we work, create, and rest in a way that honors You.
In Jesus' name, amen.

Thought: Because you are made in God's image and likeness,
you are designed to work.

Reading: **Ezekiel 24–26; 1 Peter 2**

Motivation for Work

It is through worship and communion with God that mankind receives vision, vocation, and work. Jesus, the Second Adam, seemed to have two favorite words that reflected God's purposes for mankind. One of those words was Father. He was always talking about His Father in heaven and seeking His presence in prayer. The other was work.

Jesus was intent on doing His Father's work to completion. We are to aspire to fulfill God's purposes while developing and using the gifts and talents He has given us. We aren't to be lazy; instead, we are to have visions for our lives and to be willing to work so that they can be fulfilled. Our motivation for work is to complete the purposes for which we were created.

Jesus said,

> I tell you the truth, you are looking for me, not because you saw miraculous signs but because you ate the loaves and had your fill. Do not work for food that spoils, but for food that endures to eternal life, which the Son of Man will give you. (John 6:26–27)

In other words, there's a higher reason to work than simply providing for physical needs. Again, don't work just to pay bills. Don't work only to buy food. Understand the true nature of work. In the garden of Eden, there was no supervisor, no one to hand out paychecks. Work was given to Adam because it was a natural part of his being. Through work, he fulfilled part of his purpose as a human being created in God's image.

Prayer: Father, You have revealed an exciting truth:
Work is a natural part of who we are.
As I work on this earth, I pray that Your favor would be
upon me and that You would establish the work of my hands.
In Jesus' name, amen.

Thought: Our motivation for work is to complete the purposes for which we were created.

Reading: **Ezekiel 27–29; 1 Peter 3**

The Ability to Cultivate

The third means of providing for our visions is our God-given ability to cultivate things. *"The LORD God took the man and put him in the Garden of Eden to work it and take care of [cultivate] it"* (Genesis 2:15). God prefers cultivation to barrenness and wilderness, and He has given us the ability to cultivate as one way of reflecting His image. Recall that in Genesis 1:2, God created or cultivated the earth out of a *"formless and empty"* state.

Let me tell you the story of Hog Island in the Bahamas. Years ago, people used to dump garbage on the island, and wild hogs used to scavenge through all the mess. Then, one day, a man came to the Bahamas, flew over Hog Island, and saw something there that no one else could see. He bought Hog Island for practically nothing because the seller figured, "Oh, it's just hogs. You can have it." This man, however, didn't see only hogs. He saw a resort. He cultivated Hog Island and made it productive. Today, the island is a destination for vacationers. It has a new name. It's called Paradise. What a change! All it took was someone to manage it.

You can cultivate what is around you and make it a resource for your vision. That's what we are doing at Bahamas Faith Ministries. We bought a piece of barren land in the center of the island at a very good price, and we are turning it into an international leadership center. God wants people who can dream and then act. Cultivate what you own to further your vision.

Prayer: Father, open my eyes to the possibilities around me. Show me what I can cultivate as a resource for my vision. In Jesus' name, amen.

Thought: The gift of cultivation involves the ability to see potential in what others view as wasteland.

Reading: Ezekiel 30–32; 1 Peter 4

NOVEMBER 28

The Ability to Reserve for the Future

The fourth way God provides for your vision is by giving you wisdom to preserve and reserve for the future. For example, Joseph was sent to Egypt ahead of his brothers and his father Jacob because God knew a famine was coming, and they would need to be preserved. When poverty struck the land, Joseph's family would need a place to go to survive and then prosper when times got better.

There are people whom God calls to be planters, and He will send them ahead of you to prepare the way for you. In addition, while we live on the daily bread God gives us, He also wants us to plan for things in faith. Planning destroys worry. God will teach you how to put things on reserve for the future. He gave Joseph a reservation plan during the famine. Joseph was able to harvest the grain during the seven years of abundance and store it for the years of famine so that Egypt and the surrounding lands would have food when the drought hit.

A fifth way God provides for vision is by enabling us to help future generations with their dreams. God not only wants you to enjoy the wealth, but He also wants your children and grandchildren to enjoy it, too. "A good man leaves an inheritance for his children's children" (Proverbs 13:22). What about your great-grandchildren? What is your vision of inheritance for your descendants? God wants us to think generationally. When He speaks to you, He is also talking of your descendants and the generations that will follow you.

Prayer: Father, give me the wisdom to handle all
my resources well, so I may plan for the future.
Enable me also to leave an inheritance of spiritual
and material wealth for the needs of future generations.
In Jesus' name, amen.

Thought: God wants us to think generationally.

Reading: **Ezekiel 33–34; 1 Peter 5**

Action Steps to Fulfilling Vision

A principle we talked about earlier needs to be reviewed here: whatever God calls for, He provides for. God provides what we need, but we are often involved in the process. If you are a college student, your parents may provide your tuition to go to school, but they cannot make you learn. The provision is made, but the work is up to you. Your parents cook food and put it on the table for you, but you have to eat it; you have to get the energy from it yourself. It's the same way with God. He provides, but He doesn't do the work for us. We have to go after what He has provided as our supply.

Now ask yourself the following questions: Has your definition of prosperity changed as a result of the last two weeks of readings? Why or why not? What resources do you need to fulfill your vision? List them, and then trust God to provide for all the needs of your vision as He has promised to do. Prayerfully use the knowledge you have gained to receive provision for your vision.

Let's pray together:

Prayer: Heavenly Father, You are truly
Jehovah-Jireh, our Provider. You show us that provision
and prosperity are so much more than an excess of money.
Godly prosperity includes personal peace and well-being.
It is a daily provision that reminds us not to worry about tomorrow.
Your provision involves resources that will meet
the requirements of the visions You have given us.
The provision of spiritual blessings is available for us as well.
Father, we cannot thank You enough that
Your provision not only meets our needs, but also
goes exceedingly beyond what we can ask or imagine.
In the mighty power of Jesus' name, amen.

Thought: God provides what we need, but we are
often involved in the process.

Reading: **Ezekiel 35–36; 2 Peter 1**

Principles of Provision for Vision

Today, review the following principles of provision for vision:

1. God often gives us dreams that initially confound us because He wants to make sure we don't attempt to fulfill them apart from Him.
2. God will never give you a vision without the provision for it.
3. The ability and resources are available for what you were born to do, yet your provision is usually hidden until you act on your vision.
4. God has already blessed us with every spiritual blessing in the heavenly places.
5. Prosperity doesn't mean that tomorrow's need is met today; it means that today's need is met today.
6. True prosperity means being free of worry and fear. It reflects a state of contentedness that everything necessary is being taken care of.
7. God has designed every purpose with its own prosperity.
8. Sometimes God doesn't give us all the resources we need to fulfill our visions because He has called other people to provide them for us.
9. Your obedience to your vision affects not only your life, but also the lives of those who will work with you.
10. When we go to heaven, most of us are going to be shocked at what was ours for use on earth that we never asked for.
11. Specific ways that God provides the resources to fulfill our visions are:
    - Land and its inherent wealth
    - The ability to work
    - The ability to cultivate
    - The ability to preserve and reserve for the future
    - The ability to leave wealth for future generations

Reading: **Ezekiel 37–39; 2 Peter 2**

The Tenth Principle: Use Persistence

T he tenth principle in our Twelve Principles of Vision is that we must be persistent if we are going to achieve the visions God has given us. As I wrote earlier, you must realize that obstacles are going to come against you and your vision. Even though God gave the vision, that doesn't mean it's going to be easy to obtain. Please don't think that you are exempt from this reality. When you decide to be somebody, every-thing is going to try to get in the way of your vision. You must be pre-pared for the challenges, for they are coming.

God demonstrates persistence in His very nature. One word that describes the essence of His nature is *faithfulness*. Psalm 89 declares, "*You established your faithfulness in heaven itself....O LORD God Almighty, who is like you? You are mighty, O LORD, and your faithfulness surrounds you*" (vv. 2, 8). God is faithful because He is true to what He has decided to accomplish, and nothing can stop Him. We need to manifest this characteristic in our own lives.

Another word that helps us understand God's nature in relation to persistence in purpose is the word *steadfast*. Psalm 111:7–8 says, "*The works of [God's] hands are faithful and just; all his precepts are trustworthy. They are steadfast for ever and ever, done in faithfulness and uprightness.*" To be steadfast means to stand fast or stand steady in the face of resistance. If you are steadfast, when opposition comes, you don't turn and go back where you were. You push forward. Opposition should strengthen your resolve and revive your stamina.

Prayer: Father, You are faithful and steadfast in accomplishing Your will in my life. Please give me the strength to stand fast against resistance to my vision with godly persistence.
In Jesus' name, amen.

Thought: You must be persistent if you are going to achieve the vision God has given you.

Reading: **Ezekiel 40–41; 2 Peter 3**

The Courage to Stand

C ourage is another key word in regard to persistence. It is the ability to stand up in the face of fear. In fact, it is impossible to have courage without fear. In a sense, if we don't have any fear, we're not living in faith. That may sound like a strange statement, but faith always demands that we do something we know we can't do on our own. This challenge often causes us to be fearful at first.

Many times in the Bible, God's people are encouraged to be courageous. God told Joshua,

> Be strong and courageous, because you will lead these people to inherit the land I swore to their forefathers to give them. Be strong and very courageous....Have I not commanded you? Be strong and courageous. Do not be terrified; do not be discouraged, for the LORD your God will be with you wherever you go. (Joshua 1:6-7, 9)

Why did God speak about courage several times to Joshua? Clearly, Joshua must have been scared! Fear, however, is a positive thing when it gives birth to courage. Moses also told Joshua and the Israelite people, "Be strong and courageous. Do not be afraid or terrified because of them [their enemies], for the LORD your God goes with you" (Deuteronomy 31:6).

If you're afraid to step out in your vision because it's so big, then let your courage come to life as you trust God. Courage says, "I'm afraid, but I'm still moving." Jesus loves for us to do the impossible because the impossible is always possible with God. (See Matthew 19:26.)

Prayer: Father, You have not given us a spirit of fear.
Thank you that my courage can come to life
as I trust in You and Your power.
In Jesus' name, amen.

Thought: Courage is the ability to stand up in the face of fear.

Reading: **Ezekiel 42–44; 1 John 1**

Overcoming Challenges in Life

During His time on earth, Jesus showed us how to bring a vision to pass in the midst of life's challenges and pressures. He faced problems and obstacles similar to what you and I face today, yet His vision came to pass. Jesus is our greatest Teacher when it comes to learning how to overcome challenges. No matter what your background is, your relationship with your heavenly Father will help you rise above your difficult circumstances and fulfill your purpose.

Do you feel pressured by your family's expectations to pursue a certain career or lifestyle when you know that isn't God's plan for you? You don't always have to wait until you're older or "have it all together" before you know God's will for your life. Perhaps your parents have told you, "You are going to do this," but you feel called to do something else. Jesus faced a similar challenge. When He was twelve, He knew what He was born to do. Yet Jesus' earthly parents didn't understand His vision, even when He said, *"Didn't you know I had to be in my Father's house?"* (Luke 2:49; see verse 50). Then, when Jesus grew older, His mother tried to push Him into fulfilling His vision prematurely, and He had to tell her, *"My time has not yet come"* (John 2:4). Even though Jesus respected and honored His parents (see Luke 2:51-52), He had to follow God's purpose for His life. You must follow the vision God has given you. At the same time, you should always show your family love and respect.

Prayer: Father, please give me the strength to stand
strong for what I believe You have called me to do.
Yet always help me to speak the truth to others with Your love.
In Jesus' name, amen.

Thought: Jesus is our greatest Teacher when it comes
to learning how to overcome challenges.

Reading: **Ezekiel 45–46; 1 John 2**

Is Your Vision Larger Than Your Opposition?

Jesus experienced many forms of opposition. There were people who continually schemed to make Him fail. There were those who liked to set Him up for a fall by asking Him trick questions. A crowd once tried to push Him off a cliff. The religious leaders plotted to kill Him. Do you think people call you names? They called Jesus names, too. They called Him demon-possessed, illegitimate, a glutton, and a drunkard.

How did Jesus overcome? How did He succeed in His vision? How did He finish the work the Father had sent Him to do when He faced all that opposition? Jesus was able to remain composed through all those trials because what He had in His heart was bigger than all their threats, accusations, and insults. He knew how to persevere with a dream. Likewise, the vision in your heart needs to be larger than any opposition that comes against you so you can persist in your life's purpose.

When a person knows his purpose, if trouble comes, he can smile and say, "This won't last. With God, I'm tougher than this." When you draw on God's strength, you are tougher than your trials because you see them in a different light. You realize that every point of resistance to your vision gives you the opportunity to become wiser, not weaker. Let every opposing force strengthen you rather than stop you. Peter said that trials refine our faith and make us better. (See 1 Peter 1:7.) That is why we can say, "Bring on the challenges!"

Prayer: Father, help me to persevere in my dream.
Establish the vision in my heart so that it is bigger than
any opposition that comes against me.
In Jesus' name, amen.

Thought: Let every opposition strengthen you
rather than stop you.

Reading: **Ezekiel 47–48; 1 John 3**

Destiny Demands Diligence

Destiny demands diligence. I recommend that you write that statement down on a piece of paper and put it where you can see it every day. If you are going to quit after a couple of challenges, you will never win. Persistence is withstanding all opposition.

Nehemiah could have stopped his work on the wall of Jerusalem because of all the problems, slander, and jeers, but he was persistent. He was determined to complete his vision. You will never be successful unless you have the spirit of persistence. Persistence means that you insist on having what you are going after; you stand up against resistance until you wear it down; you make people who are against you so tired of fighting that they either become your friends or leave you alone; and you stop only after you've finished.

Again, how badly do you want your vision? Jesus told a parable in Luke 18 about a persistent woman. She tirelessly appealed to the judge with her request for justice until he said, in essence, "Give it to her!" (See Luke 18:2–8.) God wants you to do the same. He wants you to say, "Life, this belongs to me." If Life refuses, go back and say the same thing every day until it eventually says, "Here, take it!" Many people lose because they quit when Life says no the first time, but persistent people win. They never take no for an answer when it comes to their visions.

Prayer: Father, I have been tempted to give up
when I have experienced resistance to my vision.
Please help me to develop persistence and determination
to see my vision through to fulfillment.
In Jesus' name, amen.

Thought: Persistence is withstanding
all opposition.

Reading: **Daniel 1–2; 1 John 4**

Jesus Encourages Persistence

T he parable of the woman and the judge that I mentioned yesterday illustrates the power that persistence can have in accomplishing what we truly desire. At another time, Jesus told a similar parable that teaches us that success comes to those who persist—not only in the natural realm, but also in the spiritual realm.

> *Suppose one of you has a friend, and he goes to him at midnight and says, "Friend, lend me three loaves of bread, because a friend of mine on a journey has come to me, and I have nothing to set before him." Then the one inside answers, "Don't bother me. The door is already locked, and my children are with me in bed. I can't get up and give you anything." I tell you, though he will not get up and give him the bread because he is his friend, yet because of the man's boldness he will get up and give him as much as he needs. So I say to you: Ask and it will be given to you; seek and you will find; knock and the door will be opened to you. For everyone who asks receives; he who seeks finds; and to him who knocks, the door will be opened.* (Luke 11:5-10)

As you develop a spirit of persistence, remember these truths about the nature of your Creator and His own persistence in carrying out His purposes for you:

- God is faithful.
- God does not lie.
- God has established His Word.
- Your purpose is already completed in Him.
- God delights in you and considers you His child.

Prayer: Father, You are persistent in carrying out
Your good purposes in my life. Please help me to be persistent
in following after You and Your Word as I pursue my dream.
In Jesus' name, amen.

Thought: Jesus' parables encourage us that success comes
to those who persist.

Reading: **Daniel 3–4; 1 John 5**

Fight Through to Victory

Once, when I was watching a boxing title match on television, one of the boxers was getting beaten badly. At the end of the sixth round, he stumbled back into his corner and sagged on the stool as if he were a sack of potatoes. In seconds, several men went to work on him. One grabbed a bucket of water and doused him with it. The next grabbed a soaking-wet sponge and squeezed water all over his face. Another applied ointment to soothe his wounds. Even though he was getting trounced, they were telling him, "You can do this. You can get back out there. You're better than he is!" One of the men said, "Keep your left hook, okay? You can get him with that left." After about two minutes, the boxer jumped up, saying, "Yeah! Oh, yeah!" He ran back out there, and everything changed in the seventh round. Guess who won? The one who had been about to quit in the sixth round won the fight and received the prize.

You may get beaten up pretty badly in life, but stay in the fight. Fight until you feel the joy of victory. When you think you're going to lose and you stumble back into the corner of life, the Lord will come and pour the cool water of His Word on your head. He will take the ointment of the Holy Spirit and bring healing to your wounds. He will rub life back into your spirit so you can get back out there and start throwing blows. Keep your left up. That's persistence.

Prayer: Father, You encourage us in Your Word
to persist in fighting the good fight of faith.
Please strengthen me to stay in the fight so I may
experience the joy of victory in You.
In Jesus' name, amen.

Thought: Fight until you feel the joy of victory!

Reading: **Daniel 5–7; 2 John**

We Are Warriors

We know that God wants us to be fighters because the Bible calls us soldiers. (See 2 Timothy 2:3–4.) We are spiritual warriors. We are people of battle. The Bible also refers to us as those who *"wrestle"* (Ephesians 6:12 NKJV). This is because we don't just receive medals from God. We earn them. If God didn't want you to fight, He would have given you the medal without the conflict.

The Bible says, *"They overcame [Satan] by the blood of the Lamb and by the word of their testimony"* (Revelation 12:11). Some people don't have a testimony of overcoming. Their testimony is, "I went through the fire, and I got burned. I went under the water and almost drowned." Other people are so spiritually "clean-cut" that you know they have never had a skirmish with the devil. Those who have a true testimony usually don't even have to talk about it because it is evident in their lives.

The fight can be tough, but God says He will stay with you and work out the steps of your vision.

> *Who shall separate us from the love of Christ? Shall trouble or hardship or persecution or famine or nakedness or danger or sword?...No, in all these things we are more than conquerors through Him who loved us* [and called us and gave us our visions]. (Romans 8:35, 37)

God has put so much in you that if you are willing to capture it, nothing can stop you. There is not enough darkness in the world to extinguish the light God has put within you.

Prayer: Father, thank You for the light of
Your Holy Spirit within me.
Thank You for Your love, which gives me
the strength to fight the battles of life.
I know that I will be victorious in Jesus' name. Amen.

Thought: God has put so much in you that if you
are willing to capture it, nothing can stop you.

Reading: **Daniel 8–10; 3 John**

Character under Pressure

Perseverance actually means "to bear up under pressure." I like this quote from Eleanor Roosevelt, which actually applies to all people: "A woman is like a tea bag. You never know how strong she is until she gets into hot water." Successful people persevere under pressure and use it for their own benefit. People who have vision are stronger than the pressure life brings.

I have discovered that sometimes you don't get the scent from the rose until you crush it. In order to draw the fragrance of His glory from your life, God will allow you to be subject to stress. We forget too easily that character is formed by pressure. The purpose of pressure is to get rid of what is not of God and to leave what is pure gold.

When God showed Abraham the land his descendants would inherit, He told him that everything as far as he could see would be his. However, the land was full of Moabites, Hittites, Canaanites, and Amorites—the Israelites' future enemies! Likewise, whenever God shows us a vision, it is full of "enemies" or opposition that we can't see at first. Initially, the vision looks great. But the enemies are still there. God doesn't show you the "ites" right away because He doesn't want to frighten you. He's building up your faith to prepare you for the time when you are ready to face the opposition and overcome it. Therefore, don't run—stay in the fight! There is no stopping a person who understands that pressure is good for him because pressure is one of the keys to perseverance.

Prayer: Father, help me to understand that character
is formed by pressure and is vital for victory.
Enable me to persevere under pressure and
to use it for the benefit of my vision.
In Jesus' name, amen.

Thought: Successful people persevere under pressure and
use it for their own benefit.

Reading: **Daniel 11–12; Jude**

Test Your Vision for Authenticity

Let me confess something to you: I wish I didn't have to be doing what I'm doing. I didn't say that I don't want to. I said I wish I didn't have to. That is not a negative statement, just a realistic one, because I know what the cost of my vision is going to be. In the next twenty or thirty years of my life, I know the cost is going to be high. That's why I thank God that, earlier in my life, I had the privilege of observing first-hand the cost to another visionary, who told me, "Myles, my son, get ready for the price." Because of that experience, I have been prepared to accept the cost.

At times, you will find it difficult to remain in your vision. I understand. At times, it's tough for me to stay in mine. The demands that God makes on my ministry are high because the call requires it. Vision always demands a cost. Someone has to pay the price. Are you willing to do it? We need to be like Paul, who was obedient to the vision God had given him, even at great sacrifice.

Every true vision will be tested for authenticity. If your vision is authentic, life is going to try it, just to make sure. Don't be afraid when you make a declaration of what you're going to do in life and difficulty follows; that opposition comes to test your resolve. If a vision is stopped by trials or tests, then perhaps it was not really a vision from God. Be careful not to become involved in superficial enterprises. Put the vision to the test.

Prayer: Father, testing my vision will make
certain that I am following Your purpose in my life.
I surrender to those tests with a heart of trust.
In Jesus' name, amen.

Thought: Every true vision will be tested for authenticity.

Reading: **Hosea 1–4; Revelation 1**

Action Steps to Fulfilling Vision

Persistence is vital for your vision to be successful. All of us will encounter opposition and crises in life, but these challenges don't have to be setbacks. They can be turning points at which our understanding of and commitment to the vision is tested and matured. A crisis can lead us to greater challenge and victory. If you are encountering resistance to your vision, be encouraged that your faith is being strengthened. God is not only enabling you to stand strong in the face of opposition to your vision, but also to overcome it—to His glory and praise.

Therefore, ask yourself the following questions: In what areas of my life and vision am I in need of perseverance? What have I given up on that I need to pick up again and continue with? Ask God to develop faithfulness, steadfastness, and courage in you.

Write down the saying "Destiny demands diligence," and put it where you can be reminded of it every day.

Let's pray together:

Prayer: Heavenly Father, You have shown us
that destiny and vision demand diligence in our lives.
You graciously provide the vision and You generously
give us the resources. Yet You have still called us
to persevere for the good things in our lives.
You urge us not become weary in doing good
with Your promise that at the proper time
we will reap a harvest if we do not give up.
Please strengthen us to be persistent.
Remind us daily that You have provided the Holy Spirit
to teach us, guide us, and give us the power to persevere.
In Jesus' name, amen.

Thought: Challenges to your vision don't have to be
setbacks—they can be turning points.

Reading: **Hosea 5–8; Revelation 2**

DECEMBER 12

Principles of Persistence in Vision

Today, reflect on these principles of persistence in vision:

1. Obstacles will come against you and your vision. You must be persistent if you are going to achieve the vision God has given you.
2. Faithfulness means being true to what you have decided to accomplish and letting nothing stop you.
3. Steadfastness means to stand fast or stand steady in the face of resistance.
4. Courage is the ability to stand up in the face of fear.
5. Fear is a positive thing when it gives birth to courage.
6. Even though there will be times of stress, disappointment, and pressure, your vision will come to pass.
7. Every point of resistance to your vision comes to make you wiser, not weaker. All opposition comes to strengthen you, not to stop you.
8. Destiny demands diligence.
9. Many people lose because they quit when life says no the first time, but persistent people win. They never take no for an answer when it comes to their visions.
10. There is not enough darkness in the world to extinguish the light God has put within you.
11. Perseverance means "to bear up under pressure."
12. Character is formed by pressure. The purpose of pressure is to get rid of what is not of God and to leave what is pure gold.
13. There is no stopping a person who understands that pressure is good for him because pressure is one of the keys to perseverance.
14. Vision always demands a cost.
15. Every true vision will be tested for authenticity.

Reading: **Hosea 9–11; Revelation 3**

The Eleventh Principle: Be Patient

Principle number eleven in our Twelve Principles of Vision is that we must be patient in seeing the fulfillment of our visions. Again, it may take a while for your vision to come to fruition, but if you are willing to wait for it (which many people are not), it will come to pass. The writer of Hebrews tells us, *"Do not throw away your confidence; it will be richly rewarded. You need to persevere* ["have need of patience" KJV] *so that when you have done the will of God, you will receive what he has promised"* (Hebrews 10:35–36). People who have steadfast patience will always win.

When some people make plans to carry out their visions, they try to force those plans into their own timetable or their own way of bringing them to pass. However, you cannot rush a vision. It is given by God, and He will carry it out in His own time. You may ask, "Then what is the reason for developing a plan in the first place?" Remember that the reason you make plans is to give you a direction to move in. You can modify the plans, as necessary and appropriate, along the way—while still keeping to the overall vision. We are not all-knowing, as God is. We need to patiently rely on His guidance every step of the way.

As I wrote earlier, when we first receive our visions, we are yet not ready for them. We must learn to follow the subtle leading of the Holy Spirit in our lives in which we *"hear a voice behind* [us], *saying, 'This is the way; walk in it'"* (Isaiah 30:21).

Prayer: Father, patience is one of the fruit
of the Spirit at work in our lives.
Please help me to wait patiently for
my vision's fulfillment as You guide me daily.
In Jesus' name, amen.

Thought: People who have steadfast patience will always win.

Reading: **Hosea 12–14; Revelation 4**

The Fullness of Time

While it is important to establish deadlines for your goals, you must also be willing to rearrange those deadlines. Be assured that the vision is coming at just the right time. God sent Jesus to be our Savior about four thousand years after the fall of man. Humanly speaking, that was a long time to wait. But He came just as predicted and at just the right time. The Bible says,

> But when **the time had fully come**, God sent his Son, born of a woman, born under law, to redeem those under law, that we might receive the full rights of sons.　　　　(Galatians 4:4–5, emphasis added)

As long as you can dream, there's hope. As long as there's hope, there's life. It's crucial that you and I maintain our dreams by patiently waiting for their fulfillment in the fullness of time. James 1:4 says, "*But let patience have its perfect work, that you may be perfect and complete, lacking nothing*" (NKJV). Others who have gone before us have had their faith tested, and it has produced patience in them (see verse 3) so that they were able to win the race. Let us do the same. The writer of Hebrews expressed it this way:

> Wherefore seeing we also are compassed about with so great a cloud of witnesses, let us lay aside every weight, and the sin which doth so easily beset us, and let us run with patience the race that is set before us.　　　　(Hebrews 12:1 KJV)

Prayer: Father, it is my desire to let patience
do a perfect work in me, to make me mature in You
and ready for my vision. Please work in my heart
and help me to develop a patient spirit.
In Jesus' name, amen.

Thought: As long as you can dream, there's hope.
As long as there is hope, there's life.

Reading: **Joel; Revelation 5**

DECEMBER 15

Patience to Overcome

When you are patient in the fulfillment of your vision, you are able to be calm in the midst of uncertainty. For example, you can be at peace when everyone else is worrying about being laid off. You can endure the cross when you have seen the joy of the end of your vision. (See Hebrews 12:2.) When you don't have vision, you complain about the cross. You become frustrated about your position. You get angry about your salary. You worry about holding on to your job.

However, when you understand vision, you remember that vision takes time and patience and often involves change. As I wrote earlier, vision may constantly keep you unsettled, but it will also keep you fluid and mobile, ready to take the next step. When you keep company with God, you have to keep moving, but you have the assurance that He is always with you along the path toward your vision's fulfillment.

Patience is also the key to power over adversity and turmoil. If you threaten a man and he just waits, your threat is going to wear off. The Bible says that a patient man is stronger than a mighty warrior: *"Better a patient man than a warrior, a man who controls his temper than one who takes a city"* (Proverbs 16:32). When I first read that verse, I found it hard to believe that patience is more powerful than might. Then I came to understand the power of patience. A patient person makes others unsettled because they want that person to react to them, to become angry—but he never does.

Do you see the fruit of patience working actively in your life?

Prayer: Father, help me to be patient in spirit
so that I can be calm in the midst of uncertainty,
and overcome the opposition of the proud in my life.
In Jesus' name, amen.

Thought: Patience is the key to power over
adversity and turmoil.

Reading: **Amos 1–3; Revelation 6**

Action Steps to Fulfilling Vision

Have you been trying to force the timetable of the fulfillment of your vision? If so, what have you learned about patience in these last few days that will enable you to trust God to fulfill the vision in His timing? Encourage your spirit as you wait for your vision to come to pass by committing these verses to memory this week:

But let patience have its perfect work, that you may be perfect and complete, lacking nothing. (James 1:4 NKJV)

We do not want you to become lazy, but to imitate those who through faith and patience inherit what has been promised. (Hebrews 6:12)

You need to persevere so that when you have done the will of God, you will receive what he has promised. (Hebrews 10:36)

Let's pray together:

Prayer: Heavenly Father, as we consider patience, we realize how often we are impatient with the pace of our lives. When we pray and You reveal our visions, we want to see them done now. Help us to understand how Your timetable is best for us, no matter how impatient we may feel. Many times, the psalmist David wrote about waiting for You, Lord, and he encourages us to do the same. We will learn to wait patiently for You, Lord, and to trust that Your timing and Your will are always perfect for our lives. In Jesus' name, amen.

Thought: *"Let patience have its perfect work."*

Reading: **Amos 4–6; Revelation 7**

Principles of Patience for Vision

Today, reflect on these principles of patience for vision:

1. We must be patient in seeing the fulfillment of our visions.
2. *"Do not throw away your confidence; it will be richly rewarded. You need to persevere ["have need of patience" KJV] so that when you have done the will of God, you will receive what he has promised"* (Hebrews 10:35–36).
3. People who have steadfast patience will always win. Patience ensures the eventual success of your vision's plan.
4. We cannot try to force our visions into our own timetables. Vision is given by God, and He will carry it out in His own time.
5. Your vision will come to pass if you are willing to progress at the vision's pace.
6. When you are patient in the fulfillment of your vision, you are able to be calm in the midst of uncertainty.
7. Vision takes time and patience and often involves change.
8. Patience is the key to power over adversity and turmoil.
9. The testing of our faith produces patience, and patience perfects our spiritual character and leads to the fulfillment of our visions. (See James 1:4.)
10. *"Wherefore seeing we also are compassed about with so great a cloud of witnesses, let us lay aside every weight, and the sin which doth so easily beset us, and let us run with patience the race that is set before us"* (Hebrews 12:1 KJV).

Reading: **Amos 7–9; Revelation 8**

The Twelfth Principle:
Have a Dynamic, Daily Prayer Life

P rinciple number twelve in our Twelve Principles for Fulfilling Personal Vision is that, if you are going to be successful in your vision, you must have a daily, dynamic, personal prayer life with God. Why? Because you need continual communion and fellowship with the Source of vision.

Remember that you were born to consult God to find out His purpose for your life so that you can discover your vision. Yet, as the *"Alpha and the Omega, the Beginning and the End"* (Revelation 1:8 NKJV), God is not only the Author of your vision, but He is also your continuing Support as you progress toward its fulfillment. You will never achieve your vision without prayer because prayer is what keeps you connected to the Vision-Giver. Jesus said in John 15:5, *"I am the vine; you are the branches.... Apart from me you can do nothing."* If you stay in touch with God, you will always be nourished in both life and vision.

Prayer is the place where you can take all your burdens to God and say, "God, I have to make it," and He will say, "I'm with you. What are you afraid of?" *"The LORD is my light and my salvation—whom shall I fear? The LORD is the stronghold of my life—of whom shall I be afraid?"* (Psalm 27:1). God will bring you through your difficulties and give you the victory through prayer based on His Word.

Prayer means getting away from the noise and confusion of life, but if you will let God encourage and refresh you, by the time you have finished praying, you will be saying, "I'm ready to go again!"

Prayer: Father, those whom we love, we want to see daily.
I want to fellowship with You each day and to have communion
with you in prayer. I know that You are my lifeline.
In Jesus' name, amen.

Thought: You must have a daily, dynamic, personal
prayer life with God.

Reading: **Obadiah; Revelation 9**

Encouragement for the Fight

Through our prayers, God encourages us to get back out into the fight of faith. Isaiah 40:31 says, *"Those who hope in the LORD will renew their strength. They will soar on wings like eagles; they will run and not grow weary, they will walk and not be faint."* Yes, you will become tired, and sometimes you will want to quit. However, if you are willing to bear up in prayer and stand before God and say, "God, I'm hoping in You," He will give you strength.

A real fighter doesn't wear his medals on his chest. He wears them on his back. They are his scars. Only a few people will know what it took for you to achieve your vision. Yet you must be willing to take the scars if you want to wear the crown.

Believe me, a champion does not win every round, but if he perseveres, he wins the match. Since prayer is where you receive the ability to continue the fight, it is crucial for you to find times during the day when you can go to God and say things like, "God, I'm scared," so that He can reassure you that He is with you. He says, *"Surely I am with you always"* (Matthew 28:20). When you hear that, it is enough. You are able to say, "Let's go back, Lord, and fight one more day." You can be victorious if you are willing to take what you are afraid of to God in prayer.

Prayer: Father, like the apostle Paul, help me to
fight the good fight of faith. It is a fight that I believe
I can win because You are always there
to provide the power for victory.
Thank You. In Jesus' name, amen.

Thought: Every champion does not win every round,
but if he perseveres, he wins the match.

Reading: **Jonah; Revelation 10**

Prayer Is the Essential Resource

Without prayer, you cannot get where you want to go. There will be times when all you'll have is prayer. You won't have any money, people, or resources—just prayer. Yet that is all you need. God will see you through.

When all the trouble and opposition came to Nehemiah, he said to God, *"Remember Tobiah and Sanballat, O my God, because of what they have done; remember also the prophetess Noadiah and the rest of the prophets who have been trying to intimidate me"* (Nehemiah 6:14). Nehemiah took all his troubles and enemies to God in prayer. He didn't write a letter of complaint to the editor of the newspaper. He didn't try to justify himself. He prayed, and God answered his prayer to deliver him. (See verses 15–16.)

Likewise, when people attack your dream, go to God. Don't try to explain and give an answer for everything because you can't explain anything to critics. Their motives are already contaminated, and they'll use your words against you. Instead, stay connected to your Source for the renewal of your purpose, faith, and strength, and you will be able to persevere to victory.

There are many days (and nights) when I stumble into my prayer room and say, "God, if You won't help me in this, I want You to take me home to You." Visions can be very demanding. Sometimes you will wonder, "Am I ever going to make it?" That's a good time to run to God. *"If the LORD delights in a man's way, he makes his steps firm; though he stumble, he will not fall, for the LORD upholds him with his hand"* (Psalm 37:23–24).

Prayer: Father, thank You that when things are difficult
and people attack my dream, I know I can run to You
for purpose, faith, strength, and protection.
In Jesus' name, amen.

Thought: When people attack your dream, *go to God.*

Reading: **Micah 1–3; Revelation 11**

Attached to the Power Supply

I n the Bahamas where I live, we are located in an area called the "hurricane zone." During a monster storm in 2004, the electricity went out, and my wife and I were left sitting in darkness. I reached for the flashlight and surveyed the room. Then I took a walk through the darkened house and checked everything to make sure the shutters were holding. As I examined the rooms with the flashlight, I noticed the many items we had accumulated that had become so important to us, but that now were completely useless: the large-screen television, VCR, CD players, air conditioners, computers, printers, and other high-tech "toys" we had purchased.

I stood there in the dark for a moment and thought about all the power, potential, benefits, pleasure, and untapped functions trapped in each of these items that were completely useless to me at that moment. These things existed, but they could not contribute to my present situation and life. The items were filled to capacity with possibility, but they could not deliver. Why? Because they were cut off from their source, their power supply.

I then saw a true picture of mankind: a powerful creature full of divine potential, talents, gifts, abilities, untapped capacity, creativity, ingenuity, and productivity. But unless man is connected to God, his true abilities lie dormant inside him. Man can fulfill his true potential and maximize his full capacity only by remaining connected to his Creator. Prayer and communion with God give us the power we need to fulfill our purposes in Him. Stay connected to your power supply.

Prayer: Father, thank You for creating me
with the potential to accomplish great things.
Please help me to recognize You as my only true power supply.
In Jesus' name, amen.

Thought: Stay connected to your power supply.

Reading: **Micah 4–5; Revelation 12**

Action Steps to Fulfilling Vision

There is nothing more important in life than establishing a daily prayer time or communion with God through Christ. God should be the Source of all that we do and are in life. Jesus reminded us that without Him we can do nothing. (See John 15:5.) Committing everything in our lives to God and maintaining our relationship with Him through prayer is the only way we can have true meaning in our lives and fulfill the purposes for which we were created.

Have you established a daily prayer time with God? In what ways are you relying on God for your life and vision? In what ways aren't you relying on Him? Commit to prayer the areas in which you aren't currently relying on Him. Be honest with Him about how you are feeling and allow Him to strengthen, sustain, and encourage you through His presence and His Word.

Let's pray together:

Prayer: Heavenly Father, we want to meet with You
in prayer every day. Help us to know in our hearts
that throughout the day, we can bring our prayers
before You and know that You hear us.
May we never forget that You are always ready
to listen to our hearts' cries.
Help us to remember to bring our needs to You first,
before we complain to others, or before we
allow our fears to discourage our hearts.
You are the One who gives our visions meaning and purpose.
May we long for communion
with You more and more each day.
In Jesus' name, amen.

Thought: God should be the Source of all
that we do and are in life.

Reading: Micah 6–7; Revelation 13

Principles of Prayer for Vision

Today, reflect on these principles of prayer for your vision:

1. To be successful in your vision, you must have a daily, dynamic prayer life with God.
2. God is not only the Author of your vision, but also your continuing Support as you progress toward its fulfillment.
3. You will never achieve your vision without prayer because prayer is what keeps you connected to the Vision-Giver.
4. If you stay in touch with God, you will always be nourished in both life and vision.
5. Prayer sustains us in the demands of vision. God will bring you through your difficulties and give you the victory through prayer based on His Word.
6. Prayer encourages us to get back in the fight of faith.
7. Since prayer is where we receive the ability to continue the fight, it is crucial for us to find times during the day when we can go before God.
8. Prayer is the essential resource of vision. When people attack your dream, go to God. Remain connected to your Source for the renewal of your purpose, faith, and strength, and you will be able to persevere to victory.
9. Prayer and communion with God give us the power we need to fulfill our purposes in Him.

Reading: **Nahum; Revelation 14**

Seasons under Heaven

Ecclesiastes 3:1 says, *"There is a time for everything, and a season for every activity under heaven."* Like the calendar year, our lives have four seasons, and each of those seasons must come to pass.

The first season is birth and dependency. All of us go through this season in which we must rely totally on outside help, particularly our families, for survival. We need to be taught and trained in what is right and wrong and what is important in life.

The second season is one of independence, in which we capture what we were born to do. We no longer depend on other people to give us a vision for life or to help us survive. We focus in on our own goals.

The third season is interdependence. In this stage, we have become so free in our visions that we can give our dreams to other people. We can now pass on our visions to the next generation.

The final season is death, where our lives become the nourishment for other people's dreams in succeeding generations. If people can't receive life from the legacy you leave when you die, then you really didn't live effectively. People should be able to flourish on the fruit of the vision you leave behind on earth.

Vision gives us assignments that will impact the earth. We must be able to say we have changed the world in some way while we were here and that we have left a mark for those who will come after us. Let's discover and pursue the visions God has placed in our hearts.

Prayer: Father, there is a time for everything,
and our times are in Your hands.
You are Lord over all the seasons of our lives.
May each one of them bring glory to You.
In Jesus' precious name, amen.

Thought: Like the calendar year, our lives have four seasons,
and those seasons must come to pass.

Reading: **Habakkuk; Revelation 15**

Realizing Your Vision

The ability to dream is the greatest power on earth. The ability to see your hope is the greatest motivator of humanity. Without hope, life has no positive future, and disillusionment becomes a way of life. The ability to dream is the greatest power on earth because it is the essence of true faith.

If you have a dream, or if you want to discover your vision, remember this: God loves dreamers. He gives visions, and He is attracted to people who love to dream big. In Genesis 37, God introduces us to one of the biggest dreamers in the Bible. Joseph had a dream from God that he was destined to be a ruler or leader among men. Joseph may not always have handled his vision correctly, but he trusted God, moved toward the dream, and saw it come to pass. God loves a dreamer who is surrendered to Him.

What is the difference between the dreamer who realizes his dream and the dreamer whose dream becomes a nightmare of unfulfilled hopes? The dreamer who succeeds is someone who has a clear vision and acts on it. As long as a person can hold on to his vision, then there is always a chance for him to move out of his present circumstances and toward the fulfillment of his purpose.

Be encouraged—God wants to see your dreams fulfilled in Him!

Prayer: Father, the life of Joseph has always been
an excellent example of Your faithfulness.
It is also an example of a vision that comes alive in a
person's life and is fulfilled through faith and perseverance.
I trust You that my vision will come alive
in my life and will be fulfilled as well.
In Jesus' name, amen.

Thought: The ability to dream is one of
the greatest powers on earth.

Reading: **Zephaniah; Revelation 16**

Draw Solid Blueprints for Your Life

C ommit to the LORD *whatever you do, and your plans will succeed"* (Proverbs 16:3). Most of us are trying to construct our lives without any real thought or planning. We are like a contractor who is trying to construct a building without a blueprint. As a result, our lives are out of balance and unreliable.

Discovering and implementing your personal vision is a process of learning about yourself, growing in your relationship with and knowledge of the Lord, and continually fine-tuning your understanding of the vision God has given you. It would be a good idea to review your personal vision on a regular basis. At least every six months to a year, set aside a block of time to pray and reevaluate where you are in relation to your vision. You will add to or take away from certain elements of your plan as God refines your understanding of His purpose. Eventually, you will begin to see, "This is the real thing!" However, if you never write out a life blueprint, then God will have nothing to direct you in.

My prayer is that you will stop the construction of your life right where it is and go back and draw solid blueprints that will lead you where you want to go in life through the vision God has put in your heart. Over the next several days, we will look at guidelines for discovering and developing your personal vision plan. I encourage you to use these last few days of this year to write a plan for your life.

Prayer: Father, guide me as I write down
the vision for my life. I commit my plans to You.
Please help me to continue to fine-tune them
as I seek Your direction in prayer.
In Jesus' name, amen.

Thought: When you write your vision,
realize that it won't be a finished product, but it will
be refined as God makes your purpose clearer.

Reading: **Haggai; Revelation 17**

How to Write Your Personal Vision Plan

I t is time to write down your personal vision plan, perhaps for the very first time. Even if you are revising your plan, complete the following steps. God has a wonderful blueprint to reveal to you.

Step One: *Eliminate Distractions.* Sit down somewhere by yourself, away from any distractions and responsibilities, and allow yourself some uninterrupted time to think and pray. Do this as often as you need to as you develop your plan.

Step Two: *Find Your True Self.* Until you know who you are, why God created you, and why you're here, life will simply be a confusing experiment. Answering the following questions will help give you clarity and confidence in regard to your personal identity. Write down your answers to these questions, taking the time to answer them with much thought. You may also want to review the previous devotionals on finding out who you are in God.

- Who am I?
- Who am I in relation to God?
- Where do I come from as a person?
- How have I been created like my Source? (See Genesis 1:26–28.)
- Why am I here?

Write out your personal purpose statement. Ask yourself, "What is my reason for existence as a human being and as an individual?" (You may be able to answer this question only after you have completed the other steps. However, you may also want to write an answer now and then compare it with what you think after you have gone through the rest of the questions.)

Prayer: Father, I am trusting You for Your clear guidance in developing my vision plan. Reveal my true self to me as You have designed me. Thank You for leading me in the way I should go. In the precious name of Jesus, amen.

Thought: God has a wonderful blueprint to reveal to you.

Reading: **Zechariah 1–4; Revelation 18**

Finding Your True Vision

Let us continue with the steps in writing your personal vision plan.

Step Three: *Find Your True Vision.* Prayerfully answer the following questions, and you'll be amazed at the way God will begin to open your mind to His purpose and vision for you. You'll begin to see things that you've never seen before. Write them down, read them over, think about them, pray about them, and begin to formulate ideas of what you want out of life. Ask yourself the following:

- What do I want to do with my life?
- What am I inspired to do?
- What would I want to do more than anything else, even if I was never paid for it?
- What do I love to do so much that I forget to eat or sleep?

Allow yourself to think freely. Don't put any limitations of time or money on your vision. Because many of us are influenced by others' opinions of us and by our own false expectations for ourselves, it may take you a little time to discover what you really want. Persevere through the process and dig down deep to find your true desires.

Step Four: *Discover Your True Motivation.* A vision from God is never selfish. It will always help or uplift others in some way. It is designed to make the lives of mankind better and to improve society. It inspires and builds up others. Ask yourself the following and write down your answers:

- How does my vision help others?
- What is the motivation for my vision?
- Why do I want to do what I want to do?
- Can I accomplish my vision and still have integrity?

Prayer: Father, open my heart and my mind to Your purpose and vision for my life. Give me a heart to uplift others in all that I do. In Jesus' name, amen.

Thought: A vision from God is never selfish.

Reading: **Zechariah 5–8; Revelation 19**

Principles for Life

Today, we will look at steps five and six to writing down your personal vision plan.

Step Five: *Identify Your Principles.* Your principles are your philosophy of life. In other words, they are how you intend to conduct yourself during your life. You must clarify what you will and won't do. These principles are your guides for living, doing business, relating to other people, and relating to life. You must settle them in your heart and mind so that you will have standards to live by.

The Ten Commandments are great principles and a good starting point for developing your own principles. For example, you could write, "On my way to my vision, I will not steal, lie, or bear false witness; I won't worship any god but God Almighty; I will not commit adultery; I will not covet," and so on. Write out your life principles.

Step Six: *Choose Your Goals and Objectives.* Goals are the steps necessary to fulfill your vision. What practical things do you need to do to accomplish your dream? Goals are clear markers that indicate where you need to go. Write out your goals.

Objectives are the detailed steps of your goals. They determine when you want things to happen. You must clearly delineate what you need to do and when you need to do it in order to get to where you want to go. For example, if you want to open a mechanics shop, and one of your goals is to go to school to learn mechanics, some of your objectives will be to choose a school, fill out an application, and start classes. Objectives should include specific timetables. Write out your objectives.

Prayer: Father, put Your laws in my mind and write them in my heart as my standard of conduct and living. In Jesus' name, amen.

Thought: Goals are clear markers that indicate where you need to go, the steps necessary to fulfill your vision.

Reading: **Zechariah 9–12; Revelation 20–21**

Identifying Resources

Here is the seventh step to take when writing down your personal vision plan.

Step Seven: *Identify Your Resources.* You now need to identify all the resources you will need to accomplish your vision.

Identify your human needs. What help do you need from others to fulfill your vision? What kind of personal associations do you need to have—and not have?

Identify your resource needs. What kinds of resources do you need to fulfill your vision? Don't worry about how large they may seem. Write them down.

Write down your strengths. What are your gifts? What do you know you are good at? Write down your answers, and then make plans to refine your strengths. For example, if your vision requires that you must speak before large groups of people, you have to start stepping out and doing it. You don't know what you can do until you have to do it. Some amazing gifts come out of people when they are under pressure.

Write down your weaknesses. What does your vision need that you aren't good at? Don't be ashamed of your weaknesses, because everyone has something he is not good at. However, you must identify them because God will supply other people to do what you cannot do toward your vision. Remember, you need other people in your life because your vision cannot be fulfilled by you alone.

Prayer: Father, show me my strengths and weaknesses,
and where I need others to help fulfill
the vision You have given me.
Thank You for supplying all of my needs, including people,
even before I knew I had need of them.
In Jesus' name, amen.

Thought: Some amazing gifts surface and develop
only when people are under pressure.

Reading: **Zechariah 13–14; Revelation 22**

Commit to Your Vision

On this last day of the year, we come to the concluding step in writing out your vision plan.

Step Eight: *Commit to Your Vision.* You will never fulfill your vision if you are not committed to it. You will need to make a specific decision that you are going to follow through, acknowledging that God may refine your plans as He leads you through the process. Also, commit your vision to God on a regular basis. Proverbs 16:3 says, *"Commit to the LORD whatever you do, and your plans will succeed."*

- Commit to your vision.
  - Commit your vision to God.
    - Remember, God will bring
      your vision to fulfillment!

I have shared my vision openly in these devotional pages. My purpose is to inspire and encourage leadership and vision in the lives of people all over the world, and I am especially committed to doing so with the people of Third-World developing nations.

Life was designed to be lived intentionally and on purpose, but most of the people of the world exist under circumstances beyond their control. They live by duress rather than destiny. For most, history has robbed them of the capacity to dream and to live with hope for a better future. *"Where there is no vision, the people perish"* (Proverbs 29:18) could describe many of the developing Third-World nations, where a lack of national pride, a poor work ethic, a culture of corruption, and the citizenry's loss of hope are pervasive. We need the emergence of leadership that can see beyond their personal gain and capture a God-inspired vision of their nations that incorporates the aspirations of the people and their right to pursue their personal dreams and visions. I believe the key is visionary leadership. May the principles in this book be a source of igniting the passion of purpose in the hearts of this very special and unique group of people.

Reading: **Malachi; Revelation 23–24**

My Prayer for You

Heavenly Father,
In Your abundant grace, inspire these readers to discover,
pursue, and fulfill the visions in their hearts and
maximize the potential trapped within them, potential
that was buried in the historical grave of low self-esteem
and self-doubt. May they dream dreams that inspire their
children to dream and have visions of a better world. May
their visions become reality and impact those who are
not yet born. May the Third World live up to its destiny
and set an example for all the world to see. May each and
every one see farther than their eyes can look.
In the powerful, matchless name of Jesus, amen.

March 31 Lord pray

JOURNAL

JOURNAL

JOURNAL

JOURNAL

JOURNAL

Journal

JOURNAL

Virginia Starke
410 625-3878

About the Author

D r. Myles Munroe is an international motivational speaker, best-selling author, educator, leadership mentor, and consultant for government and business. Traveling extensively throughout the world, Dr. Munroe addresses critical issues affecting the full range of human, social, and spiritual development. The central theme of his message is the maximization of individual potential, including the transformation of followers into leaders and leaders into agents of change.

Dr. Munroe is founder and president of Bahamas Faith Ministries International (BFMI), a multidimensional organization headquartered in Nassau, Bahamas. He is chief executive officer and chairman of the board of the International Third World Leaders Association and president of the International Leadership Training Institute.

Dr. Munroe is also the founder and executive producer of a number of radio and television programs aired worldwide. In addition, he is a frequent guest on other television and radio programs and international networks and is a contributing writer for various Bible editions, journals, magazines, and newsletters, such as *The Believer's Topical Bible, The African Cultural Heritage Topical Bible, Charisma Life Christian Magazine,* and *Ministries Today.* A popular author of over forty books, his works include *The Most Important Person on Earth, The Spirit of Leadership, The Principles and Power of Vision, Understanding the Purpose and Power of Prayer, Understanding the Purpose and Power of Woman,* and *Understanding the Purpose and Power of Men.*

Dr. Munroe has changed the lives of multitudes around the world with a powerful message that inspires, motivates, challenges, and empowers people to discover personal purpose, develop true potential, and manifest their unique leadership abilities. For over thirty years, he has trained tens of thousands of leaders in business, industry, education, government, and religion. He personally addresses over 500,000 people each year on personal and professional development. His appeal and message transcend age, race, culture, creed, and economic background.

Dr. Munroe has earned B.A. and M.A. degrees from Oral Roberts University and the University of Tulsa, and he has been awarded a number of honorary doctoral degrees. He has also served as an adjunct professor of the Graduate School of Theology at Oral Roberts University.

Dr. Munroe and his wife Ruth travel as a team and are involved in teaching seminars together. Both are leaders who minister with sensitive hearts and international vision. They are the proud parents of two college graduates, Charisa and Chairo (Myles, Jr.).